Born Twice, Built Once

A GUIDE TO INNER AWAKENING & PURPOSEFUL LIVING

SIDDHARTH SHARMA

INDIA · SINGAPORE · MALAYSIA

ISBN 979-8-89929-346-7

CONTENTS

INTRODUCTION

Some lives begin twice—once when we arrive in the world, and again when we finally begin to understand who we are and what we're here for. *Born Twice, Built* Once is a story of that second beginning, a quiet yet powerful turning point that transforms everything.

In the early chapters of life, not every page was easy to read. I grew up in an environment filled with noise—some of it loud, some of it silent. There were lessons in those days that came not through words, but through the spaces between them. Family, though full of tradition and togetherness, sometimes carried unspoken tensions. Childhood friendships and early relationships, though hopeful at first, often left behind unanswered questions and a longing to belong.

Like many, I sought my place in the world—sometimes trying to fit in, sometimes choosing to disappear. Along the way, the weight of expectations, misunderstandings, and personal struggles led me down a path I didn't fully recognize. It became easier to retreat into the familiar than to confront the unknown. And yet, something within me quietly resisted. There was always a small voice, almost imperceptible, that kept asking: *Is this all there is?*

The answer came not in a moment of grand clarity, but through the steady presence of a mentor—a guide who didn't give me answers, but helped me ask better questions. Through spiritual reflection, honest self-inquiry, and the gift of grace, I began to rebuild—not from scratch, but from truth. Not to become someone new, but to return to someone I had almost forgotten.

This book is not about what went wrong, but about what can go right—when we choose to see ourselves not as victims of circumstance, but as architects of meaning. It's about the quiet strength that emerges when we accept responsibility, the calm that follows the storm, and the joy that grows from living with intention.

Everyone, at some point in life, will encounter moments that challenge them deeply. But in those very moments lies the invitation to begin again—not with regret, but with reverence. That is the heart of being *born twice.* And when we commit to building ourselves with care, clarity, and courage, we need only build once.

WHAT'S IN THIS BOOK

In a world full of noise, distractions, and relentless pressure to perform, true success is no longer just about skills—it's about mastering the inner game. This transformative book is a practical and profound guide to personal and professional excellence, crafted from years of deep study, real-world application, and the wisdom of great minds across time.

Drawing from the fields of leadership, time management, stress mastery, communication, relationship building, project management, and the evolving world of network marketing, this book distils complex life skills into simple, actionable insights. Whether you're an entrepreneur, a leader, a student, or someone striving for personal growth, this book meets you where you are—and helps elevate you to where you truly belong.

Each chapter is a deep dive into timeless principles backed by modern psychology, personal reflections, and stories of achievers from diverse walks of life. From building strong habits and managing your time with intention, to leading with authenticity, handling pressure with calm, and nurturing powerful human connections—this book offers a roadmap to build not just success, but a meaningful life.

What sets this book apart is its holistic view—success isn't fragmented; it's integrated. You'll discover how leadership is built on self-awareness, how managing time is really about managing energy, how stress can be transformed into strength, and how network **marketing is not just a business, but a mirror of your inner growth.**

ACKNOWLEDGEMENTS

Writing this book has been a journey of growth, reflection, and purpose—and I could not have walked this path alone.

First and foremost, I bow my head in deep gratitude to my parents, whose values, sacrifices, and blessings have laid the foundation of my life. Your love is my anchor and your faith, my fuel.

To my loving wife, your unwavering support, silent strength, and constant encouragement gave me the space and courage to create. This book carries your fingerprints in every chapter.

To my dearest friends, thank you for standing by me, lifting my spirits, and believing in my dreams. Your presence is a reminder that I'm never walking alone.

A heartfelt thank you to Yogesh Srivastava, Anas, and Vikas Raheja—your friendship and belief in me have been instrumental in this journey.

To my mentor and guide, Mr. Surender Siddhanti, your wisdom, discipline, and spiritual insight have deeply influenced my thought process and values. You have shown me the power of clarity and direction.

To my leader and source of inspiration, Mr. Anil Blaggan, your leadership, vision, and faith in me have shaped my growth. Your encouragement gave me the confidence to dream bigger.

And finally, to all the thinkers, leaders, authors, and human beings whose lives I have learned from—whether through books, conversations, or observations—this work is the result of standing on the shoulders of giants. This book is not just mine—it belongs to all of you.

PREFACE

For many years, I've been a part of the dynamic world of network marketing, and along this journey, I've had the privilege of training individuals across India on essential skills such as communication, leadership, and business ethics. These teachings, which I have shared with countless people, have allowed me to witness firsthand the power of transformation that comes from the right mindset and skill set. Yet, as I look back, I have often wondered whether I was truly "enough" to guide others.

I didn't walk the traditional path as my education didn't come from a regular college. Instead, my learning came from within. Through self-study, I immersed myself in books, courses, and personal development resources. I have read extensively, gathering wisdom from the sages of all ages, absorbing timeless teachings, and reflecting on my own experiences. This book is the result of that journey—a culmination of the knowledge I have acquired and the lessons I have learned along the way.

While the wisdom and insights shared here are vast, they are only as valuable as the actions we take. Knowledge is powerful, but it truly comes to life when it's put into practice. This is why I encourage you, dear reader, to not just read but to apply the lessons contained in these pages. It is through practical action that real change occurs—whether in business, leadership, or personal growth.

As you embark on your own journey with the tools and insights I've shared, I invite you to reflect on the wisdom that resonates most with you and challenge yourself to take the necessary steps toward growth. We all have the potential to achieve greatness; it's not about the credentials we hold but the commitment to learning and the courage to take action.

This book is my gift to you—a collection of reflections, experiences, and timeless wisdom that has shaped my journey. I hope it inspires you to step into your own potential and take meaningful action toward your success. Here is to your journey of growth, both personal and professional. Let's get started.

Topic 1
LEADERSHIP & ENTREPRENEURSHIP

In today's ever-evolving world, leadership and entrepreneurship are no longer limited to titles or business cards—they are mindsets. Whether you're a network marketer building a team from scratch, a startup founder disrupting an industry, a team leader guiding professional, a corporate employee navigating change, or a traditional business owner striving for growth—the principles of leadership and entrepreneurship apply to you.

We live in a world where change is constant, where old systems are collapsing, and new opportunities are emerging every day. In this landscape, those who think like leaders and act like entrepreneurs thrive. They don't wait for permission. They take initiative. They embrace uncertainty. They find solutions where others see problems.

Leadership is no longer about authority—it's about influence. It's about taking ownership of outcomes, inspiring trust, and setting an example. It means thinking long-term, acting with integrity, and making decisions that elevate the team and the mission.

Entrepreneurship, too, is not just about starting a company—it's about being a creator. Entrepreneurs see gaps and build bridges. They innovate. They dare. They execute with speed. They learn from failure. Whether you're launching a product, growing a team, or turning ideas into income streams, an entrepreneurial spirit helps you stay agile, adaptable, and alive to possibility.

In the direct selling world, this mindset is essential. A network marketer is not merely a salesperson—they are a leader, a coach, a brand builder, and a visionary. The same applies to professionals in any field today—the ability to lead with clarity and act with courage is what separates the ordinary from the extraordinary.

"The following nuggets are powerful insights distilled from real-world leadership and entrepreneurial experience. Each one is designed to inspire action, spark reflection, and awaken the leader and creator within you."

1. Leadership, Vision, and the Power of Visualization

For many years, I was unknowingly trapped in a cycle of negative visualization. My mind would often drift into dark places—thoughts of dying unexpectedly, losing my loved ones, or suddenly being fired from my job. These weren't fleeting worries; they were recurring fears that took hold of my imagination and grew stronger the more I entertained them. I lived under a cloud of "what ifs" that drained my energy, dulled my confidence, and kept me playing small in life.

But something shifted when I started to understand the power of the mind. I realized that **visualization is a tool—neutral in nature—but incredibly powerful**. And like any tool, how we use it determines the result. I had been using it unconsciously to visualize loss, fear, and failure. What if, I thought, I could use the same mind to visualize strength, calm, and success?

It started small. Before an important meeting, I would take a few quiet moments to **visualize myself walking in confidently**, greeting everyone with poise, sharing my thoughts clearly, and being well-received. Before delivering a speech, I would close my eyes and picture the entire room—how I'd Walk up to the stage, how my voice would sound steady, how the audience would nod and smile. I began to **experience success internally before it happened externally**.

And slowly, things started to change. My voice grew stronger. My body language shifted. My confidence became real—not because I had faked it, but because I had already lived it in my mind.

As I deepened my understanding, I found that **great leaders all share one common trait—they carry a strong vision**. But more than that, they make that vision **visible**—to themselves and others. They **see it in their minds before others can see it in the world**. Whether it's building a company, transforming a team, or shaping a culture, leadership begins with the ability to imagine something better, something brighter, something bolder.

Visualization is not wishful thinking. It is **mental rehearsal for the life we are building**. Olympians use it. Entrepreneurs use it. Artists use it. And so must leaders.

Because leadership is not just about guiding others—it's about guiding your own mind first. When your inner world is clear, focused, and filled with empowering images of what's possible, your outer world begins to align with it.

So, ask yourself:

- What do you see when you close your eyes?
- Is it fear? Or is it the future you're excited to create?
- Are you rehearsing your doubts? Or are you practicing your dreams?

Your vision as a leader starts from within. And **visualization is the bridge between belief and achievement**. Use it wisely. Use it daily. Use it boldly.

2. Use the "Replace" Function for Negative Thoughts

Just like Microsoft Excel's "Replace" function swaps out specific words, **leaders can do the same with their thoughts**. It's said that we think about 90,000 thoughts a day, and 95% of them are the same as the day before. As leaders, it becomes essential to **think about our thoughts**—are they ***True, Helpful, Inspiring, Necessary, and Kind?*** This is not just a mental exercise but a leadership strategy. A leader's mindset determines the culture they cultivate—both within themselves and their teams.

The quality of your thoughts directly impacts your actions and, by extension, the results you achieve. For example, consider how you respond when a team member misses a deadline or fails to answer your call. As a leader, you have the choice to assume the worst—believing that they're being negligent or avoiding responsibility. Or you can **choose to believe** they might be overwhelmed, busy with another project, or facing challenges that you aren't aware of. **Leaders replace negative assumptions with constructive ones**. By consciously replacing negative thoughts with positive, action-oriented ones, we don't just improve our mindset; we **shape a healthier, more productive team culture**.

Nature abhors a vacuum—we can't simply eliminate negative thoughts without replacing them with better ones. In leadership, this is a key practice: *cultivate positive, empowering thoughts that align with your values, vision, and team goals*. This mental shift doesn't just enhance your leadership effectiveness; it inspires your team to think and act in the same way.

3. Be Impractical

I've encountered a few people in my life who always focus on why something shouldn't be done. They often justify this mindset by claiming they are just being practical. While I agree that practicality is important, being too practical can actually hold us back. People who are overly practical often avoid taking bold steps—and without boldness, it's hard to achieve anything extraordinary. Sometimes, a touch of impracticality is essential to do something great.

Take **Steve Jobs**, for example. He was known for his "reality distortion field," and many people around him thought he was impractical. Yet, he was one of the rare individuals who changed history. The same can be said for **Elon Musk**, the **Wright brothers,** and **Thomas Edison**. All of them were considered impractical at some point, but their willingness to dream beyond limitations led to real, lasting impact.

So, don't be afraid to be a little impractical—sometimes, that's exactly what it takes to create meaningful and practical change.

4. Don't Worship or Copy—Learn from Others

We all have role models, and it's natural to admire them. But sometimes, we get so influenced—or even infatuated—that we either start worshipping them or doubting ourselves for not being like them. The truth is, we can't be them. They are unique, just as we are.

When I used to write poetry, I had a role model whose work deeply inspired me. But I found myself constantly comparing my progress to his achievements, wondering if I could ever reach that level. Eventually, I realized—I'm not meant to be him. I'm meant to be the best version of myself.

Every successful person—whether it's **Steve Jobs, Sachin Tendulkar,** or anyone else—got there by following a focused, persistent path. I can't be another Steve or Sachin, but I can become a better Siddharth by staying committed to my own journey.

Trying to be like someone without putting in the time, effort, and dedication leads us nowhere. The road to success is never a straight line—it's full of curves, setbacks, and challenges. Every role model you admire has been through that. Learn from their journey, but walk your own path.

5. Goal-Getting Is Different from Goal-Setting

Setting goals is important—but achieving them is a different game altogether. We all know that goals should be SMART: Specific, Measurable, Attainable, Realistic, and Time-bound. They should be written down and have clear deadlines. But the real key to goal getting is consistent, focused action—daily action.

Big goals are achieved by meeting small, daily milestones. Your monthly, quarterly, and yearly results are built one day at a time. That's where the Here & Now principle comes in: focus on what needs to be done today—not tomorrow, not someday. Success is the result of small, repeated wins. Each task you complete today builds momentum and confidence for the journey ahead.

Don't wait for the perfect time or circumstances. Use every day as a building block. One powerful day, repeated with intention, becomes a powerful life.

Also, avoid vague goals—define specific outcomes. Here are a few examples

- ✗ I want to get fit → ✅ I will lose 10 kg in the next two months.
- ✗ I want to be rich → ✅ I will earn ₹1 lakh per month by May 2025.
- ✗ I want to improve my relationships → ✅ I will sit with Mr. A to understand his perspective and resolve our differences by next Saturday.

6. The Staircase Approach Is Better Than the Elevator Approach

In today's fast-paced world, many people seek the elevator—quick fixes or shortcuts to success. Quick commerce, for instance, has made it easier than ever to buy almost anything in minutes, and platforms like TikTok and YouTube Shorts emphasize fast consumption of content, where everything happens in seconds. We've become accustomed to immediate gratification: faster food delivery, rapid results in social media engagement, and instant communication. But real growth and success don't work like this.

The staircase approach—climbing one step at a time, with consistency and effort—remains a more effective and sustainable way to achieve meaningful goals. Success that's built step by step is solid and lasting. Consider how athletes train: while shortcuts like performance-enhancing drugs might promise quick results, the staircase approach—rigorous training, diet, and perseverance—leads to long-term success and true mastery.

Look at successful entrepreneurs like Elon Musk or Jeff Bezos. They didn't launch multi-billion-dollar companies overnight. They built their businesses by taking one calculated decision at a time, facing numerous setbacks and challenges along the way. Their success came not from rushing, but from taking steady, focused steps over the years.

Even in the world of personal finance, **the "get-rich-quick**" schemes often fail. True wealth is accumulated through disciplined saving, investing, and gradual growth, much like climbing a staircase. Compare that to the rise and fall of many cryptocurrencies "get-rich-quick" stories—where people hoped to make instant profits but faced massive losses because they skipped the foundational steps.

While the elevator may look attractive, it skips over the critical lessons and resilience built with each step. Quick fixes may provide temporary satisfaction, but the staircase approach offers lasting growth, deeper satisfaction, and meaningful achievement. Slow and steady really does win the race.

7. Change Your Locus of Control

For a long time, I blamed my family for not sending me to a regular college or for not being born into a wealthy family. I thought my circumstances were holding me back. But life taught me a crucial lesson: my happiness and success are not determined by external factors—they are in my hands. This realization led me to change my locus of control.

Locus of control refers to the belief about the extent to which we have control over the events that affect our lives. People with an internal locus of control believe they can influence their outcomes through their actions, decisions, and mindset. On the other hand, those with an external locus of control believe that external forces, like luck, other people, or circumstances, control their fate.

When I shifted my focus from blaming external factors to taking responsibility for my own life, everything changed. Despite not attending a regular college, I took up online courses, studied through distance education, and read countless books to educate myself. I realized that education doesn't come from a traditional classroom alone—it comes from the desire to learn and grow. One quote by Mark Twain really inspired me: "*I have never let my schooling interfere with my education.*"

The moment I embraced an internal locus of control; I stopped seeing limitations and began seeing opportunities. I understood that true happiness comes from within and that by focusing on what I can control—my effort, my mindset, and my choices—I can shape my future.

Remember, you are the creator of your destiny. When you take control of your own life, you stop being a passenger and start being the driver.

8. Change from Within

For a long time, I wanted love and affection from others, so I tried everything to earn it—dressing well, always being the "Yes Man," trying to please everyone, and even buying expensive gifts. Despite my efforts, I found myself being taken for granted and still not receiving the kind of love I was desperately seeking. That's when I realized something was wrong.

To truly change my circumstances, I had to start by changing myself. I had to dig deep and confront some hard truths. I understood that I couldn't make everyone happy, and more importantly, I had to focus on changing my core beliefs—about both myself and others. I needed to examine my habits, my personality, and my outlook on life. This shift was inspired by the **Inside-Out Approach by Stephen Covey,** *which emphasizes that change must begin within. It's about transforming your own mindset, behaviours, and attitudes before you can expect change in your external relationships.*

I realized that I had been hurting people, not intentionally, but through some bad habits I had failed to address. People weren't rejecting me—they were reacting to the way I was presenting myself, and I wasn't making the changes that mattered most. Once I made the decision to improve from within, everything shifted. I began to change the way I approached life and how I interacted with others. Slowly but surely, I started attracting the love and affection I had been craving. It wasn't because I was trying harder; it was because I had become someone worthy of that love.

Sometimes, we don't realize how much we need to change our internal world before we can expect positive change in our external world. Love and affection are attracted to authenticity, not efforts to please. The Inside-Out Approach taught me that true transformation begins from within, and that's when the world around us begins to change.

9. Replace Unhelpful Beliefs with Helpful Beliefs

Over time, I worked on shifting my unhelpful beliefs to positive, empowering ones. The beliefs we hold are formed by repeated thoughts and experiences, ***as Tony Robbins explains in Awaken the Giant Within.*** *These beliefs are not fixed; they can be replaced through conscious effort.*

Here's how I transformed my beliefs:

1. ***Old Belief***: *I must be approved by everyone, otherwise I am not a good person.*
2. ***New Belief***: *I am enough as I am; my worth does not depend on others' approval.*
3. ***Old Belief***: *Other people must treat me nicely and fairly, or else they are bad.*
4. ***New Belief***: *I can't control others, but I can choose how I respond with kindness and understanding.*
5. ***Old Belief***: *I must have an easy, happy life, or I cannot enjoy living at all.*
6. ***New Belief***: *Life is full of challenges, and overcoming them is where true growth and happiness lie.*
7. ***Old Belief***: *I must always be a high achiever, or else I am a worthless person.*
8. ***New Belief***: *Success is not defined by constant achievement; it's about progress and learning from each experience.*

10. The Marshmallow Test – A Lesson in Self-Control

Aristotle, one of history's greatest philosophers, emphasized the virtues of wisdom, courage, and temperance as the foundation of a well-lived life. Among these, temperance—the ability to practice self-control and delay immediate pleasures for long-term rewards—holds particular significance in today's world, where instant gratification is often seen as the ultimate goal.

A famous study that highlights the power of delayed gratification is the Marshmallow Test. In this experiment, children were offered a choice: they could either eat one marshmallow immediately or wait for a short period and receive two. Those who waited tended to have better life outcomes, excelling in areas like academic success and self-discipline. This test illustrates how our ability to delay gratification can lead to greater success and fulfilment.

For a long time, I was someone who always wanted everything right now. I sought immediate rewards, whether through quick fixes or temporary pleasures, believing they would bring me happiness. However, this never truly helped me. I found that chasing instant gratification often led to short-term satisfaction but left me feeling unfulfilled in the long run.

The real lesson came when I started to embrace delayed gratification. Instead of looking for quick results, I focused on long-term goals, like investing in self-improvement, education, and building meaningful relationships. Over time, I understood that true success and happiness come from practicing temperance—the ability to wait for the right moment, to resist immediate temptations, and to work towards lasting rewards.

By developing patience and self-control, I was able to make better choices, plan for the future, and experience a deeper, more meaningful sense of accomplishment. Delayed gratification doesn't mean deprivation; it means having the wisdom to prioritize what truly matters and the courage to follow through on long-term goals. It's a shift from instant pleasure to lasting fulfilment.

11. Master Patience and Clarity

Success requires patience, clarity, and perseverance. Like the ***bamboo tree****, which spends years growing roots before rapidly shooting up, true success often requires groundwork before visible results. Similarly, the* ***butterfly cocoon*** *teaches us that growth sometimes involves periods of discomfort before transformation.*

Clarity *is just as vital. An airplane needs clear skies to take off or land, just as you need clarity of purpose to move forward. When your goals are clear, obstacles become easier to navigate. With a focused vision, distractions fade, and your path becomes more direct.*

Gaining clarity of vision requires patience, reflection, and trust in the process. When I was uncertain whether to pursue an ***LLB, MA in Philosophy****, or* ***MA in Psychology****, I struggled with decision fatigue, but by reflecting on my core values and embracing uncertainty, the path gradually became clearer. I focused on small steps and took the time to quiet the distractions in my mind, trusting that clarity would emerge. Seeking advice was helpful, but ultimately, the decision needed to come from within. Clarity takes time—like the bamboo tree, which roots itself before growing tall—and as I gave myself the space to explore and reflect, I gained the confidence to choose a path aligned with my true desires.*

12. Develop Expertise in One Area

Early in my career, I was like a butterfly, fluttering from one interest to another, eager to explore everything—whether it was law, philosophy, psychology, or various business concepts. I thought versatility would give me the edge, believing that if I could master everything, I'd be unstoppable. However, this approach left me scattered and unfocused. I wanted to do it all, but I wasn't truly excelling in anything.

It was only when I made a conscious decision to focus on ***training and development*** *that things started to shift. I realized that true success lies in developing expertise in a single area. Just like* ***Mark Manson's idea***—*"Gold is buried in the depth"—I understood that to unearth true mastery, I needed to dive deep into one field rather than spreading myself too thin.* ***Napoleon Hill, in Think and Grow Rich, emphasized the difference between generalists and specialists.*** *Generalists might have broad knowledge, but it's the specialists who stand out and become irreplaceable in their fields.*

I decided to commit fully to becoming an expert in ***training and development****, honing my skills in coaching, leadership training, and team development. With deep focus, I was able to create impactful training programs, mentor others, and continuously refine my craft. This deep commitment not only set me apart in my field but also gave me a sense of purpose and fulfilment. By specializing, I became more valuable, and the results spoke for themselves.*

13. Character Development vs. Personality Development

While personality can help you make a great first impression, it's character that sustains long-term success. As Stephen Covey emphasizes in the 7 Habits of Highly Effective People, character development is built on core values such as integrity, resilience, and humility. It's about the internal qualities that shape how you respond to challenges, make decisions, and maintain your values under pressure. Personality development, on the other hand, focuses on outward traits and behaviours that can influence how others perceive you.

In the short term, personality might win you admiration or success, but without solid character, those gains will be fleeting. As John C. Maxwell discusses in the 21 Irrefutable Laws of Leadership, true, lasting success stems from internal strength—the ability to stay true to your values, no matter the external circumstances.

For example, someone who focuses solely on charm may win others over, but if their actions don't align with honesty or responsibility, their success won't last. On the other hand, someone with a strong character—driven by values like hard work, kindness, and reliability—may not always be the centre of attention, but they will gain respect, trust, and long-term success. As Jim Collins points out in Good to Great, leadership is built on deep personal integrity, and companies (and individuals) that prioritize character will outlast those driven by short-term gain.

To develop character, focus on:

- ***Integrity**: Stick to your principles, even when it's hard, as Mahatma Gandhi said, "You must be the change you wish to see in the world."*
- ***Resilience**: Bounce back from failures with courage and optimism, as Nelson Mandela famously demonstrated in his life after imprisonment.*

- ***Humility***: *Recognize your limitations and stay grounded, a quality that Abraham Lincoln was known for throughout his leadership.*
- ***Empathy***: *Understand and support others, building deeper connections. Brené Brown speaks of the power of empathy in building meaningful relationships in her research.*
- ***Accountability***: *Own your actions and their impact, as John C. Maxwell highlights the importance of responsibility in leadership.*

14. Dream Big: Unlocking the Power of Imagination

To achieve greatness, it all starts with dreaming big. Your dreams, fueled by imagination, set the direction for your future. Ask yourself these six simple yet powerful questions:

a. *What do I want to be?*

b. *What do I want to do?*

c. *What do I want to give?*

d. *What do I want to have?*

e. *How do I want to spend my time?*

f. *With whom do I want to spend my time?*

These questions are the foundation of building a vision that aligns with your true desires. As George Bernard Shaw famously said, "Some people see things as they are and say, 'Why?' I dream things that never were and say, 'Why not?'"

Before achieving anything, you must first see it in your mind. As Alex Morrison wisely put it, "You must first see a thing in your mind, before you can do it." Your imagination shapes your reality, as Albert Einstein emphasized, "Imagination is more important than knowledge." When you control the pictures in your mind, you control your path to success, as Jeff Keller reminds us, "You have control over the pictures that control your mind."

Imagination allows you to see opportunities others may miss. Jonathan Swift said it best: "Vision is the art of seeing things, invisible to others." If you can dream it, you can do it, as Walt Disney famously proclaimed.

Dream big, think beyond what's possible, and let your imagination guide you to what others may deem impossible. The path to success begins in the mind. If you can envision it, you can achieve it.

15. Take Responsibility and Be Accountable

Success isn't determined by how easily you can achieve your goals, but by your ability to persist in the face of challenges. As Napoleon Hill said, "Effort fully releases its reward, when a person refuses to quit." The road to success is often difficult, but perseverance is the key that unlocks victory. Winston Churchill's famous words, "Never, Never, never give up," remind us that persistence is the most important trait on the path to success.

Sir Thomas Buxton encapsulated this truth perfectly when he said, "With ordinary talent and extraordinary perseverance, all things are attainable." While talent may open doors, it is perseverance that keeps us moving forward when the going gets tough. Ted Engstrom further emphasizes that "The rewards for those who persevere far exceed the pain that must precede the victory." The struggles you face today are the stepping stones to tomorrow's success.

Mistakes are not failures but valuable lessons. Benjamin Franklin wisely said, "Things which hurt, instruct." Each setback or mistake is an opportunity to learn, grow, and adjust your approach. Seneca also reminds us that "It is a rough road, that leads to the heights of greatness." The greatest achievements often come from enduring the most difficult paths.

Lastly, as Elbert Hubbard pointed out, "The greatest mistake one can make is to be afraid of making one." Mistakes are inevitable, but they should never deter you. Embrace them, learn from them, and keep moving forward. Never give up. The rewards of perseverance and learning from mistakes are far greater than the pain of the journey.

16. Live with Purpose and Service to Others

True leadership is not about power or personal gain; it's about serving others. Swami Vivekananda's quote, "They alone live, who live for others," captures this essence perfectly. Effective leaders focus on empowering those around them, not seeking recognition or control. When leaders prioritize the collective good, they foster a culture of collaboration, trust, and growth.

Examples of serving others in leadership include:

- A manager who takes time to mentor employees, helping them grow professionally and personally.
- A community leader organizing initiatives that provide resources and support to those in need.
- A business owner who prioritizes employee well-being and development over short-term profits.

This approach leads to lasting influence, as those empowered by such leadership often go on to inspire others. The impact extends far beyond the leader, creating a ripple effect of positive change. Ultimately, the most successful leaders are those who serve others, creating a legacy that strengthens individuals and communities alike.

17. Purpose Over Pay check: Leading with Meaning

Leadership in the modern workplace has undergone a profound transformation.

Today's employees, especially millennials and Gen Z, aren't just clocking in hours for a pay check—they are seeking meaning, connection, and alignment with a higher purpose. This shift requires leaders to evolve. It's no longer enough to offer competitive salaries or perks; people want to feel that their work matters and contributes to something bigger than themselves.

A wise leader recognizes this and communicates the organization's purpose with clarity and passion. During interviews or onboarding, don't just talk about the job—talk about the mission.

Ask potential team members if they feel emotionally connected to the company's vision. Do they believe in the impact you're trying to create? Are they excited to be part of the journey?

Leadership today is about helping people see that they are not just employees, but co-creators of a meaningful legacy.

When people align with a purpose, they bring their heart to work—and those changes everything.

18. The Power of Clear Expectations

The most underrated yet powerful leadership practices is setting clear, consistent expectations. Teams don't stumble because they lack talent—they stumble when they lack clarity. Great leaders articulate exactly what success looks like, and more importantly, why it matters.

For example, a team leader might clearly explain that the goal is to increase customer satisfaction by 10% over the next quarter, and break this down into smaller, achievable steps like improving response times or offering personalized services. Expectations should be specific, tied to outcomes, and repeated often.

Don't assume people "get it" after one discussion—revisit expectations at each milestone. Use simple language. Break down complex goals into smaller, understandable chunks.

Link each goal to the broader customer or business impact so team members understand the "why" behind the "what."

When expectations are ambiguous, confusion spreads; when they're crystal clear, confidence and ownership grow. A team that knows what's expected—and why—becomes more focused, collaborative, and empowered

19. Developing People Through Targeted Training

Training your team—it's a core responsibility of leadership.

True leaders don't just assign tasks; they build capabilities. Today, with access to courses, books, podcasts, and expert videos, the possibilities for development are endless.

But rather than overwhelming the team with information, smart leaders curate learning. Use microlearning techniques—quick snippet trainings or 10-minute skill boosts—to make development consistent and digestible. Show your team what excellence looks like.

Demonstrate real examples, not just theories. Decide what you want your team to know, and what you want them to do—and give them the context behind it.

Training should be about empowerment, not instruction. Let your team see that learning is part of your culture, not just a checkbox on a form. Invest in your people's growth, and they will invest in your vision.

20. Make Meetings a Leadership Masterclass

Meetings are often seen as a time-waster—but under effective leadership, they become energizing and purposeful.

The difference lies in preparation and structure.

Share agendas in advance so everyone arrives ready to contribute. Begin meetings not with dry numbers, but with stories of customer impact or a team win. Get people engaged emotionally before moving to data. Encourage active participation—every voice matters.

Make sure each meeting ends with clarity: decisions made, action items assigned, and timelines agreed upon. Don't let meetings become monologues or status dumps. Instead, make them decision-making platforms where energy rises, alignment sharpens, and people leave with a renewed sense of direction. Meetings done right reflect a team's culture and a leader's intent.

21. Culture is Created in Micro-Moments

Culture is not a strategy slide—it's how your team behaves when no one is watching. It's the subtle moments of laughter, learning, support, and shared reflection. Leadership plays a crucial role in shaping this daily culture.

Schedule an hour at the beginning of the year for a "Culture Brainstorm" session—invite the team, grab some post it notes, and create space for personal sharing and professional dreaming.

Ask each person to share one personal and one professional goal, and then as a group, brainstorm how the team can support each other in achieving them. This creates a bond that transcends tasks. Celebrate team wins—even small ones. Take five minutes in each meeting to recognize someone's contribution or share a story of a challenge overcome.

Culture is not about posters; it's about practices. Great leaders lead culture by being intentional in the little things, every day.

22. Building a Culture of Growth and Mobility

A thriving team is a learning team. As a leader, your responsibility is to cultivate a culture where development is not occasional but continuous. Start by identifying skill gaps through observation, peer feedback, or client suggestions.

Break down job roles into specific skill sets and compare them to top performers or industry benchmarks. Encourage cross-functional training, job shadowing, and knowledge-sharing sessions across departments. Make learning part of the workflow, not something extra. Recommend relevant podcasts, articles, or webinars.

Join industry associations and invite your team to do the same. Promote internal mobility by helping team members see opportunities for advancement or lateral moves. When people feel they are growing and learning, their loyalty increases. A leader who creates an environment where curiosity is celebrated and development is expected builds a team that can adapt, evolve, and lead from the front.

23. Reframe Failure as a Learning Strategy

Failure is not the enemy of success—fear of failure is. In high-performance teams, leaders normalize the idea that mistakes are inevitable and even valuable.

Instead of assigning blame, they ask, "What did we learn from this?"

By treating failure as data, leaders create psychological safety—a space where innovation can thrive. Celebrate the lessons, not just the wins.

Publicly appreciate the efforts behind a bold attempt, even if the result wasn't ideal. This sends a message: it's okay to try, even if you fall short. When your team knows they won't be punished for honest mistakes, they stop playing small. They think creatively, speak up bravely, and take ownership fully.

Failure is not a setback when it becomes a stepping stone—and that transformation begins with leadership.

24. Build Relationships First, Then Results

Strong leaders understand that results are built on relationships.

Before people commit to a task, they need to feel connected to the team and the leader.

Make time for informal, human conversations. Schedule coffee chats or team lunches.

Share your story—not just your achievements, but also your struggles, lessons, and values.

When leaders show vulnerability, they invite authenticity.

Be curious about your team members—ask about their interests, passions, and goals.

Listen actively—not just hearing, but understanding. Use eye contact, ask thoughtful questions, and follow up meaningfully. Gratitude also strengthens bonds—a simple thank-you note or a moment of appreciation in a meeting can lift spirits for days.

Relationships are the invisible glue that holds high-performing teams together. When people feel known and appreciated, they give their best.

25. Stay Interviews: A Leader's Secret Weapon for Retention

Waiting for an exit interview to understand why someone left is reactive.

Great leaders are proactive—they conduct "stay interviews" to understand what's working, what's frustrating, and how to keep good people engaged.

A stay interview is a structured conversation where the manager listens deeply and responds intentionally. Ask questions like:

What do you look forward to when coming to work?

What would make your job more enjoyable?

What talents are we not using enough?

These insights reveal small changes that can make a big difference. Stay interviews build trust, demonstrate care, and help leaders act before it's too late. They show that retention is not a strategy—it's a relationship.

26. Leadership Starts with Self-Belief

To lead others, you first must believe in yourself. I struggled with self-doubt for many years, but I realized that unless I trusted my own abilities, I couldn't expect others to trust me.

Leadership begins from within. As a leader, your self-belief sets the tone for your entire journey. It's your internal belief that drives you to take risks, face challenges, and motivate those around you. When you trust yourself, others will follow your lead with the same confidence.

History offers countless examples of this truth—one of the most powerful being the story of **Mahatma Gandhi**. Despite being soft-spoken, modest, and often underestimated, Gandhi's unwavering belief in nonviolence and justice allowed him to lead an entire nation toward independence. His self-confidence in his ideals remained firm even when he faced opposition, imprisonment, and doubt from others. That inner conviction inspired millions to follow him and adopt his methods of peaceful resistance.

Like Gandhi, when you lead from a place of inner certainty, your belief becomes contagious—it strengthens the vision, unites people, and turns challenges into opportunities

27. The Power of Vision

Leaders don't just manage—they create a vision of a better future. Visionary leadership is about seeing what others can't and motivating your team to work toward that vision. I learned the hard way that without a clear vision, leadership becomes reactive rather than proactive.

When you have a purpose-driven vision, you can guide your team through challenges with clarity and confidence. Leadership requires a long-term perspective, not just focusing on immediate results.

Like an eagle that flies high and sees its target from miles away, visionary leaders rise above the noise and stay focused on the bigger picture. That sharp, long-range vision keeps the team aligned, motivated, and moving forward—no matter the obstacles.

28. Effective Communication

The ability to communicate effectively is one of the cornerstones of leadership. I used to think that leadership was all about making decisions, but I realized that how you communicate your vision, goals, and decisions is what really matters. Whether through one-on-one conversations, team meetings, or public speaking, clear and open communication helps build trust and understanding.

A leader who communicates well ensures their message is received, understood, and acted upon. I once conducted a training session where I explained a new process in great detail—only to discover later that half the team thought it was optional and the other half thought it was a game! One even asked, "So, do we win something if we finish first?" That's when I realized: if communication isn't clear, training turns into comedy. Effective communication isn't just about speaking—it's about ensuring the message actually lands where it's supposed to.

29. Lead by Example

As a leader, your actions speak louder than words. I once had a mentor who always told me,

"People will do what you do, not what you say."

This has stuck with me throughout my leadership journey.

Leading by example means demonstrating the values and behaviours you expect from your team.

When you embody the qualities, you want to see in others—such as hard work, integrity, and responsibility—your team will follow suit. Your leadership will inspire them to rise to the occasion.

30. Empower Others to Lead

True leadership is about developing other leaders.

In my early years, I focused so much on proving myself that I overlooked the potential in others. As I matured in my leadership role, I realized that my job was not only to lead but to empower others to lead as well.

By giving people, the tools, resources, and autonomy to lead themselves, you create a ripple effect that strengthens the entire team.

Leadership is about creating more leaders, not followers.

31. Build Trust Through Integrity

Without trust, leadership crumbles.

I've learned that leadership is rooted in integrity.

When you consistently act in ways that align with your values and principles, you build trust with your team.

This trust becomes the foundation for effective collaboration, innovation, and long-term success.

As a leader, it's essential to be honest, transparent, and accountable, even when it's difficult. Trust isn't given—it's earned through consistent, ethical Behaviour.

32. The Importance of Emotional Intelligence

Leadership is not just about strategy and execution; it's about understanding and managing emotions.

Emotional intelligence (EI) has been one of the most critical factors in my leadership development.

A leader who understands their own emotions and those of others can manage relationships more effectively, resolve conflicts, and foster a positive work environment. Developing EI requires self-awareness, empathy, and the ability to regulate emotions, all of which are key to building strong teams.

There was a time early in my leadership journey when I believed strategy and execution were the only things that mattered. I focused on goals, timelines, and KPIs, thinking those were the keys to success. But one day, during an important project, things didn't go as planned. A team member, usually reliable, missed a deadline, and I could feel the frustration building in the room. I was ready to step in with a firm "solution-oriented" approach, but then I paused.

Instead of reacting immediately, I took a moment to reflect on how I was feeling—frustrated, yes, but also anxious about how this could affect the project. I decided to approach my team member with understanding, asking what had caused the delay. It turned out, there were personal challenges that had impacted their performance.

By showing empathy and listening, we not only found a way forward but also built a stronger rapport. That experience taught me that emotional intelligence (EI) is what makes leaders truly effective. A leader who understands their own emotions and those of others can manage relationships better, resolve conflicts with empathy, and create a positive work environment. Since then, I've prioritized EI in my leadership development, realizing that self-awareness, empathy, and emotional regulation are key to building strong, successful teams.

33. Adaptability is Key to Leadership

The world is constantly changing, and so must leadership. One of the most valuable lessons I've learned is the importance of adaptability. Leaders who can pivot when faced with change, uncertainty, or adversity are the ones who thrive. Whether it's adapting to new technology, shifting market dynamics, or adjusting team strategies, flexibility is essential. Being rigid or set in your ways limits growth. True leaders embrace change and lead their teams through it with confidence and innovation.

In today's environment, we are navigating a **VUCA world**, which stands for **Volatility, Uncertainty, Complexity, and Ambiguity**. This term describes a rapidly changing world full of unpredictable challenges that require leaders to be agile and resilient. Here are four quick tips on how to adapt:

1. **Embrace Continuous Learning**: Stay curious and commit to constant learning. In a VUCA world, the more knowledge you have, the better prepared you'll be to deal with unexpected changes.
2. **Develop a Growth Mindset**: Emphasize adaptability and resilience. When faced with uncertainty, view challenges as opportunities for innovation and growth rather than setbacks.
3. **Foster Strong Communication**: In times of ambiguity, clear and transparent communication is key. Keep your team informed, encourage feedback, and ensure alignment to maintain morale and focus.
4. **Encourage Collaboration**: Acknowledge that no one person has all the answers in a VUCA environment. Foster teamwork and collaboration so that you can pool resources and expertise to tackle challenges effectively.

34. The Power of Listening

Leadership is not about talking all the time—it's about listening. I used to think that as a leader, I had to have all the answers, but I soon realized that listening is just as important as speaking. When you listen to your team, you gain valuable insights, build stronger relationships, and make more informed decisions. Active listening also makes your team feel valued and heard, which leads to higher morale and engagement.

A historical example of the power of listening comes from **Abraham Lincoln**. During the American Civil War, Lincoln faced a divided country and many difficult decisions. He was known for his ability to listen to everyone—his generals, advisors, and even his political opponents.

There's a story about Lincoln during a time of war when he listened carefully to his war secretary, Edwin Stanton, who had criticized him publicly. Rather than dismiss Stanton's frustrations or shut him down, Lincoln took the time to understand his concerns and communicated openly with him. This led to a strong working relationship, where Stanton's insight became invaluable to Lincoln's decision-making.

By listening, even to critics, Lincoln built trust and strengthened his leadership, ultimately guiding the nation through its darkest period. This shows how listening, rather than just talking, can help leaders make the best decisions for their teams and organizations.

35. Decisiveness: Making Tough Calls

In leadership, the ability to make decisions swiftly and confidently is crucial. When I first started leading, I hesitated in making decisions, afraid of making mistakes. However, I quickly learned that indecision can paralyze progress. As a leader, you need to assess situations, gather necessary information, and make decisions quickly. Even if the decision isn't perfect, moving forward is better than standing still. Being decisive builds confidence in your leadership.

Leadership often requires making decisions that are difficult and unpopular. I faced many tough calls during my leadership journey, from reallocating resources to letting go of underperforming team members. I learned that the ability to make tough choices, even when faced with emotional challenges, is an essential leadership trait. These decisions may not always be easy, but they are necessary for the long-term health of the organization. Leaders who can make hard decisions with confidence and integrity gain the respect of their team, even if they don't always agree with the outcome.

A great example of making tough calls comes from **Winston Churchill** during World War II. In 1940, as Britain faced the threat of Nazi Germany, Churchill had to make one of the most difficult decisions of his leadership—whether to negotiate peace with Hitler or continue fighting. Despite overwhelming pressure to surrender, Churchill chose to stand firm and lead Britain in defiance, rallying the nation with his famous speeches and commitment to victory.

His decisive stance not only kept Britain in the fight but ultimately played a critical role in the Allied victory. Churchill's ability to make tough decisions, even in the face of uncertainty, demonstrated the power of leadership through action. When you are decisive, your team trusts your judgment, even during the toughest

36. Lead with Empathy

Empathy is one of the most powerful leadership tools. I once led a team where the focus was only on outcomes, but I realized that understanding and addressing the needs of my team members led to better results. Leaders who show empathy can connect with their teams on a deeper level, foster trust, and create a supportive environment. By considering people's emotions, challenges, and aspirations, leaders can build more cohesive and motivated teams.

A great illustration of empathy comes from the ancient story of **the blindfolded men and the elephant**. In the story, a group of blind men each touches a different part of an elephant's body. One feels the tusk and says the elephant is like a spear. Another touches the trunk and believes it's like a snake. The one who feels the leg thinks the elephant is like a tree, while another, touching the tail, says it resembles a rope.

Each man was right in his own experience, but none of them could understand the full picture because they didn't consider the perspectives of the others. This story perfectly illustrates how empathy works in leadership: by understanding different viewpoints and experiences, you can form a more complete picture and make better decisions. As leaders, when we take the time to truly understand our team members' feelings and perspectives, we foster stronger connections and create a more unified team.

37. Delegate, Don't Micromanage

One of the biggest mistakes I made early in my leadership journey was trying to do everything myself. I quickly learned that leadership isn't about controlling every task, but about empowering others. Delegating allows your team to take ownership and develop their skills while freeing you up to focus on higher-level strategic decisions. Micromanagement undermines trust and stifles creativity. Effective delegation is a hallmark of great leadership.

I remember a time early in my career when I was leading a project and tried to micromanage every aspect. I would check on my team's work constantly, give detailed instructions, and take over tasks when I thought they weren't being done my way. I thought I was being efficient, but in reality, I was overwhelming myself and frustrating my team. They felt disempowered and started second-guessing their decisions, which led to a drop in morale and productivity.

Through this experience, I realized that micromanagement kills innovation and trust. Here are key points for effective delegation:

a. **Set Clear Expectations**: Clearly communicate the goal, deadlines, and parameters of the task. Make sure your team knows what success looks like.

b. **Trust Your Team**: Believe in their abilities. Let them take ownership and make decisions within the scope of their responsibilities.

c. **Provide Support, Not Control**: Be available for guidance, but avoid stepping in unless absolutely necessary. Trust that they'll find solutions on their own.

d. **Give Constructive Feedback**: Once the task is completed, provide feedback that focuses on growth and development, not just the outcome.

38. Resilience: Bouncing Back from Setbacks

Every leader faces setbacks—what matters is how you respond. I've had my fair share of challenges, from business losses to personal failures. However, resilience is what allowed me to bounce back stronger each time. As a leader, you need to model resilience for your team. Show them that setbacks are not permanent and that persistence will ultimately lead to success. A resilient leader doesn't give up, no matter how tough things get.

39. Stay Focused on the Big Picture

As a leader, it's easy to get bogged down in daily tasks and small details. However, staying focused on the big picture is essential for long-term success. I learned the hard way that losing sight of the bigger vision can lead to burnout and inefficiency. Great leaders keep their eye on the long-term goals, even when dealing with day-to-day challenges. This helps them make decisions that align with their vision and inspire their teams to do the same.

Steve Jobs at Apple

Steve Jobs is a prime example of a leader who maintained a clear vision despite challenges. When he returned to Apple in 1997, the company was struggling. Instead of getting bogged down in the day-to-day issues, Jobs focused on transforming Apple into a company that created groundbreaking products. He famously cut down the company's product line, emphasizing simplicity and design excellence, ultimately leading to the iPod, iPhone, and iPad—products that revolutionized technology and led to Apple's massive success.

40. Foster Collaboration, Not Competition

Leadership isn't about pitting people against each other. I've seen teams struggle when there's a competitive atmosphere that pits individuals against one another. True leaders foster a culture of collaboration, where team members work together towards common goals. Collaboration creates synergy, innovation, and trust. A leader who values teamwork over individual performance can create a more effective, harmonious work environment.

The COVID-19 Vaccine Development

During the COVID-19 pandemic, pharmaceutical companies and research organizations worldwide collaborated to develop vaccines at an unprecedented speed. Rather than competing, entities like Pfizer, Moderna, and AstraZeneca worked alongside governments, research institutions, and even their competitors to share data, knowledge, and resources. This collaboration, driven by the shared goal of ending the pandemic, led to the rapid development of effective vaccines that have saved millions of lives. This example highlights how working together, rather than against each other, can lead to remarkable breakthroughs.

These examples show that when teams collaborate, sharing knowledge and resources for a common purpose, they can accomplish extraordinary results. Leadership that promotes teamwork and mutual support ultimately fosters a more productive and innovative environment.

41. Celebrate Successes, Big and Small

Leaders who fail to acknowledge and celebrate their team's achievements risk losing morale and motivation. I used to focus solely on the areas that needed improvement, but I now realize the importance of celebrating successes. Recognizing even small wins boosts morale, reinforces positive behaviours, and motivates the team to keep striving. Great leaders make sure to give credit where credit is due.

Celebrating Small Wins in the Office

I once led a team working on a long-term project with tight deadlines. While the end goal was a huge milestone, I made sure to celebrate smaller achievements along the way—like completing a major phase of the project or meeting an important deadline. We'd have a short team lunch, send out a thank-you email, or give a shout-out during team meetings. These small celebrations kept the team energized and reminded everyone that progress, no matter how small, was valued.

Celebrating a Big Win with a Team Outing

For a major success, such as completing a year-long project or hitting a significant sales target, we organized a team outing or a dinner at a nice restaurant. This not only showed appreciation for the hard work but also helped strengthen team bonds. In one instance, after a successful Training Launch, we held a "launch party" where everyone shared their experiences and successes. It helped the team unwind, reflect on the hard work, and recharged them for the next challenge.

Public Recognition in Meetings

Another way to celebrate both big and small successes is through public recognition. During weekly team meetings, I'd make it a point to highlight individual or team achievements. Whether it was someone staying late to meet a deadline or a department hitting its target, acknowledging their efforts in front of peers created a culture of appreciation. It made the team feel valued, and others were motivated to contribute as well.

Celebrating both big and small successes builds a culture of appreciation and keeps motivation high, reinforcing the notion that every contribution counts toward the overall success of the team.

42. Inspire Others to Dream Big

As a leader, your role is not only to achieve your own goals but to inspire others to pursue theirs. I've found that leadership is about fostering an environment where people feel empowered to dream big. When you believe in your team's potential, you motivate them to aim higher and take bold actions. Inspiring others to believe in their own capabilities creates a culture of achievement and growth.

Encouraging a Team Member to Lead a New Initiative

One time, I had a team member who was initially hesitant about taking on a leadership role for an upcoming project. Instead of focusing solely on the challenges, I encouraged them to see it as an opportunity to create something new. I shared a story of a company that had transformed its business model by taking a bold step. I made sure to express my confidence in their abilities, and I gave them the autonomy to define the vision for the initiative. By showing trust and encouraging them to think beyond their comfort zone, they stepped up, and the project became a resounding success. The team saw this example of thinking big and became inspired to pursue their own ambitious goals.

43. Prioritize Self-Care and Well-Being

A leader who neglects their own well-being risks burning out. I've had times when I was so focused on work that I ignored my physical and mental health, but I soon learned that true leadership requires balance. When you take care of yourself, you're better equipped to lead others effectively. Leadership is not just about what you do for your team—it's about being a role model for self-care and showing that personal well-being is just as important as professional success.

Here are some ways on how a leader can do self-care and well-being

- Prioritize Regular Exercise: Physical health is the foundation for mental clarity and energy.
- Practice Mindfulness: Take time to meditate or reflect to manage stress and maintain emotional balance.
- Set Boundaries: Ensure work doesn't overwhelm personal time by creating clear boundaries.
- Take Breaks: Short breaks throughout the day can refresh your mind and boost productivity.
- Sleep Well: Rest is crucial for both physical health and decision-making clarity.
- Nurture Relationships: Spend quality time with family and friends to recharge emotionally.
- Seek Support: Don't hesitate to talk to a mentor or coach for guidance and perspective.

44. Be Humble and Open to Feedback

Even the best leaders are always learning. I've found that the most effective leaders are those who are open to feedback, no matter their level of experience or success. Humility is a powerful trait in leadership. When you are willing to listen to others, acknowledge your mistakes, and make adjustments, you set an example for continuous improvement. A leader who is open to feedback fosters a culture of openness and growth.

- **Acknowledge Your Limitations:** Recognize that no one knows everything and there's always room to grow.
- **Listen Actively:** Give your full attention when receiving feedback, without interrupting or becoming defensive.
- **Value Constructive Criticism:** See feedback as an opportunity to improve, not as a personal attack.
- **Express Gratitude:** Thank others for their input, regardless of how difficult it may be to hear.
- **Stay Curious:** Approach feedback with an open mind, seeking to understand different perspectives.
- **Admit Mistakes:** Own up to errors and learn from them, showing vulnerability and growth.
- **Encourage Regular Feedback:** Create a culture where feedback is welcomed and appreciated from all levels.

45. Be Strategic with Your Time

As a leader, time is one of your most valuable resources. I've learned that how I use my time is a direct reflection of my priorities. Effective leaders are strategic with their time, focusing on tasks that drive the most significant results. Time management is a skill every leader must master. Prioritizing tasks, delegating effectively, and maintaining a balance between short-term goals and long-term vision are essential for sustainable success.

- ∢ **Prioritize High-Impact Tasks:** Focus on activities that align with long-term goals and business outcomes.
- ∢ **Delegate Effectively:** Empower others by assigning tasks that allow you to concentrate on leadership priorities.
- ∢ **Set Clear Boundaries:** Protect your time by saying no to distractions that don't contribute to your objectives.
- ∢ **Plan Ahead:** Use tools like calendars and to-do lists to map out time for key tasks and strategic thinking.
- ∢ **Batch Similar Tasks:** Group related tasks together to maximize efficiency and reduce cognitive overload.
- ∢ **Review and Adjust Regularly:** Continuously evaluate how your time is spent and adjust based on what's driving the most value.

46. Maintain Consistency in Your Leadership Style

Consistency in leadership builds trust and credibility. I realized that when I changed my leadership style frequently, it confused my team and reduced their confidence in my decisions. A consistent approach helps team members understand what to expect from you, which makes it easier to follow your lead. While flexibility is important, a leader's core values and approach should remain steady to maintain trust and stability.

- **Define Core Values:** Stick to your core principles to guide your decisions and actions consistently.
- **Communicate Clearly:** Regularly communicate your vision, expectations, and goals to ensure alignment with your team.
- **Be Predictable in Behaviour:** Act with reliability by maintaining a steady demeanor and approach, even in challenging situations.
- **Lead by Example:** Model the behaviours and attitudes you want your team to adopt, setting a consistent example.
- **Evaluate and Reflect:** Regularly assess your leadership style and make intentional adjustments while staying true to your core values.

47. Cultivate a Strong Sense of Purpose

A strong sense of purpose is the foundation of effective leadership.

I learned that without a clear, compelling purpose, it's easy to lose direction and become overwhelmed by challenges. Leaders who are driven by purpose inspire others to contribute to something bigger than themselves.

When you know why you're leading and what you're striving for, you make decisions with clarity, and your team will rally behind that vision.

Purpose-driven leadership fuels motivation and resilience, helping both the leader and the team persist through tough times.

48. The Importance of Building a Supportive Team

Leadership is not about being the lone star; it's about creating a team that complements each other's strengths.

I realized that a leader's success is directly tied to the effectiveness of their team.

Investing in building strong relationships and developing a supportive culture within your team can lead to greater collaboration, innovation, and success.

A supportive team doesn't just help you achieve goals—it helps you push boundaries and reach new heights. As a leader, your role is to cultivate an environment where every team member feels valued and empowered.

The following actions would lead to a more collaborative and supportive environment in any team-

- **Foster Open Communication:** Encourage team members to share ideas, concerns, and feedback openly without fear of judgment.
- **Recognize Contributions:** Regularly acknowledge and celebrate individual and team achievements to boost morale.
- **Provide Growth Opportunities:** Offer training and development to help team members enhance their skills and confidence.
- **Encourage Collaboration:** Promote a culture where team members help and support one another to achieve common goals.

49. Offering constructive feedback

Giving feedback is an essential leadership skill that helps individuals grow and improve. It's important to be specific, focusing on clear examples of Behaviour rather than personal traits. Feedback should be constructive, offering both praise for strengths and suggestions for improvement. Timing is key—providing feedback soon after the event ensures its relevance and impact. When delivered in a positive, solution-oriented manner, feedback becomes a tool for growth and strengthens trust between leaders and team members. Encourage open dialogue to ensure understanding and promote a culture of continuous improvement. A Few suggestions on offering feedback-

Be Specific: Focus on clear examples and actionable behaviours rather than general comments.

Stay Positive: Frame feedback constructively, highlighting strengths alongside areas for improvement.

Be Timely: Offer feedback as soon as possible after the event to ensure it's relevant and fresh.

Focus on Solutions: Provide suggestions for improvement rather than just pointing out mistakes.

Encourage Dialogue: Allow the recipient to ask questions and discuss the feedback to ensure understanding.

50. Lead with a Servant's Heart

Leadership is not about asserting power but about serving others. I found that when I shifted my focus from "What can I get from this?" to "How can I help others succeed?"

it changed the dynamics of my leadership.

Servant leadership focuses on the well-being and growth of your team, ensuring they have the resources and support needed to thrive.

When your team feels genuinely cared for and supported, their loyalty and motivation to perform at their best grow exponentially.

True leadership is about lifting others up, not elevating oneself.

51. Drive Change with Confidence

Change is inevitable, and successful leaders know how to navigate it effectively. I used to resist change, thinking that stability was key to success. Over time, I learned that change presents opportunities for growth and innovation. A leader who drives change with confidence inspires others to embrace it. Leading through change involves clear communication, transparency, and a calm demeanor that reassures the team. When you lead with confidence through transitions, your team will trust the process and remain focused on the end goals. This is how we can drive change-

- **Communicate a Clear Vision:** Articulate the reasons for change and how it aligns with the team's long-term goals.
- **Involve the Team Early:** Engage team members early in the process to gather input and create buy-in.
- **Lead by Example:** Be the first to embrace change, demonstrating commitment and enthusiasm.
- **Foster a Growth Mindset:** Encourage team members to view change as an opportunity for growth, not a threat.
- **Provide the Necessary Resources:** Ensure your team has the tools, training, and support they need to succeed with the change.
- **Set Milestones:** Break down the change process into manageable steps to create a sense of progress and achievement.
- **Address Resistance Openly:** Listen to concerns and address resistance with empathy and transparency.
- **Celebrate Small Wins:** Acknowledge and celebrate progress along the way to keep morale high.
- **Empower Leaders Within the Team:** Identify champions of change within the team who can help spread the vision and motivate others.
- **Be Patient and Persistent:** Understand that change takes time, and maintain focus and persistence to drive long-term transformation.

52. Leverage Diversity for Strength

Diversity isn't just a buzzword—it's a strategic advantage. I realized that a diverse team brings different perspectives, skills, and ideas to the table. Embracing diversity in all its forms—whether it's cultural, gender, or cognitive diversity—can drive innovation and problem-solving.

As a leader, I learned to value the unique contributions of each team member and foster an inclusive environment where diverse viewpoints are heard and respected.

By leveraging diversity, leaders create a stronger, more adaptive team that can tackle challenges from multiple angles.

53. Prioritize Results Over Activity

Not all actions lead to progress. In my leadership journey, I learned that it's easy to get caught up in being busy, but true leadership is about being effective, not just active. Leaders must focus on results, not on checking off tasks or looking busy. Effective leaders measure their success by the impact they create and the progress they make toward their goals. To drive meaningful results, it's essential to prioritize high-impact tasks that directly contribute to the organization's vision and objectives, rather than getting lost in the daily grind. This is what we can do as a leader to ensure productivity in place of activity in our team-

- **Focus on Output, Not Hours:** Prioritize tasks that contribute to tangible outcomes rather than spending time on busywork.
- **Measure Impact, Not Effort:** Shift the focus from how much work is done to how much progress is made towards goals.
- **Avoid Multitasking:** Concentrate on completing one task at a time for better results instead of jumping between multiple activities.
- **Evaluate Task Relevance:** Regularly assess if activities align with your goals and eliminate tasks that don't directly contribute to meaningful results.

54. Nothing in Leadership Is to Be Feared; It Is Only to Be Understood

"Nothing in leadership is to be feared; it is only to be understood." – This powerful quote by **John F. Kennedy** reminds us that fear is often a product of the unknown.

As leaders, it's natural to feel apprehensive when facing unfamiliar situations or difficult decisions. However, fear diminishes when we pause, understand the cause, and confront it head-on. For instance,

Elon Musk faced significant fears when he invested in SpaceX and Tesla, companies that many thought were bound to fail. Instead of letting fear of failure consume him, he embraced the challenges, learned from his mistakes, and eventually turned these companies into industry leaders.

In leadership, we can follow this approach by not allowing fear to drive us. Instead, take time to analyse situations, gather knowledge, and face uncertainties with a clear, strategic mindset. This transforms fear into an opportunity for growth, making us better equipped to lead our teams through tough times.

55. Reflect on Your Present Leadership Blessings, Not on Past Misfortunes

During the COVID-19 pandemic, many leaders around the world faced unprecedented challenges, yet they also had the opportunity to focus on their current blessings rather than past misfortunes.

For instance, **Jacinda Ardern**, the Prime Minister of New Zealand, faced immense pressure when COVID-19 hit. Instead of focusing on the initial setbacks or the economic downturn, she led with a focus on the health and well-being of her citizens. She celebrated New Zealand's success in quickly containing the virus, turning the collective efforts into a unifying source of pride for the country. Her leadership style, which emphasized clear communication and empathy, kept the country united in the face of adversity.

Similarly, **Satya Nadella**, CEO of Microsoft, found opportunity during the pandemic. While many companies struggled, Nadella focused on the blessings of Microsoft's strong cloud services and remote working tools. He accelerated the company's growth in these areas, enabling businesses to adapt to remote work. Rather than dwelling on challenges, he looked to what was working and invested in the future.

These examples show how focusing on the present strengths and blessings can help leaders navigate even the toughest challenges, like those posed by the COVID-19 pandemic. Leaders who reflected on the positive progress—whether it was public health success or business adaptability—were better equipped to keep moving forward with hope and purpose.

56. As a Leader, know what you can control, and what you can't control

Leadership is about focus, and there are three areas where leaders have total control: their actions, their thoughts, and their reactions. While external circumstances may be beyond a leader's control, the way they respond to situations is always within their grasp.

Leaders who focus on controlling these three areas maintain composure even during turbulent times.

By keeping their thoughts positive, actions purposeful, and reactions measured, leaders can create a stable foundation for success, regardless of the chaos around them.

Leadership is a delicate balance of action and trust. While it's important to take initiative and put in the effort, effective leaders know when to delegate and trust others to carry out tasks beyond their control. No leader can do everything themselves, and recognizing the need for collaboration strengthens the entire team. Delegating tasks not only helps the leader stay focused on their strengths but also empowers others to contribute meaningfully to the organization's success.

57. Press Against Pressure to Grow Stronger

Just as diamonds are formed under immense pressure, so too are leaders forged through challenges and adversity. The tough moments, the high-stress situations, and the obstacles we face are the crucibles that refine leadership skills. Rather than avoiding pressure, leaders should embrace it as a means of personal and professional growth. It is through these trials that leaders develop resilience, creativity, and problem-solving abilities that help them shine in the face of adversity.

"Press against the pressure," as Joyce Meyer wisely said, is a reminder that pressure, though uncomfortable, is one of the most powerful forces for growth. In leadership, pressure can arise from various sources: tight deadlines, difficult decisions, or managing crises. However, great leaders understand that embracing pressure rather than avoiding it can lead to extraordinary growth.

Vinod Dham (Entrepreneur and Innovator): Known as the "Father of the Pentium Chip," Vinod Dham is an Indian-American entrepreneur who has faced significant pressure in the highly competitive world of technology. In recent years, he has shifted his focus to supporting startups in India, helping drive innovation and entrepreneurship. His leadership is a prime example of pressing against the pressure of global competition and continually pushing for technological advancement. He continues to inspire a new generation of Indian entrepreneurs to innovate and think big

58. "Reactive People Are Shaped by External Forces; Proactive Leaders Create Their Own Weather"

Leadership is not merely about taking charge of situations; it's about taking control of your own responses to whatever the external circumstances are. Reactive leaders are often swayed by the turbulence around them, their mood and actions dictated by external events. In contrast, proactive leaders take charge of their reactions, maintaining composure and clarity in chaotic circumstances, which in turn sets the tone for their teams. Proactive leaders define the environment, rather than letting the environment define them.

As Stephen Covey wrote in his book *The 7 Habits of Highly Effective People*, "Between stimulus and response, there is a space. In that space is our power to choose our response. In our response lies our growth and our freedom." This quote underscores the power of choice and how proactive leaders harness it to shape their reactions and outcomes.

A Proactive Leader- Oprah Winfrey: Oprah, often hailed as one of the most influential women in the world, exemplifies proactive leadership. Despite facing numerous setbacks and obstacles—ranging from a troubled childhood to early career failures—she consistently chose how to respond. Oprah focused on fostering an environment of growth, compassion, and empowerment, inspiring millions. Her proactive leadership has created an expansive and lasting impact, not only in entertainment but also in social change.

59. Leadership Will Be Tested to See How Committed You Are to Your Goals

"The journey of leadership is filled with tests that challenge a leader's commitment and resolve."

Leadership is often defined by how a leader navigates through setbacks and challenges, not by how they manage during times of ease. It's easy to lead when everything is going according to plan, but the true test of leadership comes when obstacles arise. How a leader responds to adversity is what truly shapes their ability to inspire and guide others.

As **John C. Maxwell** once said, "A leader is one who knows the way, goes the way, and shows the way." This quote emphasizes that a true leader's strength is tested when faced with adversity. It's not just about knowing what needs to be done but also leading by example through tough times.

A prime example of this is **Sylvester Stallone**. Before achieving fame with the *Rocky* series, Stallone faced numerous rejections from Hollywood. In fact, he was even homeless at one point. But instead of giving up, he persevered. Stallone wrote the script for *Rocky* in just a few days and was determined to star in the film, despite being told he was too unknown. His unwavering belief in his vision, despite setbacks, ultimately led to the movie's success, cementing his place as a symbol of perseverance in the face of adversity.

Stallone's journey is a powerful testament to how a leader's resolve is forged through trials, demonstrating that commitment and resilience are key to overcoming challenges and inspiring others to do the same.

Greatness is often achieved through struggle. The path to success is rarely smooth, and it is the rough roads that provide the greatest lessons. As leaders, it's essential to recognize that each challenge faced is an opportunity to develop resilience, creativity, and problem-solving skills. The tougher the journey, the more profound the growth. These rough roads, though difficult, ultimately lead to higher levels of leadership and achievement.

60. The Language You Use Shapes Your Leadership Destiny

The words we choose not only convey information but also shape the way we think and act. In leadership, language has a powerful impact on the energy we create within ourselves and within our teams. The language leaders use can either build an atmosphere of positivity and growth or create an environment that holds people back. Positive language encourages progress and fosters motivation, while negative language can suppress creativity and enthusiasm. Leaders who speak in empowering, uplifting ways help to create a culture of success and development.

As **Tony Robbins** wisely says, "The way we communicate with others and with ourselves ultimately determines the quality of our lives."

10 Phrases of Positive vs. Negative Language in Leadership

Positive Language

a. "I believe in your abilities, and I'm here to support you."
b. "Let's focus on solutions and what we can do next."
c. "We can overcome this challenge together."
d. "Your contribution is valuable and makes a difference."
e. "We are constantly learning and improving as a team."
f. "I trust you to handle this responsibility."
g. "Let's work together to find the best approach."
h. "I see potential in this idea—let's explore it further."
i. "We have the resources we need to succeed."
j. "This is an opportunity for growth and innovation."

Negative Language

a. "I'm not sure if you can handle this."
b. "We've tried that before, and it didn't work."

c. "This problem is too big to solve."
d. "I don't think this is going to work."
e. "I'm not sure we'll ever get better at this."
f. "You're on your own with this one."
g. "This is a mistake we can't recover from."
h. "Your idea doesn't seem practical."
i. "We'll never have enough resources to succeed."
j. "We've hit a dead end; there's no way forward."

By choosing positive, empowering language, leaders can foster a culture of motivation, growth, and trust, helping their teams navigate challenges with a sense of purpose and optimism.

61. The Power of Long-Term Commitment

True leadership isn't defined by quick wins or short-term accomplishments. It's about long-term commitment to a vision, a cause, or a team. Leaders who demonstrate unwavering dedication over time—who remain focused and resilient through setbacks—are the ones who truly make a lasting impact. **Thomas Edison**, for example, spent decades working on the lightbulb, enduring countless failures. But it was his long-term commitment to his inventions, despite repeated setbacks, that ultimately changed the world.

Amitabh Bachchan is an exemplary figure in Indian cinema who has demonstrated long-term commitment as a style of leadership. Over the decades, Bachchan has not only remained relevant but has continued to evolve with changing times. Despite facing career downturns, including a brief period in the 1990s where he stepped away from films, Bachchan's return to the screen marked a new era of success. He embraced new technology, took on varied roles, and mentored younger generations of actors, showcasing a leadership style rooted in dedication and resilience.

His leadership goes beyond his films; Bachchan's perseverance in adapting to the digital age, hosting television shows, and engaging in philanthropic work reflects a vision built on long-term impact, not just immediate success. His journey demonstrates that true leadership requires sustained effort, growth, and an unwavering commitment to one's craft.

62. Paradox of Choices and Focused Leadership: Stay Focused

In today's world, the paradox of choice looms large. The more options we have, the more we question our decisions. This leads to dissatisfaction and indecision. For leaders, it's essential to embrace focus. Steve Jobs, known for his obsession with simplicity, often spoke about limiting choices to maximize impact. By narrowing options, leaders not only enhance productivity but also clarity of vision, guiding their teams toward meaningful achievements with fewer distractions.

M.S. Dhoni: Known for his calmness under pressure, M.S. Dhoni has exemplified how focus and leadership can drive success. As captain of the Indian cricket team, Dhoni led with a clear vision, never allowing distractions or the weight of expectations to affect his decisions. His focus was evident when he guided India to victory in the 2007 ICC World T20, the 2011 ICC World Cup, and the 2013 ICC Champions Trophy. Dhoni's ability to remain composed and focused on the game, even in high-pressure situations, is a hallmark of his leadership style.

63. The Four Levels of Action in Leadership

The Four Levels of Action

Leaders often face four levels of action in their decision-making process:

a. **Doing Nothing**: This is the most passive form of leadership. In times of crisis or uncertainty, some leaders choose to avoid making decisions, hoping that the situation will resolve itself. This approach leads to stagnation and missed opportunities.

b. **Retreating**: Leaders may sometimes choose to step back from challenges. This retreating action is often a form of self-preservation but can ultimately lead to loss of confidence from the team and a failure to navigate critical situations.

c. **Normal Action**: This represents a routine response—leaders take standard, measured steps to handle day-to-day challenges. While normal action keeps things steady, it doesn't propel the team or the organization toward extraordinary achievements. Leaders who rely only on normal action may maintain the status quo but fail to achieve breakthrough results.

d. **Massive Action**: The most impactful leaders take bold, decisive steps, particularly in times of great challenge. This is the level of action that creates momentum, inspires teams, and leads to monumental results. Leaders like **Winston Churchill** exemplified this during World War II. When the world was on the brink of destruction, Churchill didn't shy away from taking bold action. His speeches, determination, and relentless pursuit of victory energized the British people and united them against a common enemy. His ability to act decisively, even when the stakes were highest, showed true leadership.

You can overcome fears by only taking action.

Motivation does not lead to action, but action leads to motivation.

64. The Role of Obsession in Success

Obsession, when channeled toward a clear purpose, separates good leaders from truly great ones. **"I'm convinced that about half of what separates the successful entrepreneurs from the nonsuccessful ones is pure perseverance,"** observed Steve Jobs—a testament to how relentless focus fuels breakthrough results. Obsession isn't about mindless repetition; it's about an unshakable commitment to delivering value, refining every detail, and pushing boundaries long after others have stopped.

Elon Musk exemplifies this principle. From founding SpaceX in a bid to colonize Mars, to transforming Tesla into the benchmark for electric vehicles, Musk's leadership is rooted in an almost singular fixation on innovation. When rockets failed to land, he personally reviewed every test; when production bottlenecks threatened Tesla's viability, he slept on the factory floor. His obsession with excellence—regardless of skepticism or risk—has driven two industries forward and inspired tens of thousands of engineers, marketers, and policymakers worldwide.

In **network marketing**, this same engine powers transformational leaders:

- **Deep Product Mastery:** Top distributors obsessively learn every ingredient, benefit, and usecase of their portfolio, so their recommendations are never generic but tailored and insightful.
- **Relentless FollowUp:** Rather than accepting "no" as final, they craft thoughtful, valuedriven touchpoints—email, calls, or personal meetups—demonstrating genuine care and building trust over time.
- **Continuous SelfImprovement:** They consume books, podcasts, and trainings voraciously, then apply—and teach—new tactics to their teams, creating a culture of perpetual growth.

In **corporate leadership** and **entrepreneurship**, obsession shows up as:

a. **Uncompromising Standards:** Championing quality over convenience, even if it delays launch or increases cost.
b. **Iterative Experimentation:** Rapid prototyping and datadriven pivots, fueled by a refusal to accept "good enough."
c. **Visible Commitment:** Leaders who work shouldertoshoulder with their teams send a powerful signal: "These matters to me, so it must matter to you."

Why Obsession Matters

- **Creates Momentum:** When a leader's energy is visibly focused, it ignites passion in others.
- **Drives Innovation:** Obsession compels you to ask "What if?" and "Why not?" more often than "What works already?"
- **Builds Credibility:** Teams trust leaders who demonstrate through action that they won't settle for mediocrity.

Turning Obsession into Action

a. **Define Your NonNegotiables:** Identify the 2–3 areas where your obsession will have the greatest impact.
b. **Set MicroGoals:** Break your big vision into daily, hyperfocused tasks—then track progress relentlessly.
c. **Model the Behaviour:** Share your process—and setbacks—with your team. Transparency fuels collective obsession.

65. The Danger of Negative Self-Talk in Leadership

Leaders who are trapped in negative self-talk often limit their potential. In history, many leaders have faced public criticism and doubt, but their internal dialogue made all the difference. Franklin D. Roosevelt, despite his physical disabilities, maintained a strong belief in his abilities. Leaders must focus on cultivating positive affirmations and avoiding the trap of self-doubt. What we say to ourselves directly influences the outcomes we achieve.

Examples of Negative vs. Positive SelfTalk in Leadership

Leaders often face high stakes and heavy responsibilities, and the way they talk to themselves under pressure can make or break their effectiveness. Below are common patterns of negative selftalk, how to reframe them into empowering, positive selftalk, and why this shift is critical for leadership success.

Negative SelfTalk	Positive Reframe
"I'm not good enough to lead this team."	"I have the skills and experience to guide this team—and I will learn more as I go."
"If I make a mistake, everyone will think I'm a failure."	"Mistakes are opportunities to learn and grow—my team respects me for my honesty."
"I can't handle this level of pressure."	"I've faced challenges before and succeeded; I can navigate this one too."
"I shouldn't ask for help; it shows weakness."	"Asking for support builds collaboration and shows I value others' expertise."
"I'm too inexperienced to make this decision."	"I can gather input, trust my judgment, and adjust as needed."

How to Turn Negative SelfTalk into Positive SelfTalk

a. **Recognize the Voice**

Notice when your inner dialogue takes a pessimistic turn. Pause and label it ("That's selfdoubt talking.").

b. **Challenge the Evidence**

Ask yourself: "What proof do I have that I can't succeed?" versus "What successes have I had?"

Replacing overgeneralizations ("I always fail") with facts ("I overcame X challenge last year") breaks the cycle of negativity.

c. **Reframe with Growth Mindset Language**

Swap fixedmindset phrases ("I'm not a natural leader") for growthmindset affirmations ("I can develop leadership skills through practice")—a technique championed by psychologist **Carol Dweck.**

d. **Use "I Can" Statements**

Replace "I can't" with "I can learn to," or "I will." This subtle shift empowers you to see obstacles as surmountable.

e. **Anchor in Purpose**

Remind yourself of your mission and values ("I lead to help my team grow") to replace fearbased thoughts with purposedriven motivation. Accountable for progress.

Why Positive SelfTalk Is Crucial for Leaders

- **Boosts Confidence & Resilience**

  Positive selftalk strengthens selfefficacy, making you more likely to tackle challenges headon and rebound from setbacks.

- **Improves DecisionMaking**

  Calm, encouraging inner dialogue reduces stress and prevents overreacting, helping you make clearer, more strategic choices.

- **Sets the Tone for Your Team**

  Leaders' selftalk isn't just internal—it influences body language, tone, and behavior. Optimistic selftalk fosters a culture of trust and psychological safety, encouraging team members to speak up and innovate.

- **Enhances Emotional Regulation**

  Replacing catastrophizing thoughts ("This is a disaster") with balanced ones ("We have a plan and resources to address this") helps you stay composed under pressure.

- **Drives Continuous Growth**

  Positive selftalk aligns with lifelong learning. By viewing setbacks as feedback rather than failures, you remain curious and committed to improvement.

"Whether you think you can, or you think you can't—you're right."

– Henry Ford

By consciously shifting from negative to positive selftalk, leaders can harness the full power of their mindset to inspire action, foster team cohesion, and achieve sustainable success.

66. Shifting Mindsets from Victimhood to Ownership

What Is a Victim Mindset?

- **Blame & Excuses**: "I can't succeed because of…"
- **Helplessness**: Belief that circumstances or other people control your outcomes.
- **Fixed Thinking**: "This is just the way things are."
- **ShortTerm Focus**: Seeking immediate relief over longterm solutions.

"Victims make excuses. Winners make things happen."

– John C. Maxwell

Impact on Leadership

Victimminded leaders avoid accountability, dampen team morale, and erode trust. Their teams learn to expect handholding, become riskaverse, and stop innovating.

What Is a Winner Mindset?

- **Ownership & Accountability**: "What can I do to move forward?"
- **Empowerment**: Belief that with effort and creativity, you shape your destiny.
- **Growth Thinking**: "I can learn, adapt, and improve." (Carol Dweck)
- **LongTerm Vision**: Embracing challenges as opportunities to build resilience.

"Whether you think you can, or you think you can't—you're right."

– Henry Ford

Impact on Leadership

Winnerminded leaders inspire confidence, encourage autonomy, and foster innovation. Their teams feel psychologically safe to experiment, give feedback, and strive for excellence.

SidebySide Comparison

Aspect	**Victim Mindset**	**Winner Mindset**
Responsibility	"It's not my fault."	"I own the outcome."
Response to Failure	"I'll never succeed."	"What can I learn?"
Approach to Risk	Avoids risk; stays in comfort zone.	Embraces calculated risks.
Team Impact	Creates dependency and fear of failure.	Builds autonomy and courage.

How to Shift from Victim to Winner

1. **Spot the Story**

   Notice when you default to "poor me" thinking. Label it as "victim talk."

2. **Reframe the Challenge**

   Ask, "What's one small step I can take right now?"

3. **Anchor in Purpose**

   Remind yourself of your "why"—your deeper vision for the team or organization.

4. **Celebrate Agency**

   Acknowledge even small wins to reinforce your power to influence outcomes.

Why It Matters

A leader's mindset cascades through every decision, every conversation, and every crisis response. By embracing a **winner mindset**, you model resilience, accountability, and optimism—qualities that transform individual performance into collective greatness.

67. The Role of Ethical Leadership in Organizational Success

Ethical leadership is not just a moral choice—it is essential for long-term success. Leaders like Mahatma Gandhi demonstrated that ethical leadership transcends personal gain and aims to serve the greater good. Ethical leaders establish trust within their teams, foster a culture of fairness, and ensure that their actions align with their values. This trust fuels higher levels of engagement and productivity within organizations, including network marketing. Here is a list of ethics which any leader should follow-

a. **Lead with integrity:** Always align your actions with your stated values.

b. **Practice transparency:** Share information openly and honestly with your team.

c. **Own your mistakes:** Admit errors promptly and take responsibility for correction.

d. **Champion fairness:** Treat everyone equally and make unbiased decisions.

e. **Respect individuality:** Honor diverse perspectives and backgrounds.

f. **Foster accountability:** Hold yourself and others responsible for commitments.

g. **Demonstrate empathy:** Listen actively and consider others' feelings and needs.

h. **Maintain confidentiality:** Protect private information entrusted to you.

i. **Uphold justice:** Advocate for what is right, even when it's unpopular.

j. **Promote humility:** Give credit where it's due and remain open to feedback.

k. **Encourage ethical courage:** Support team members in speaking up against wrongdoing.

l. **Value sustainability:** Make decisions that benefit both current and future generations.

68. The Influence of Self-Image in Leadership

A leader's self-image directly impacts their effectiveness. Leaders who believe in their capabilities, like Theodore Roosevelt, are more likely to inspire confidence in their teams. Building a strong, positive self-image requires continuous self-assessment and a commitment to personal growth. By embodying the qualities, you wish to see in your team, you lead by example and set the standard for excellence. Do the following to build a positive self- image-

- **Master Your Craft**

  Commit to continuous learning—read, attend workshops, or find a mentor. Expertise breeds selfrespect and projects confidence to your team.

- **Develop a Strong Physical Presence**

  Stand tall, make deliberate eye contact, and use open gestures. Embodied confidence influences both how you feel and how others perceive you.

- **Solicit and Embrace Constructive Feedback**

  Actively ask trusted colleagues what you do well and where you can grow. Demonstrating that you can hear—and act on—feedback bolsters your selfrespect.

- **Align Actions with Core Values**

  When your daytoday choices reflect what matters most to you, you reinforce trust in yourself. Integrity is the cornerstone of a positive selfimage.

- **Practice SelfCompassion**

  Treat yourself with the same kindness you'd offer a team member. Acknowledge mistakes as learning steps rather than proof of inadequacy.

≺ Visualize Success

Spend a few minutes each morning imagining yourself handling challenges with poise. Visualization primes your mind to act in alignment with that confident image.

≺ Surround Yourself with Supportive Peers

Engage a peeradvisory group or mastermind. Being part of a network that celebrates your growth and holds you accountable strengthens how you see yourself.

69. The Value of Courageous Conversations in Leadership

Leadership often involves difficult conversations. Historical leaders like Abraham Lincoln faced moments where hard truths had to be spoken to their teams or constituents. These moments define leadership. Whether it's addressing a failing project or giving critical feedback, courageous conversations are essential for growth and alignment. Leaders who shy away from these conversations risk stagnation within their teams.

- Embrace difficult dialogues to foster transparency and trust.
- Address issues early to prevent team stagnation and misalignment.
- Speak hard truths with empathy to drive collective growth.
- Provide candid feedback to uphold standards and accelerate improvement.
- Model courage by initiating conversations others avoid.
- Use honest dialogue to reinforce accountability and shared vision.

70. Resilience in Leadership

Resilience is a core trait of any successful leader. Leaders like Mahatma Gandhi showed incredible resilience through years of nonviolent protest, leading to the independence of India. Resilience allows leaders to stay focused on their goals despite setbacks. Building resilience within your team strengthens their resolve, helping them push through challenges and emerge stronger.

- Embrace setbacks as learning opportunities to strengthen your resolve.
- Cultivate a growth mindset by viewing challenges as paths to development.
- Maintain a support network to share burdens and gain new perspectives.
- Practice regular selfreflection to identify and leverage personal strengths.
- Prioritize selfcare—sleep, nutrition, and exercise—to sustain mental toughness.
- Set adaptive goals that allow flexibility in the face of change.
- Develop stressmanagement rituals like mindfulness or deep breathing.
- Celebrate small wins to build confidence and momentum.
- Seek feedback to coursecorrect early and avoid compounding errors.
- Anchor yourself in purpose to navigate uncertainty with clarity.

71. Building Trust as a Foundation of Leadership

Trust is the cornerstone of effective leadership. Leaders like Abraham Lincoln built trust by consistently making decisions that prioritized the greater good. Trust is earned through integrity, consistency, and a commitment to doing what's right. Building trust within your team ensures that they will follow you through challenges and support you in achieving the organization's goals.

- Lead by example—demonstrate the Behaviour you expect from others.
- Keep your promises, even in small matters.
- Be transparent with your intentions and decisions.
- Communicate consistently and honestly, even when the news is tough.
- Admit mistakes and take responsibility without blame.
- Listen actively and make people feel heard and valued.
- Treat everyone with fairness, respect, and dignity.
- Recognize and appreciate contributions openly and sincerely.
- Be consistent in your actions, not just your words.
- Create a safe space where people feel comfortable sharing concerns.

72. The Balance Between Confidence and Humility in Leadership

Great leadership is a fine balance between **confidence** and **humility**, and mastering this balance sets apart truly exceptional leaders from the rest. Confidence is the fuel that enables a leader to take risks, make decisions under pressure, and stand firm in the face of adversity. It gives the team a sense of direction and security, especially during uncertain times. People are drawn to leaders who believe in themselves, their vision, and the capacity of their team. However, when confidence is not grounded in humility, it can become arrogance—blinding a leader to feedback, disconnecting them from reality, and creating a toxic culture where others feel unheard or undervalued.

On the other hand, humility keeps the leader open, teachable, and connected to the people they serve. It is not about thinking less of oneself, but about thinking of oneself less. Humble leaders listen more than they speak, acknowledge the contributions of their team, and are quick to admit when they are wrong. They create psychological safety where innovation and honesty thrive. As leadership expert Jim Collins puts it, Level 5 leaders “blend extreme personal humility with intense professional will.” They are fiercely committed to results, yet their egos do not get in the way of collaboration and growth.

When a leader pairs **bold vision** with **quiet strength**, they earn the loyalty, trust, and respect of those around them. They don’t need to shout to be heard. Their presence speaks through their consistent actions, emotional intelligence, and unwavering integrity. In essence, confidence is what gives a leader their voice, and humility is what ensures people are willing to listen. Together, they create a leadership style that is both powerful and deeply human.

73. Networking as Leadership

Building relationships and expanding your network is not just a social skill—it is a strategic necessity for effective leadership. Great leaders like Andrew Carnegie famously said, "It marks a big step in your development when you come to realize that other people can help you do a better job than you could do alone." True networking goes beyond collecting business cards or LinkedIn connections; it's about fostering genuine, value-based relationships that are mutually beneficial. For leaders, networking provides access to diverse perspectives, industry insights, opportunities for collaboration, and even crisis support during tough times. Attending industry conferences, participating in mastermind groups, hosting roundtables, or simply reaching out for a virtual coffee with peers are excellent ways to stay connected. Volunteering to mentor others or inviting feedback from external stakeholders can also strengthen credibility and trust. Most importantly, leaders who invest in their networks with authenticity—by being helpful, respectful, and curious—build a strong circle of influence that fuels long-term growth. In today's interconnected world, the quality of your network often determines the scale of your impact.

74. The Role of Innovation in Leadership

Innovation is the engine of sustainable leadership, and great leaders continuously push their teams to think beyond the status quo and discover uncharted territory. In highly competitive "Red Oceans," where markets are saturated and rivals fight over limited demand, innovation becomes a survival tool. However, true visionary leaders shift their teams toward "Blue Ocean" thinking—creating new markets with little to no competition. Consider how **Apple**, under Steve Jobs, moved away from competing in the traditional PC market and instead created a new category with the iPod and later the iPhone—redefining entire industries. Or look at **Reed Hastings** of Netflix, who transitioned the company from DVD rentals to streaming, and then into content creation, outpacing the competition by innovating at each stage. Leaders who foster innovation don't wait for disruption—they **become** the disruption.

- Encourage divergent thinking by asking "what if" questions in meetings.
- Reward experimentation and normalize failure as a step toward success.
- Challenge the team to find solutions that don't yet exist in the market.

In India, **Anand Mahindra**'s support of projects like the e-rickshaw and local electric mobility solutions reflects a leader who nurtures grassroots innovation. Similarly, **Narayana Murthy** and the Infosys team reimagined IT services by offering quality solutions from India to the world, creating a global footprint. These leaders didn't just optimize what existed—they **redefined** it. Innovation leadership involves more than creativity; it demands the **courage to act on unconventional ideas**, the **clarity to prioritize what's meaningful**, and the **persistence to push through uncertainty**.

- Avoid micromanagement—give your team space to explore and experiment.
- Promote cross-functional collaboration to break silos and spark creativity.
- Shift focus from competition to value creation—ask, "How can we make this 10x better?"

In network marketing and direct selling too, innovation is the difference between fading into obscurity and building a legacy. Whether it's leveraging digital tools, gamifying training systems, or crafting new incentive models—leaders must constantly push boundaries. Remember, innovation isn't a department—it's a culture, and the leader's mindset sets the tone.

75. Leadership Through Self-Discipline

Self-discipline and integrity are the invisible pillars that uphold great leadership. Without them, even the most charismatic or intelligent leader will eventually fall. **Self-discipline** is the ability to control one's impulses, stay focused on long-term goals, and do what needs to be done—even when it's hard, inconvenient, or unrewarded in the short term. **Integrity**, on the other hand, is the consistency between what you say and what you do—acting ethically even when no one is watching.

History has shown us that the leaders who are admired across generations are those who held themselves to the highest standards. **Mahatma Gandhi** displayed extraordinary self-discipline through his commitment to non-violence and simplicity, even in the face of extreme provocation. His integrity won the trust of millions, turning him into a moral force much stronger than any army. In the corporate world, **Ratan Tata** is another example—his integrity in business decisions, his humility, and his sense of responsibility have made him one of the most respected leaders in India and globally.

- A disciplined leader sets the pace for the team's habits and focus.
- Integrity builds trust—a non-negotiable foundation for effective leadership.
- Discipline ensures consistency; integrity ensures credibility. Together, they create impact.

Leaders are constantly watched, whether they realize it or not. When they show up on time, follow through on commitments, stay true to their word, and handle tough situations with ethical clarity, they lead by example. This modelling encourages others to raise their standards too. Without self-discipline, a leader becomes reactive; without integrity, a leader loses moral authority. Both are essential for long-term influence, especially in uncertain or high-pressure environments where the temptation to cut corners is high.

Ultimately, leadership is not just about results—it's about the **way** those results are achieved. Self-discipline helps a leader stay the course; integrity ensures that the course is right.

76. Transparent Leadership: Honesty That Builds Loyalty

The strongest leaders lead with transparency, understanding that honesty, even when uncomfortable, is the cornerstone of trust and loyalty. **Indra Nooyi**, former CEO of PepsiCo, exemplified transparent leadership during her tenure. She communicated openly with both her team and the public, even about challenges the company faced, such as shifting market trends and health-focused product development. Her approach didn't shield the organization from tough times; rather, it built trust with employees, stakeholders, and consumers, as they saw her unwavering honesty and commitment to long-term goals.

Transparency in leadership means addressing uncomfortable truths and sharing information that may not be convenient. **Howard Schultz**, the former CEO of Starbucks, led with transparency when he openly acknowledged the company's challenges during the 2008 recession, which led to store closures and layoffs. Rather than hiding these tough decisions, he communicated them directly, ensuring that his employees and customers understood the vision and why difficult choices had to be made. This approach not only garnered respect but also deepened loyalty, proving that being open about challenges makes teams feel included and valued.

In contrast, leaders who shy away from transparency risk eroding trust. **Elizabeth Holmes**, the founder of Theranos, is a cautionary tale of the dangers of concealing the truth. Her leadership lacked transparency, leading to public trust being broken and a collapse in the company's reputation. In the end, her dishonesty didn't protect her company—it destroyed it.

True leadership shines brightest in the moments of struggle, not just success. When a leader is open, vulnerable, and honest with their team, clients, and stakeholders, it strengthens their credibility and fosters an environment of loyalty and respect. Transparency doesn't weaken leadership—it **empowers** it, creating a solid foundation for lasting influence.

77. Vulnerability in Leadership: The Power of Being Real

True leadership doesn't demand perfection; rather, it requires the courage to be vulnerable. Leaders who embrace vulnerability—whether by admitting their mistakes, asking for help, or acknowledging their uncertainties—create authentic connections that foster trust and growth. Take **Brene Brown**, whose work on vulnerability has redefined leadership. She emphasizes that leaders who show their authentic selves, including their imperfections, not only build stronger relationships but also cultivate a culture where others feel safe to be real. Brown's research shows that when leaders model vulnerability, they empower their teams to take risks, innovate, and grow without the fear of failure.

Satya Nadella, CEO of Microsoft, is another example of a leader who turned vulnerability into strength. Upon taking the helm, he openly acknowledged the company's past challenges and recognized the need for a cultural transformation. He wasn't afraid to express the uncertainties of leading a massive company in the face of rapid technological change. By doing so, he invited his team to embrace a growth mindset, encouraging openness, learning from mistakes, and fostering a culture of collaboration. Under his leadership, Microsoft thrived by shifting away from a fixed mindset to one that encouraged innovation through failure.

In contrast, leaders who resist vulnerability often create environments of fear and stagnation. The inability to admit mistakes or seek help prevents growth, both for the leader and the team. Vulnerability in leadership doesn't signal weakness—it reflects courage and emotional strength. It's through vulnerability that leaders build trust, foster creativity, and inspire loyalty. By embracing their imperfections, leaders become relatable, and in turn, their teams feel empowered to push boundaries and achieve greatness.

78. Empowering Leadership: Decentralizing to Unlock Potential

Top-down leadership often stifles growth, as it centralizes decision-making in the hands of a few, leaving little room for others to contribute their ideas and leadership. **Empowering leadership**, however, decentralizes authority, creating an environment where everyone has a stake in the organization's success. By entrusting team members with responsibility, leaders not only amplify their own impact but also unlock the full potential of their teams. One example is **Richard Branson**, founder of the Virgin Group, whose leadership philosophy emphasizes delegating responsibility to employees and giving them the autonomy to make decisions. Branson believes that empowering others to lead fosters creativity and drives innovation, enabling the organization to grow in new and unexpected ways.

Decentralization through delegation, accountability, duplication, and systems is essential to building this empowering culture. Leaders like **Jack Welch** of GE were pioneers in delegating authority and creating systems that allowed team members to take ownership of projects. Welch encouraged his managers to make decisions without constant oversight, giving them both the freedom and accountability to drive results. This trust not only boosted morale but also created a ripple effect of innovation throughout the organization.

Decentralization doesn't mean abandoning control; it's about creating systems where decisions can be made at multiple levels, allowing leaders to focus on the bigger picture while empowering others to take initiative. **Delegation** ensures that tasks are spread across the team, while **accountability** ensures everyone is responsible for their outcomes. **Duplication** allows leaders to build scalable systems where successful strategies and initiatives can be replicated across teams or locations.

By creating these systems and fostering a decentralized approach, leaders encourage ownership, which builds confidence and drives accountability. In such an environment, leaders don't just manage; they inspire others to lead, creating a culture where everyone's contribution counts and the organization thrives collectively.

Delegation is not about offloading tasks—it's about empowering your team to take ownership and grow. Leaders who delegate effectively recognize the strengths and skills of their team members and match tasks to their abilities. Effective delegation builds trust, increases efficiency, and helps team members develop new skills. For example, a leader might delegate a high-stakes project to a rising star on the team, giving them a chance to showcase their skills while providing guidance and support. Through delegation, leaders cultivate a culture.

79. Coaching for Development: Unlocking Potential in Others

Great leaders are not just managers—they are coaches who inspire, guide, and elevate their teams. The role of a leader as a coach goes beyond delegating tasks and providing direction; it is about nurturing growth, unlocking potential, and empowering others to excel. **Phil Jackson**, one of the most successful basketball coaches in history, exemplified this coaching leadership style. Known as the "Zen Master," Jackson led the Chicago Bulls and Los Angeles Lakers to multiple NBA championships. His approach wasn't just about strategy and technique, but about understanding his players' individual strengths, weaknesses, and mindsets. By coaching his players on mental toughness, self-discipline, and teamwork, he helped them realize their full potential both on and off the court.

In the corporate world, **Narayana Murthy**, the co-founder of **Infosys**, adopted a coaching leadership style that helped transform Infosys into one of India's most successful IT companies. Murthy emphasized mentorship and leadership development from the very beginning, promoting a culture of learning and growth. His approach focused on empowering employees by providing them with the resources and training they needed to excel. He recognized the importance of fostering a sense of ownership among employees and ensured that leadership was not confined to senior executives, but was encouraged at all levels. Under his leadership, Infosys became a global leader in technology and consulting, a testament to the power of coaching leadership.

As a coach, leaders help team members develop their skills, navigate challenges, and identify opportunities for improvement. They offer feedback that is constructive, not critical, and create an environment where mistakes are seen as learning opportunities rather than failures. For example, **Steve Jobs** was known for his tough-love approach with his teams at Apple, constantly pushing them to be innovative and think differently, but also fostering a sense of ownership and personal growth.

Coaching leaders also focus on **active listening** and **emotional intelligence** to understand their team's needs and motivations. **Ravi Venkatesan**, the former chairman of Microsoft India and an influential business leader, embraced a coaching style in his leadership. He focused on building long-term relationships, helping his team align with a clear vision, and encouraging them to grow into their leadership roles.

In essence, a leader as a coach isn't just about achieving business goals—it's about helping individuals grow, making them feel empowered to take ownership, and building a high-performing team. Leaders who adopt a coaching mindset inspire loyalty, drive innovation, and create a culture where everyone thrives. This approach goes beyond traditional management and fosters an environment where both individuals and the organization can reach new heights together.

80. Leadership with Integrity

Personality integrity in leadership is the cornerstone of authentic and ethical leadership. It means a leader consistently acts in accordance with their values and principles, regardless of external pressures or temptations. For example, consider a manager who discovers a mistake in a financial report that could cost the company a major client. Instead of covering it up to protect the team's reputation or their own image, the leader takes responsibility, informs the stakeholders, and works toward a transparent resolution. This act of honesty not only maintains trust but sets a powerful example for the team.

Another example can be seen in how a leader treats their team members. A leader with integrity doesn't show favoritism or bend rules for convenience. Suppose a high-performing employee violates a company policy. Rather than ignoring it due to their past contributions, an integrity-driven leader addresses the issue fairly, demonstrating that principles are upheld consistently for everyone. In contrast, a lack of integrity—such as saying one thing in meetings and doing another behind closed doors—quickly erodes credibility.

True leadership integrity is visible in small, everyday decisions: keeping promises, admitting mistakes, giving credit where it's due, and standing firm for what's right, even if it's unpopular. Leaders like Mahatma Gandhi and Nelson Mandela embodied personality integrity by remaining steadfast in their values of nonviolence, equality, and justice, even when facing immense personal hardship. Their character became a beacon of inspiration because their actions were a clear reflection of their beliefs. In business and life, this alignment between inner values and outward Behaviour creates trust, strengthens relationships, and builds lasting influence.

Topic 2
TIME MANAGEMENT

Time is a constant, impartial force that continues regardless of our actions, emotions, or circumstances. It neither accelerates nor slows down for anyone—it remains neutral, flowing steadily, day in and day out. Yet, what truly shifts is how we respond to time, how we manage it, and how we direct our focus. Time itself does not change; what changes is how we engage with it. Mastering time, therefore, isn't about trying to manipulate its passage or outpace it, but about mastering ourselves. It's about learning to manage our energy, shaping productive habits, cultivating a mindset of focus and discipline, and making conscious, purposeful decisions. Each decision we make reflects our internal state—our character, the clarity of our goals, and our willingness to stay aligned with our deeper values. In moments of indecision or distraction, we may waste time, but in moments of clarity and intentionality, time becomes an ally. When we take full responsibility for how we spend each moment, we move closer to achieving our highest potential. Mastering time, ultimately, is not just about being efficient—it's about being intentional with who we are and who we are becoming. The way we manage time is a direct reflection of our personal growth, resilience, and the alignment between our actions and our vision for the future. In this sense, time is not just a resource—it is a mirror of our self-mastery.

1. Prioritize – Focus on What Truly Matters

One of the biggest mistakes we make is confusing *being busy* with *being productive*. True time mastery begins with **prioritization**—learning to identify what deserves our attention and energy. I've been personally practicing writing a **daily and weekly to-do list**, categorizing tasks into personal and professional buckets, and then asking: *Is this really important?*

A simple tool that changed my life was this three-column activity filter:

- **YES** – Very Important
- **NO** – Not Important
- **MAYBE** – Somewhat Important

I eliminate all the "NO" and "MAYBE" tasks and only work on what's in the "YES" list.

U.S. President **Dwight D. Eisenhower** used a prioritization method (later popularized as the **Eisenhower Matrix**) that divided tasks into four categories—Important/Urgent, Important/Not Urgent, Not Important/Urgent, and Not Important/Not Urgent. This approach empowered him to focus on strategic decisions, not just daily noise.

→ **Action Step**: Before starting your day, sort your to-do list using this method. Watch how much clarity it brings.

2. Stop the Delay – Procrastination is the Silent Killer

Procrastination doesn't feel dangerous—until days become weeks and progress stalls. I used to delay difficult tasks too, until I trained myself with a simple technique: **write everything down the night before**. Every task, whether personal or professional, gets a spot on the list. And once it's on paper, I don't argue with it—I act.

Leonardo da Vinci, though a genius, struggled with procrastination. It took him **16 years** to complete the Mona Lisa. Imagine what more he could have achieved with better planning systems. Learning from him, we must recognize the cost of delay—even to the most brilliant minds.

→ **Action Step**: Choose one task you've been delaying. Break it into three small actions. Do the first one now—momentum builds motivation.

3. Start Strong – How You Begin the Day Shapes It All

How do you begin your day? If your morning starts with scrolling on your phone or reacting to messages, you've already surrendered control of your time. I follow a ritual—before bed, I write what I need to do the next day. When I wake up, I already know my *mission*.

Benjamin Franklin, one of America's founding fathers, began each day by asking, "*What good shall I do this day?*" He had a structured daily routine that included planning, deep work, and reflection. No wonder he was a prolific writer, scientist, and statesman.

→ **Action Step**: Write your top three goals the night before. In the morning, tackle the hardest one first. That's your real victory.

4. Buffer Time is Not a Luxury – It's a Leadership Discipline

Many of us cram our schedules back-to-back, hoping to squeeze in more productivity. But I've found that **leaving buffer time between tasks and meetings** is a superpower. It gives me space to breathe, think, reset, and show up fully present in the next task. This habit changed how I work—and how I feel at the end of the day.

Seneca, the Roman Stoic philosopher, wrote about *time as our most precious commodity*. He warned that people "guard their property" but waste time "as if it were nothing." Creating space between commitments is how we start respecting our own time.

Protect the White space in your calendar is like silence in music—it gives meaning. Don't cram every hour. Leave room to think, to shift, to breathe. Overstuffed schedules leave no space for spontaneous brilliance.

→ **Action Step**: Add 15-20 minute buffers between meetings or tasks. Use that time to reflect, prepare, or just breathe.

5. Multitasking is a Myth – Focus Wins the Game

For years, I believed multitasking made me efficient—until I noticed how often it led to mistakes, mental fatigue, and missed deadlines. Now, I schedule **single-task focus blocks** where I tackle one task at a time. I turn off distractions, close other tabs, and give my full energy to what's in front of me.

Historical Evidence: **Steve Jobs**, known for his laser focus, once said, "People think focus means saying yes to the thing you've got to focus on. But that's not what it means at all. It means saying **no** to the hundred other good ideas." That focus helped him revolutionize entire industries.

→ **Action Step**: Block out 60 minutes today for deep work. No distractions, no multitasking—just full engagement. Notice the difference.

6. Write it to Remember it – The Power of Pen and Planning

There's something magical about **writing things down**—not just in our phones or apps, but on paper. Every night, I sit with my notebook and write all the tasks I must complete—personal, professional, family, and social. It clears my mind and sets the tone for the next day. This simple habit has brought immense clarity and control to my life.

Thomas Edison, one of history's most prolific inventors, kept detailed notebooks throughout his life. His ideas, plans, and experiments were all written down—over **5 million pages** in total. That habit of writing wasn't just about memory—it was a system for innovation and action.

⇥ **Action Step**: Start a time journal for one week. Write your daily to-do list, and track how much you actually completed. Reflect and improve.

7. Declutter to Take Control – Apply the 5S Rule to Time

Just as we clean our rooms or workspaces, we must also declutter our **mental and time spaces**. I use a version of the **5S system**—originally from Japanese manufacturing—for organizing my time:

1. **Sort** – Remove unnecessary tasks.
2. **Set in order** – Schedule tasks clearly.
3. **Shine** – Refine your routine.
4. **Standardize** – Stick to a planning method.
5. **Sustain** – Make it a daily habit.

The **Toyota Production System**, built on the 5S principle, revolutionized the global automobile industry. Its emphasis on eliminating waste and improving flow applies perfectly to how we should manage our time.

→ **Action Step**: Review your calendar and eliminate one non-essential activity per day for the next 5 days. You'll feel lighter and more focused.

8. Meetings Are Time Eaters – Learn to Lead Them Right

We all attend meetings—but how many of them are truly effective? Over the years, I've realized that **bad meetings** are the biggest time wasters. So now, I lead with **purpose, agenda, preparation, and outcomes**. Every meeting must be worth everyone's time.

Peter Drucker, the father of modern management, once said, "Meetings are a symptom of bad organization. The fewer meetings the better." Yet, when used well, meetings can be powerful decision-making tools.

→ **Action Step**: Before your next meeting, ask: *Do we need this? Is there a clear agenda? What result are we expecting?* Only then proceed.

9. Handle Interruptions Like a Leader – Master the Unexpected Visitor

Time thieves often come disguised as *friendly interruptions*. A surprise visitor, a phone call, or a chatty colleague can derail a focused hour. That's why I block specific hours where I'm not available, and I gently communicate that to others. Standing up when someone enters signals, you're not fully available—yet you're still respectful.

Winston Churchill, during WWII, famously protected his work time. He would retreat into his study and wouldn't take any unscheduled visitors, even during crisis. He believed in the sanctity of deep, uninterrupted thought for making critical decisions.

⇥ **Action Step**: Identify your most productive 2 hours daily. Block them out. No calls, no meetings. Defend them like treasure.

10. Make Time Visual – Use a Time Budget Like a Financial Budget

Just like we track expenses to manage money, we must track **how we spend our time**. I use a **personal time budget** divided into:

- Personal
- Family
- Social
- Professional

Every week, I review this "time spend" to see if I'm living in alignment with my values. It's eye-opening—and empowering.

Charles Schwab, a steel magnate, once asked productivity consultant **Ivy Lee** for advice. Lee told him to plan the next day's six most important tasks each evening. Schwab paid Lee **$25,000 (in 1918!)** after seeing productivity skyrocket.

Create a "time spending pie" for the past week. Where did your time go? Is it aligned with what matters most to you?

11. Mastering Time Management Through Productive Meetings

"Time isn't the main thing. It's the only thing."

– Miles Davis

In today's fast-paced world, **meetings can either be the heartbeat of collaboration or a drain on time and morale**. For a leader, mastering the art of meetings is not just about time efficiency—it's about **clarity, impact, and leadership presence**. A well-run meeting is a mirror of a well-run organization.

I. The Purpose of a Meeting: Never Meet Just to Meet

Before calling a meeting, ask: *Is it necessary? What is the intended outcome?*

Many organizations fall into the trap of holding habitual meetings without real necessity. A staggering **two-thirds of professional's report that many meetings are a waste of time**. Instead, every meeting should answer these key questions:

- Do we need to collaborate or simply communicate?
- Are we solving a specific problem?
- Is synchronous discussion required, or can this be handled asynchronously (email, message, video updates)?

II. The Six Pillars of Successful Meetings

1. **Purpose** – Clearly define why the meeting is happening.
2. **Time** – Decide the optimal duration. Respect everyone's hours.
3. **Agenda** – Share it in advance and stick to it.
4. **Preparation** – Encourage participants to come ready with data, questions, and contributions.

5. **Focus on Outcomes** – Avoid distractions and side conversations.
6. **Leadership** – Appoint a facilitator to guide the meeting and maintain flow.

III. The Rhythm of Meetings: Know the Right Frequency

- **Daily Meetings** – Quick, standing briefings focused on updates (ideal for team alignment).
- **Weekly Meetings** – Structured, collaborative, and ideal for decision-making and planning.
- **Monthly or Annual Meetings** – Reserved for strategy, vision, and long-term goal setting.

Pro tip: Schedule meetings **outside peak productivity hours**. Avoid interrupting deep work or focus time. **Virtual attendance options** increase flexibility and participation.

IV. Time-Smart Meeting Design: Structure is Power

Here's a suggested time allocation for a **60-minute meeting**:

- Welcome & Set Tone – 2 minutes
- Training Moment – 3 to 5 minutes
- Reports/Updates – 5 minutes
- Each Member's Contribution – 5 minutes per person
- Wrap-Up & Commitment Recap – Last 5 minutes

Use **timers** to maintain flow. A simple 4–5-minute slot with a 1-minute buffer helps avoid overruns.

V. Leading the Meeting: Everyone Has a Role

- Rotate the **facilitator role**—this builds leadership across the team.
- **Start on time**. This trains punctuality.

- **Welcome all participants warmly.**
- Keep the meeting focused. If the discussion strays, gently remind the team of the purpose.
- **Everyone gets a chance to speak**—encourage quieter team members and politely manage those who dominate or interrupt.

VI. Incorporate a "Training Moment"

A 3-minute inspirational or skill-based input to energize and educate:

- **What**: A concept worth sharing (e.g., customer care, ownership, teamwork)
- **How**: Through stories, visuals, questions, or brief videos
- Keep it **relatable, focused, and action-driven**

VII. Managing Online and Hybrid Meetings

Use the right format:

- **Video** – For introductions, collaboration, and new ideas
- **Audio** – Ideal for check-ins and longer updates
- **Hybrid** – Balance attention between in-office and remote participants

Challenges like reduced mobility, distractions, and cognitive load should be acknowledged. Train your team to **look at the camera**, minimize self-view distractions, and **stay engaged**.

VIII. The Art of Following Up

Every meeting should end with a **clear recap of "Who will do What by When."**

- Email the **minutes of meeting** promptly
- Create personal or team **reminders** for action items

- If someone misses a deadline, ask: "What got in the way?" (Not "Why?")—and support them to follow through
- Close the meeting with **encouragement and positivity**, not pressure

IX. Feedback, Conflict & Listening

- **Feedback** should focus on actions, not personalities
- Use softening language: "*It appears…*" or "*What I noticed…*"
- If conflict arises, suggest a **1-on-1 follow-up meeting**—keep the team space safe
- Praise contributions and revisit ideas in a dedicated forum if not discussed in full

X. Post-Meeting Habits: Where Real Impact Happens

- Review your personal commitments and **schedule action time**, not at the last moment
- Follow up with those you delegated to— **"How is it coming along?"** builds gentle accountability
- Track progress on long-term projects through meeting agendas and regular check-ins

Historical Wisdom on Meetings

Peter Drucker, the father of modern management, once said,

"Meetings are a symptom of bad organization. The fewer meetings the better."

But when done well, meetings **don't just manage time—they multiply energy, ideas, and ownership.**

If you host a **1-hour meeting with 10 attendees**, it's not a 1-hour cost—it's **10 hours of collective time**. That's the real weight of a meeting.

Respect it. Design it. Lead it well.

12. Prioritize Your Most Important Tasks

It's easy to get caught up in the urgency of small tasks that don't actually move the needle in your life. These tasks can create a sense of busyness without meaningful progress. The key to mastering time is learning to identify and focus on the tasks that bring you closer to your long-term vision.

As Dwight D. Eisenhower famously said, "What is important is seldom urgent, and what is urgent is seldom important." This insight led to the development of the **Eisenhower Matrix**, which categorizes tasks into four quadrants:

1. **Urgent and Important**
2. **Not Urgent but Important**
3. **Urgent but Not Important**
4. **Neither Urgent nor Important**

Your goal is to spend as much time as possible in the **"Not Urgent but Important"** quadrant. These tasks, though not pressing, will have the biggest impact on your long-term success. Eisenhower's principle reminds us that by prioritizing these important but not urgent activities, we can focus on strategic growth rather than reacting to emergencies.

Examples of Tasks in Each Quadrant

I. Urgent and Important (Crisis Mode)

These tasks require immediate attention and are critical to your goals or responsibilities.

a. A deadline for a major project that affects your team's results or a client-facing crisis that needs resolution within hours.

b. Handling an emergency situation like a product defect that needs immediate customer communication.

II. Not Urgent but Important (Strategic Focus)

These activities are not time-sensitive, but they are crucial for long-term growth and success. As Eisenhower emphasized, focusing on important but not urgent tasks allows us to stay proactive and plan ahead.

a. Planning your career development by enrolling in a course or acquiring new skills.

b. Setting long-term business strategies, nurturing relationships with key clients, or improving personal habits like exercise and reading.

III. Urgent but Not Important (Distractions)

Tasks in this quadrant seem urgent but don't significantly contribute to your goals. They can easily derail you from what matters.

a. Responding to non-urgent emails that could be delegated, or attending meetings that don't align with your core responsibilities.

b. Spending time on social media notifications or chatting with coworkers about non-work-related topics.

IV. Neither Urgent nor Important (Time Wasters)

These tasks don't contribute to your goals and don't need immediate attention. They are often time drains.

a. Watching TV or scrolling through your phone during work hours without any productivity or purpose.

b. Over-organizing your workspace or engaging in excessive administrative tasks that could be automated or delegated.

By identifying and focusing on **"Not Urgent but Important"** tasks—like strategic planning, skill development, and relationship-building—you can make significant strides toward your long-term goals. As Eisenhower wisely suggested, focusing on these activities before they become urgent allows you to maintain control over your time and ultimately work more effectively.

13. Embrace the Power of Focus

In our modern, digitally-driven world, distractions are constant. Notifications, emails, and endless multitasking pull our attention in multiple directions, often resulting in fragmented work and mediocre outcomes.

One of the most powerful tools for effective time management is *single-tasking*—the art of deep focus. When you commit to one task at a time, you give that task the full attention and mental presence it deserves. This not only improves the quality of your work but also increases your efficiency.

True productivity isn't about rushing through your to-do list—it's about the depth and quality of your output. And in today's world, the ability to focus without interruption has become a rare and highly valuable skill.

- **Work Projects:** Instead of answering emails while preparing a presentation, block a 90-minute window with all notifications off, and work solely on the presentation. You'll finish faster and with higher quality.
- **Study Sessions:** A student studying for an exam can use the Pomodoro Technique—25 minutes of focused study followed by a 5-minute break. This helps maintain concentration while avoiding burnout.
- **Creative Work:** Writers, designers, or content creators often produce their best work during uninterrupted blocks of time. One writer might schedule early morning hours with no phone or internet access just to write 1,000 words of meaningful content.
- **Meetings:** During a one-on-one conversation or a team meeting, putting your phone away and being fully present allows for better understanding, quicker decisions, and deeper collaboration.

Practicing focused work not only boosts your performance but also trains your brain to resist distractions. Over time, it becomes your superpower in an age of noise.

14. Set Boundaries to Protect Your Time

Your time is one of your most valuable assets, and setting boundaries is essential to preserve and manage it wisely. Without clear boundaries, other people's demands and expectations will begin to fill your schedule—often at the cost of your own priorities.

This may mean saying no to meetings that don't align with your goals, declining social invitations that distract from your vision, or limiting time spent on activities that don't support your well-being or success. Setting boundaries isn't always comfortable—it requires discipline and self-respect—but it is crucial for leading a focused, balanced, and fulfilling life.

As the saying goes, "*If you don't prioritize your life, someone else will.*"

Imagine you're working on launching a new business, and a friend frequently calls you during your peak work hours to chat. If you don't set boundaries, these interruptions can derail your focus and progress. A simple boundary might be saying, "*Hey, I'd love to catch up, but I'm working heads-down between 10 AM and 2 PM. Can we talk in the evening instead?*" This small step protects your productivity while still honoring your relationships—just on your terms.

15. Plan Your Day the Night Before

One of the most effective strategies for time management is to plan ahead. Take just a few moments at the end of each day to map out your top priorities for the next day. This simple habit helps you start your morning with a clear sense of direction, eliminating the mental clutter that often accompanies unstructured days.

By outlining your tasks in advance, you can enter each day with focus and clarity—ensuring that you tackle the most important things first instead of getting lost in distractions. This small yet powerful practice can turn chaotic mornings into calm, purposeful starts.

- **Daily Planning:** Before going to bed, list your top 3 tasks for the next day. For instance, if you're preparing for a client meeting, block time for reviewing notes, preparing your pitch, and finalizing the presentation first thing in the morning.
- **Time Blocking:** If you're a student with assignments due and exams coming up, block out specific hours for focused study and others for revision, so you're not scrambling at the last minute.
- **Morning Routine:** For parents or working professionals, planning the next day's meals, clothes, and commute the night before can eliminate stress and save valuable decision-making energy in the morning.
- **Workplace Efficiency:** A manager might review the team's progress at the end of the day and schedule quick check-ins or delegate tasks for the next day, ensuring a smooth workflow.

Planning ahead is like laying tracks before the train arrives—it ensures a smoother, more efficient journey through your day.

16. Break Large Projects into Smaller Tasks

Large tasks often feel like monumental obstacles, causing us to feel overwhelmed, which in turn leads to procrastination and delays. The sheer size and complexity of a big project can create a mental block, making it difficult to take that first step. This is where the strategy of breaking down a large task into smaller, more manageable chunks becomes incredibly effective. By doing so, you transform the overwhelming project into a series of smaller, achievable steps. Each smaller task feels less intimidating and more within your control, reducing the feeling of being paralyzed by the overall scope of the work. This method not only makes the project feel more doable but also provides a clear path forward, allowing you to map out exactly what needs to be done.

Moreover, as you tackle each small step, you experience a sense of accomplishment, no matter how minor it might seem. This positive reinforcement fuels your motivation and gives you the momentum to keep progressing. The satisfaction of completing each segment gives you confidence and reduces anxiety, allowing you to focus on the next step. Over time, these small wins accumulate, bringing you closer to the completion of the entire project. By the time you've worked through all the steps, the once-daunting task is now behind you, and the sense of achievement is all the more rewarding because of the consistent, focused effort you put in. This approach, which breaks down a large task into smaller milestones, not only enhances productivity but also fosters a mindset of progress and accomplishment.

17. Learn the Art of Saying No

One of the most powerful time management tools is learning the art of saying no. While saying yes to every request might feel polite or accommodating, it often leads to burnout, stress, and a scattered focus. You end up investing your energy in things that don't truly align with your goals or values.

Saying no isn't about being rude or unkind—it's about honoring your priorities and protecting your time. When you say no to distractions and low-value commitments, you make room for what truly matters.

From my personal experience, I've learned that saying no is rarely easy—especially when it involves people we care about or want to impress. But avoiding it can create internal conflict, resentment, and even strained relationships later.

A simple but effective strategy is this: when someone makes a request, don't respond immediately. Take a pause. Give yourself time to evaluate whether it aligns with your priorities. And if you need to say no, do it with kindness and confidence. Smile. Express appreciation for the opportunity. Then, if possible, offer a helpful alternative.

If a colleague asks you to take on a last-minute project that doesn't fall under your responsibilities and you're already overwhelmed, you might respond, "*Thank you for thinking of me. I'm currently focused on completing another priority task, so I won't be able to take this on right now. However, have you considered reaching out to [Name]? They might be able to help you within your timeline.*"

Or when a friend invites you to a weekend outing while you've planned to rest or work on a personal goal, you might say, "*That sounds like a lot of fun, but I've already set aside this weekend for some personal commitments. Let's try to catch up next week instead.*"

Saying no with grace and clarity strengthens your self-respect and communicates to others that your time has value. The more you practice, the more natural it becomes.

18. Use the 80/20 Rule (Pareto Principle)

The 80/20 rule, also known as the Pareto Principle, is a powerful concept for managing time and increasing productivity. It suggests that 80% of your results come from just 20% of your efforts. In other words, a small portion of your tasks often contributes to the majority of your success.

By identifying and prioritizing those high-impact activities, you can focus your energy where it counts most—and either eliminate, automate, or delegate the rest. This principle prevents you from getting bogged down in low-value tasks and keeps you aligned with your goals.

Few Examples of the 80/20 Rule in Time Management:

- **Work Tasks**

  In many jobs, 20% of the tasks produce 80% of the value. For instance, a salesperson might find that 20% of their clients generate 80% of their revenue. By focusing more on nurturing these key relationships, they can improve results significantly.

- **Email Management**

  You might receive dozens of emails daily, but only a handful (say 20%) require real action or drive important outcomes. By identifying and responding to those first, you avoid wasting time on low-priority messages.

- **Goal Setting and Project Planning:**

  When working on a large project, often 20% of the milestones lead to 80% of the project's success. Focusing on these critical tasks first helps avoid procrastination and ensures momentum.

- **Learning and Skill Development**

  If you're learning a new skill, such as public speaking or digital marketing, 20% of the techniques or content often deliver 80% of the practical improvement. Prioritizing those can fast-track your growth.

- **Meetings**

  In team meetings, 20% of the agenda usually holds the most impactful discussions. Recognizing this helps structure meetings to be more efficient and outcome-driven.

By consistently applying the 80/20 rule, you can dramatically improve the way you manage your time, reduce stress, and amplify your effectiveness.

19. Develop a Routine to Increase Consistency

Success is often the result of consistent action over time. One of the best ways to achieve this consistency is by developing a daily routine. A routine helps eliminate decision fatigue and creates structure, allowing you to focus your energy on your most important tasks. By having a set routine, you avoid the stress of deciding what to do next, allowing your brain to focus on execution instead of the logistics of planning.

A well-designed routine can boost productivity by making important activities habitual, so they require less mental effort. The consistency that comes with a routine ensures that you are prioritizing the right actions each day, making your goals more achievable over time.

For example, you could start your day with a morning workout. This not only boosts your physical energy but also sets a positive tone for the rest of the day. You might also dedicate specific time blocks for deep work, free from distractions, to tackle your most important tasks. Over time, these actions will become ingrained in your routine, requiring less effort to initiate and offering more lasting results.

The power of routine lies in its ability to remove uncertainty and allow you to channel your energy into high-impact activities. Just like any successful person, when you create and stick to your routine, you remove distractions and optimize your time for success.

20. Practice the Two-Minute Rule

The two-minute rule is a simple yet effective time management strategy. The rule states that if a task will take two minutes or less to complete, do it immediately. This applies to small actions like responding to an email, making a quick phone call, or filing a document. By completing these small tasks right away, you prevent them from piling up and cluttering your schedule. This approach helps you stay on top of small, routine tasks without allowing them to become overwhelming.

Imagine you open your email inbox and see a short email from a colleague asking for clarification on a minor point. Instead of letting it sit and get lost among other emails, you apply the two-minute rule and respond right away. Similarly, you might have a few documents on your desk that need to be filed. Rather than letting them accumulate into a larger task, you take two minutes to file them immediately, clearing up your workspace.

By adopting the two-minute rule, you create a habit of managing small tasks efficiently, which prevents unnecessary stress and keeps you focused on more important tasks. Over time, these small actions add up, making your overall time management more effective.

21. Take Regular Breaks to Recharge

Effective time management isn't just about working hard; it's also about knowing when to rest. Research shows that taking regular breaks throughout the day can actually improve productivity and creativity. Breaks give your brain the chance to rest and recharge, preventing mental fatigue. Whether it's a short walk, a meditation session, or a few minutes of stretching, incorporating breaks into your day ensures that you stay focused and energized, rather than burning out. Remember, productivity is a marathon, not a sprint.

For instance, let's say you're working on a report that requires deep concentration. After working for 60 to 90 minutes, you decide to take a 10-minute break. You step away from your desk, go for a quick walk around the block, or simply stretch for a few minutes. When you return to your work, you feel more refreshed and are able to approach the task with a renewed focus. This short break helps prevent mental fatigue, ensuring you're more productive and creative when you resume your work.

By regularly incorporating breaks into your day, you optimize your energy levels, reduce stress, and increase your overall efficiency. It's about working smarter, not just harder.

22. Batch Similar Tasks Together

Task batching is a technique that involves grouping similar tasks together and completing them in one dedicated block of time. This eliminates the mental effort required to switch between different types of tasks and helps you stay focused. By batching tasks, you reduce the need for constant task switching, which can otherwise lead to burnout and decreased productivity.

Instead of checking emails sporadically throughout the day—each time getting distracted from your main task—designate a specific time block, say from 10:00 AM to 10:30 AM, to respond to emails. By focusing solely on emails during this dedicated time, you can handle them more quickly and efficiently, without losing focus on other critical tasks.

If you're a manager, you can batch meetings. Rather than attending meetings at random intervals, schedule all your meetings for specific days or times of the week. For example, you could hold meetings only on Tuesday mornings, ensuring that the rest of the week is reserved for focused, uninterrupted work. This way, you reduce the mental load of constantly preparing for or transitioning between meetings and work tasks.

If you have multiple phone calls to make, batch them together during a certain time in the afternoon, such as from 2:00 PM to 3:00 PM. Instead of interrupting your workflow by making calls whenever they come up, you concentrate on one task (making calls) during a specific time frame.

Batching tasks like this can significantly improve your efficiency, reduce distractions, and help you maintain a smooth workflow. Over time, this practice frees up more mental space, allowing you to focus on high-impact activities that drive results.

23. Focus on Outcomes, Not Just Activities

It's easy to get caught up in a flurry of activity and convince yourself that you're being productive simply because you're busy. However, true productivity comes from focusing on outcomes, not just activities. Ask yourself: What is the result of the work I'm doing right now? Does this activity move me closer to my personal or professional goals? Instead of filling your day with endless to-dos, focus on achieving measurable outcomes that matter. This mindset shift will ensure that every action you take brings you closer to your ultimate purpose.

Let's say you're working on a project, but you spend a lot of time reading emails, replying to non-urgent messages, and attending meetings that aren't directly related to your goal. While you're busy, these activities aren't moving you forward. Instead, if you focused on drafting key sections of the project or conducting research for the deliverables, your time would be spent more productively, as these tasks contribute directly to the outcome you're aiming for.

If you're a sales professional, rather than spending hours organizing your CRM or making small talk with colleagues, ask yourself: "What actions will lead to closing deals?" Perhaps that means focusing on calling high-potential leads, preparing tailored pitches, or following up on previous conversations—activities that will directly impact your sales numbers and bring you closer to your targets.

When you're working on personal development, don't just spend time reading self-help books or attending webinars. Instead, ask: What actionable steps can I take from this knowledge? For example, after attending a leadership seminar, you might set a goal to practice specific leadership skills like delegation or feedback in your next team meeting, ensuring the knowledge translates into meaningful growth.

By focusing on outcomes rather than just activities, you ensure that every task you engage in moves you closer to your long-term vision. This shift in mindset transforms busy work into productive action that directly contributes to your success.

24. Eliminate Time Drainers

Time drainers are those activities or habits that suck up your time without giving you anything meaningful in return. These can include excessive social media scrolling, watching TV, or engaging in unnecessary meetings. Identifying your time drainers is key to improving your time management. Once you recognize them, you can take steps to eliminate or limit their impact.

Reduce the following

- **Social Media Scrolling:** Set a timer to limit your social media usage to 15 minutes a day.
- **Unnecessary Meetings:** Decline meetings without clear agendas or objectives.
- **TV Watching:** Replace mindless TV watching with more productive or relaxing activities like reading or exercising.
- **Email Checking:** Set specific times during the day to check emails, instead of checking them constantly.
- **Over-committing:** Learn to say no to requests that do not align with your priorities.

25. Create a "Do Not Do" List

We often focus on what we should do, but sometimes the most powerful strategy is identifying what we should not do. Creating a "Do Not Do" list helps you outline actions, habits, or commitments that are counterproductive to your goals. For example, "Do not multitask with unrelated activities that split your attention." Multitasking can seem like a time-saver, but it often leads to lower quality work and slower progress. Instead of juggling multiple tasks, focus on one thing at a time to complete it with full attention and quality. A "Do Not Do" list serves as a reminder to steer clear of activities that waste your time or energy, allowing you to direct your efforts toward what truly matters.

26. Learn to Delegate Effectively

No one can do everything themselves, and trying to do so is a surefire way to burn out. The key to effective time management is learning to delegate tasks to others. When delegating, focus on the strengths and expertise of your team members, ensuring that tasks are assigned to the right person. For example, if you're managing a project and someone on your team excels at graphic design, delegate the task of creating visuals to them. Provide clear instructions, set expectations, and trust others to carry out the tasks. By delegating effectively, you free up your own time for higher-value activities and empower others to grow in their roles, creating a more efficient and collaborative team.

27. Break Free from Perfectionism

Perfectionism can be a major time-sink. Striving for perfection in every task often leads to overthinking, procrastination, and missed deadlines. For example, if you spend hours revising a report that's already solid, you're wasting valuable time that could be spent on other important tasks. Understand that perfection is not always the goal—progress is. Strive for excellence rather than perfection, and set realistic standards for yourself. For instance, when writing an email, focus on delivering your message clearly rather than obsessing over every word. Remember that completing a task and learning from it is often more valuable than obsessing over every detail. By letting go of perfectionism, you'll reduce the stress and time lost in trying to achieve an unattainable ideal, freeing up time for more productive endeavors.

28. Create Time Blocks for Focused Work

Time blocking is a powerful time management tool. It involves scheduling specific blocks of time to focus solely on one task or set of tasks. By allocating dedicated time for focused work, you reduce the chances of distractions and create periods where you can immerse yourself in deep work. For instance, you could allocate 9 AM to 11 AM for writing, 2 PM to 3 PM for meetings, and so on. During these time blocks, commit to being fully present and avoid switching between tasks. This technique helps you maintain momentum and productivity throughout the day.

29. Use Technology Wisely

Technology can either help or hinder your productivity. The key is using technology wisely. Tools like calendars, project management software, and note-taking apps can streamline your workflow and help you stay organized. For example, using Google Calendar to schedule your tasks and set reminders ensures you never miss important deadlines. Apps like Trello or Asana can help you manage projects by breaking them down into manageable tasks and tracking progress. However, it's important to avoid being distracted by notifications, social media, or unnecessary apps. Set boundaries around your use of technology—for example, turn off non-essential notifications, designate specific times for checking emails, and use apps like Freedom or Cold Turkey to block distracting websites during work hours. By using technology mindfully, you enhance your efficiency rather than letting it drain your time.

30. Prioritize Self-Care to Maintain Energy

Productivity isn't just about work; it's also about maintaining your energy levels. Taking care of your physical, mental, and emotional well-being is crucial for sustained performance. Regular exercise, such as a 30-minute walk in the morning or a yoga session to stretch and relieve tension, helps boost circulation and mental clarity. Healthy eating, like fueling your body with nutrient-dense meals—such as a balanced breakfast with oats, fruits, and protein—can provide sustained energy throughout the day. Adequate sleep, ensuring you get at least 7-8 hours of rest each night, is the foundation for sharp focus and mental agility. Additionally, carving out time for relaxation, whether it's a five-minute meditation during your lunch break or reading a book before bed, can help reset your mind. When you prioritize your health and well-being, you ensure that you have the energy and focus to tackle your tasks with clarity and enthusiasm. A well-rested, healthy mind and body are far more productive than one that is overworked and drained, giving you the power to excel in both your professional and personal life.

31. Eliminate the Need for Constant Decision-Making

Constantly making decisions throughout the day can be exhausting and time-consuming. One way to combat decision fatigue is by eliminating the need for constant choices. Streamline your daily decisions by creating routines and habits. For instance, plan your meals for the week in advance to avoid the daily question of what to eat, saving time each evening by simply following your pre-planned menu. You could create a set morning routine—such as waking up at 6 AM, exercising for 20 minutes, having a healthy breakfast, and reviewing your day's priorities—to jump-start your day with minimal decisions. Additionally, set specific times for certain tasks, like designating 9 AM to 11 AM for focused work, and 2 PM for administrative tasks such as responding to emails. When you reduce the number of decisions you need to make, you conserve mental energy for the important decisions that matter most, leaving you with more time and focus for your high-priority tasks.

32. Focus on What You Can Control

Often, we spend valuable time worrying about things that are beyond our control. Whether it's stressing over an unexpected delay in a project, worrying about a colleague's opinion, or feeling overwhelmed by tasks outside of our scope, this kind of mental energy is wasted and counterproductive. Instead, focus on what you can control—your actions, your time, and your reactions. For instance, if you're managing a project and a deadline is pushed back, instead of focusing on the delay, focus on optimizing your remaining time and adjusting your schedule accordingly.

By setting specific goals each day, you can keep your efforts aligned with what's achievable within your control, like prioritizing tasks that directly contribute to your long-term objectives. Similarly, you can control how you react to challenges—by adopting a calm, solution-oriented approach rather than stressing over obstacles.

This mindset aligns with the **Serenity Prayer**, famously penned by theologian Reinhold Niebuhr, which asks for:

"God, grant me the serenity to accept the things I cannot change,

Courage to change the things I can,

And wisdom to know the difference."

By applying this prayer to time management, you're reminding yourself to focus only on what is within your control—your time, your actions, and your approach to challenges. This mindset helps to clear away distractions, reduce stress, and keep you focused on what matters most, improving both productivity and overall well-being.

Focusing on what you can control not only empowers you, but it also helps you use your time effectively, setting you up for success rather than wasting energy on the uncontrollable.

33. Use Downtime Effectively

Downtime doesn't have to be wasted time. Whether you're commuting, waiting for a meeting to start, or taking a break, you can use these moments to make progress on smaller tasks, learn something new, or simply reflect. For instance, you can listen to an educational podcast during your commute, write notes or ideas in your phone during downtime, or review your to-do list while waiting for an appointment. By using your downtime effectively, you maximize your productivity and make the most of every moment.

Here are some examples of how to use downtime effectively:

- **During commutes**: Listen to educational podcasts, audiobooks, or language learning materials to make productive use of the time.
- **While waiting for meetings**: Review your to-do list, prep for upcoming meetings, or jot down ideas in your phone or notebook.
- **Taking a break**: Practice deep breathing or mindfulness exercises to recharge your mental energy.
- **During lunch breaks**: Read a few pages from a book on personal development or business.
- **While in waiting rooms**: Organize your phone or emails, or respond to non-urgent messages.
- **During downtime at home**: Engage in hobbies that help you relax but also provide growth, like learning to cook a healthy recipe or practicing a new skill.
- **While doing household chores**: Listen to motivational talks, podcasts, or a business webinar to stay inspired.

By consciously using these pockets of time, you can keep your productivity high and ensure you're always moving forward, even during those seemingly idle moments.

34. Develop a Morning Routine for PEAK Performance

How you start your day sets the tone for the rest of it. A strong morning routine can help you enter your day with purpose, energy, and focus. Start by identifying key activities that align with your goals, whether it's exercise, journaling, meditation, or setting your priorities for the day. Consistency is key—when you begin each day with intention and clarity, you're more likely to stay on track throughout the day. A productive morning routine helps to reduce decision fatigue and ensures that you're mentally prepared for the challenges ahead.

P - Prepare: Begin your morning by preparing your mind and body for the day. This can involve meditation, deep breathing, or reviewing your goals. Preparation sets the tone for mental clarity and calmness throughout your day.

E - Exercise: Physical activity boosts your energy levels, improves mood, and enhances focus. Even a short walk, stretching, or yoga can get your blood flowing and clear your mind for the tasks ahead.

A - Affirmations: Set a positive intention for your day. Affirmations or journaling help you cultivate a mindset of success and self-belief. For instance, you can affirm: "I am focused, disciplined, and capable of achieving my goals today."

K - Keen Planning: Take a moment to plan your day. Prioritize your most important tasks and align them with your long-term vision. Having a clear roadmap for your day helps you stay focused on what truly matters.

Time management isn't about squeezing in more. It's about flowing with purpose. Create routines. Weekly rhythms. Morning rituals. They reduce decision fatigue and stabilize performance.

35. Time is a Mirror of Your Values

What you give your hours to reflects your true values—not your intentions. You may say health is important, but if there's no time blocked for workouts, that belief is hollow. Review your calendar often. Let your time reflect the life you want to lead.

Health and Fitness: If you truly value your health, ensure that you dedicate specific hours each week to exercise. For example, blocking out 30 minutes each morning for a workout or a run ensures that your actions reflect your belief in the importance of staying fit.

Family and Relationships: If spending time with loved ones is a priority, schedule regular family dinners or weekend outings. By blocking out time for relationships, you demonstrate that they are an essential part of your life.

Personal Growth: If learning and personal development are important to you, set aside time every day for reading, courses, or self-improvement exercises. For example, committing to reading a chapter a day or enrolling in an online course shows your commitment to continuous growth.

Career Advancement: If professional success is a priority, dedicate focused time to improving your skills, networking, or working on projects that move you forward in your career. This could mean setting aside an hour every evening for deep work or taking a course to enhance your skills.

Mental Well-being: If peace of mind is important, allocate time each day for relaxation and mindfulness activities, such as meditation or journaling. This could involve spending 10 minutes each morning practicing mindfulness or using your lunch break for a calming walk.

36. Minimalism Multiplies Time

The fewer decisions you make, the more energy you conserve. Simplify your routines. Reduce possessions. Remove digital clutter. As *REWORK* suggests, "The more stuff you have, the more time you waste managing it." This aligns with the ideas of Tim Ferriss in his book *The 4-Hour Workweek*, where he advocates for eliminating distractions and focusing only on what matters most. Creating space—both mentally and physically—frees up valuable time and energy that you can invest in more important activities.

Marie Kondo's decluttering philosophy suggests, "The objective is not to declutter, but to organize your life so you can focus on what truly matters." When you cut out distractions, whether they're physical, mental, or digital, you create more room for deep work and productivity.

Mark Manson, in his book *The Subtle Art of Not Giving a* *** emphasizes the importance of choosing what to care about, stating, "You can't be available to everything. You have to learn to say 'no.'" This tie into simplifying your environment and your life choices to focus on what truly brings value, allowing you to invest your time wisely.

And sometimes, as the saying goes, "Ignorance is bliss." Not every distraction or piece of information needs your attention. The constant flow of news, emails, and social media updates can be overwhelming and time-consuming. By choosing to ignore what doesn't serve your goals, you conserve both time and mental energy, allowing yourself to focus on what matters most.

By simplifying your environment and daily tasks, you give yourself the gift of focus, leading to better time management, clarity, and a more intentional life.

37. Your Calendar is Sacred

Your time is your most valuable resource, and how you allocate it directly impacts your productivity and success. Just as you guard your wallet from unnecessary expenses, you must protect your calendar from distractions and tasks that don't align with your core values and goals. If something doesn't align with your priorities, don't hesitate to say "no" or decline. This is a powerful way to preserve your time for the things that truly matter.

For example, if you're working towards a major project or goal, such as writing a book or launching a business, it's essential to allocate dedicated time in your calendar for focused work. This means blocking off time in advance to work on your big tasks and ensuring that they come before smaller, less important tasks (the pebbles).

Stephen Covey's principle of "First Things First" emphasizes that we often get caught up in urgent but unimportant tasks, leaving the important things (like building relationships or setting long-term goals) on the back burner. By intentionally scheduling time for those "big rocks"—such as exercise, planning, strategy sessions, or personal growth—you ensure that these priorities don't get swallowed up by the busyness of everyday life.

Here are some concrete examples of how to apply this:

- **Big Rocks First:** Block out your most productive hours of the day for your most critical work. If you're a writer, for instance, designate mornings for deep work on your manuscript, leaving smaller tasks like checking emails or social media for later in the day.
- **Protect Your Time:** If a friend or colleague invites you to an event that conflicts with your core priorities, politely decline. Instead of attending every meeting or event, ask yourself: "Is this the best use of my time?" If it doesn't bring you closer to your goals, it's okay to say no.

- **Time for Yourself:** Guard time for self-care and reflection. If you're working hard to grow a business, it's easy to neglect personal well-being. Ensure you're scheduling regular breaks, time for exercise, or just a moment of rest in between tasks. By making self-care a priority in your calendar, you're also ensuring long-term productivity.
- **Delegate Low-Value Tasks:** If there are tasks that someone else can handle, delegate them. This frees up your time for higher-value activities. For example, if you're a manager, delegate administrative work or meeting scheduling to an assistant so you can focus on strategy and leadership.

By being intentional and disciplined with your calendar, you'll ensure that your time reflects the life you want to live—a life aligned with your most important goals. Just as you wouldn't let anyone waste your money, don't let anyone waste your time.

38. Create a Daily Shut-Down Ritual

A solid evening routine is just as crucial as a great morning routine. It provides closure to your day, allowing you to decompress, reflect, and prepare for the following day. The goal is to set clear boundaries between work and rest to ensure that your mind doesn't remain in a constant state of overdrive.

Here are some examples of a productive evening routine

Review Your Tasks: Before finishing your day, take 10–15 minutes to review your tasks. Check what you've accomplished and identify what needs to be done tomorrow. This prevents your brain from obsessing over unfinished work while you're trying to relax.

If you work in project management, reviewing the tasks for the next day might involve going through project timelines, ensuring you have everything ready for upcoming meetings, or preparing for any decisions you need to make.

Clear Your Workspace: A cluttered environment often leads to a cluttered mind. Spend a few minutes tidying up your desk, organizing your files, and putting things in their place. This simple act helps signal to your brain that the workday has ended, fostering a sense of closure.

If you're a writer or content creator, organizing your workspace can involve closing all your browser tabs, sorting through notes or ideas, and clearing away unnecessary papers.

Journaling or Reflection: Journaling can help clear your mind and reflect on what went well during the day. Write down your accomplishments, any challenges you faced, and set an intention for tomorrow.

A professional could journal about what went well in a client meeting and what they want to improve the next time. This process not only reflects your growth but also helps you unwind by putting your thoughts into perspective.

Prepare for Tomorrow: Set up the basics for the next day—choose your outfit, prepare any materials you'll need, and set reminders for your most important tasks. By taking these small steps in the evening, you ensure that your morning is smoother and more intentional.

If you have an early presentation, preparing the slides, reviewing your notes, and packing your materials the night before can save time and mental energy the following morning.

Unwind and Disconnect: Ensure you allow time for unwinding before going to bed. Whether it's reading, meditating, or enjoying a relaxing activity, these practices help lower stress and prepare you for restorative sleep.

A person who works in tech might disconnect from screens 30 minutes before bed, possibly listening to calming music or reading a book that has no relation to work.

By incorporating these steps into your evening routine, you create a bridge from work to rest, giving your mind the closure it needs to recharge. This will help improve both your sleep quality and your productivity in the days to come.

39. Create a Gathering Point

David Allen's "Getting Things Done" system teaches this well: never let your brain be a storage unit. Have a central place (notebook, app) to dump every task, thought, and reminder. This frees mental RAM for creative thinking.

Creating a Gathering Point is a game-changer for effective time management. David Allen's "Getting Things Done" system emphasizes that our brains are not designed to be storage units for all our tasks and thoughts. When you keep reminders, ideas, and tasks floating in your head, it's like running multiple applications on your phone without closing any. The result? Mental overload and drained energy.

a. **Notebook or Digital App**: Use a physical notebook or a digital tool like Evernote or to do list to capture every task, from work meetings to grocery lists. By writing things down or recording them digitally, you free up your mental space for deeper focus and creativity.

b. **Voice Notes**: On your commute or during meetings, use your phone's voice recorder to jot down quick thoughts, ideas, or tasks that pop into your head. This allows you to capture them instantly without interrupting your flow.

c. **Centralized Calendar**: Use a calendar app to note down appointments, reminders, and deadlines. By centralizing everything in one location, you can prevent the overwhelm of trying to remember it all.

By having a dedicated space for these thoughts, you release mental clutter and open up space for more focused, high-level thinking. It also ensures you don't forget important tasks, leading to better time management and productivity.

40. Start with Why, Not What

Before you dive into your task list, always ask yourself, *Why am I doing this?* Purpose energizes effort, and knowing your "why" transforms mundane tasks into meaningful ones. When your actions are driven by purpose, you're more likely to stay motivated and focused, especially when faced with challenging or tedious tasks.

For example, if you're organizing your workspace, instead of seeing it as just a chore, ask yourself, *why is this important?* You might realize that a clean, organized workspace fosters clarity and enhances your productivity, aligning with your long-term goal of becoming more efficient in your work.

Another example is when you're responding to emails. Instead of viewing it as a time-consuming task, ask, *why am I doing this?* You might find that responding promptly to emails fosters better communication, strengthens professional relationships, and advances your career goals.

Even with a task like grocery shopping, instead of viewing it as a mere errand, remind yourself that it's part of your bigger goal of maintaining a healthy lifestyle. This mindset shift makes the task more intentional and keeps you motivated.

As Simon Sinek famously said, "*People don't buy what you do, they buy why you do it.*" When you lead with purpose, your actions are infused with greater meaning, driving you toward success.

41. Use Deadlines to Spark Focus

Deadlines are not just time constraints; they are powerful tools for boosting productivity and focus. When you set a deadline, you essentially create a sense of urgency that helps your brain focus and organize tasks more effectively. As Parkinson's Law suggests, "work expands to fill the time available." If you give yourself a whole week to complete a task, you may find yourself procrastinating or wasting time, knowing that you have plenty of time ahead. However, if you condense that time frame into a single day or a few hours, you're forced to focus and work efficiently.

For example, if you have a report to finish, instead of planning to finish it by the end of the week, set a goal to have it done by 4 PM today. This not only reduces the chance of distractions but also increases the intensity of your effort. The pressure to meet the deadline pushes you to prioritize, avoid perfectionism, and bypass procrastination, making you more effective in completing the task.

Another example is scheduling focused work blocks in the form of deadlines for yourself. For instance, if you're working on a presentation, instead of saying, "I'll work on it this afternoon," say, "I'll complete the first three slides by 1 PM." Setting small, clear deadlines throughout the process creates a constant flow of productivity. This approach also helps break large, overwhelming projects into manageable parts.

Additionally, you can create external accountability for yourself by sharing your deadlines with others. When you know someone is expecting the task to be done within a certain time frame, it provides extra motivation to focus and get it done. You could even compete against your past self to see if you can complete the same task faster, adding a bit of healthy pressure to spark your creativity.

By using deadlines in this way, you reduce the mental drain of open-ended tasks and avoid the tendency to procrastinate, ultimately improving both the quality and timeliness of your work.

42. Use Pomodoro Technique

The Pomodoro Technique, developed by Francesco Cirillo in the late 1980s, is a time management method designed to improve focus and productivity by breaking work into short, focused intervals, typically 25 minutes in length, followed by a short break. Each of these intervals is called a "Pomodoro," after the tomato-shaped kitchen timer Cirillo originally used. The technique encourages individuals to work in concentrated bursts, which enhances concentration and minimizes the temptation of distractions.

Follow the steps

a. **Choose a task**: Select a specific task or project you want to focus on.
b. **Set a timer for 25 minutes**: Start the timer, and work on the task until it rings. During this time, give the task your full attention.
c. **Take a short break (5 minutes)**: Once the timer goes off, take a short break to relax and recharge. It's a good time to stretch, hydrate, or just rest your eyes.
d. **Repeat**: After four Pomodoros, take a longer break (15–30 minutes), which gives you more time to rest and reset before starting another cycle.

The Pomodoro Technique leverages two key psychological principles: focus and recovery. By setting a timer, you're creating a sense of urgency that helps you stay fully engaged in the task at hand. The short breaks help prevent burnout by allowing your brain to rest and recharge, ensuring sustained productivity throughout the day. The method also capitalizes on the idea of **time-boxing**—you're giving yourself permission to work intensely but only for a limited time, which helps reduce feelings of overwhelm and procrastination.

- **Studying for an Exam**: Let's say you're preparing for an exam. Instead of studying for hours on end, you can set your timer for 25 minutes to focus solely on one chapter or set of problems. After the timer goes off, take a 5-minute break and then jump into the next Pomodoro. This keeps your brain from getting fatigued and makes studying feel more manageable.
- **Writing a Report**: If you have a lengthy report to write, you can break it into smaller tasks such as gathering data, drafting sections, and editing. Set a timer for 25 minutes to focus on one part of the task, then take a 5-minute break. The structure helps avoid distractions and gives you regular opportunities to recharge.
- **Household Chores**: A task like cleaning your house can seem daunting, but with the Pomodoro Technique, you can focus on just one task at a time—cleaning the kitchen, for example. You set your timer, clean for 25 minutes, and then take a 5-minute break. This prevents the task from feeling overwhelming and helps you maintain a high level of efficiency.

Time without energy is useless. Manage your food, sleep, exercise, and mental inputs like a CEO manages budgets. What drains you? What fuels you? Guard your energy as tightly as your calendar.

43. Use Templates to Save Time and Sanity

Creating templates is a game-changer for time management, both personally and professionally. Here are some examples to help illustrate how templates can save you time and increase efficiency:

a. **Email Templates**: For professional communication, having templates for common responses (e.g., follow-up emails, meeting confirmations, or thank-you notes) can save significant time. For example, you can create a template for a weekly status update that you can easily customize each week instead of starting from scratch.

b. **Meeting Agendas**: Instead of creating a new agenda for every meeting, have a standard meeting agenda template ready. This could include sections like: meeting objectives, key discussion points, action items, and next steps. You can adjust the details based on the specific meeting, but the format remains the same.

c. **Project Reports**: For projects, create a template that includes key sections like project status, milestones, deadlines, and challenges. This way, every time you need to report on progress, you won't have to decide what information to include—it's all outlined in your template.

d. **Daily Task Lists**: For personal time management, create a daily template that includes sections for prioritizing tasks, tracking time, and allocating specific blocks for deep work. You can tweak the tasks based on your day, but the structure will remain the same, giving you clarity and focus.

e. **Budgeting**: A personal finance template can help you track your expenses, categorize them (e.g., housing, utilities, groceries, entertainment), and set monthly spending limits. Instead of tracking expenses from scratch, you simply update the numbers, and you get a clear picture of your financial health.

44. Learn the Art of Saying 'Not Now'

You don't have to say 'No' forever—sometimes 'Not now' is enough. This gentle boundary helps maintain relationships while protecting your priorities. Keep a "Later List." Revisit it weekly. It gives peace of mind and keeps the present uncluttered.

- If a colleague asks you to take on a new project that doesn't align with your current goals, instead of immediately saying "No," you could say, "That sounds interesting, but I'm focused on [current priority] right now. Let's revisit it in a few weeks."
- If a friend invites you to a social gathering, but you're swamped with work, you can respond with, "I'd love to join, but I have a lot on my plate right now. Let's plan for next month instead."
- For work meetings, when someone proposes a last-minute meeting, you could say, "I'm fully booked this week, but I'd be happy to discuss this next week."

By using a "Later List," you can place tasks, invitations, or projects that are not urgent but might be of interest at a later time. Revisiting it each week ensures you stay focused on the current priorities while keeping those opportunities on your radar. This method helps to avoid feeling overwhelmed while maintaining meaningful relationships and commitments.

45. Use Visual Timelines

Visualizing your goals can transform the way you approach time management and productivity. By creating visual representations of your goals, you bring them out of your mind and into a tangible format that keeps you accountable and focused. Here are a few examples of how to make this work:

a. **Goal Boards:** Create a vision board with pictures, quotes, or keywords that represent your long-term goals. This physical reminder can be placed where you see it daily, helping you stay aligned with your purpose. For example, if one of your goals is to improve health, you might add images of healthy food, a person working out, and inspiring health-related quotes.

b. **Timelines:** Write out a detailed timeline for your projects. For instance, if you're launching a new product, break down all the steps—market research, product development, testing, marketing, and sales—then allocate specific deadlines to each phase. This makes it easier to stay on track and evaluate progress as you go.

c. **Digital Tools:** Use widely known tools like **Google Calendar** for setting reminders and organizing deadlines or **Microsoft Outlook** to schedule and track meetings, tasks, and events. For example, you can set recurring events to block time for specific tasks or set alarms for when certain deadlines approach. With these tools, you can easily keep all your goals and to-do lists in one place.

d. **Gantt Charts in Excel:** For more complex projects, **Microsoft Excel** can be used to create Gantt charts with simple templates available. This allows you to map out the tasks, dependencies, and deadlines visually. If you're working with a team, you can use Excel to indicate who's responsible for what and when specific tasks should be completed.

By making your goals visible, you break down the barriers that often cause procrastination and ambiguity. Visibility creates clarity, and clarity motivates action. The more consistently you can see your goals and track your progress, the easier it becomes to stay on task and keep moving forward.

46. Don't Just Schedule Tasks—Schedule Thinking Time

Thinking is work, and clarity is its reward. In leadership, it's easy to confuse busyness with progress. Meetings, messages, and multitasking can create the illusion of productivity, but real breakthroughs often arise in moments of deep, intentional thought. Wise leaders carve out protected time weekly—sometimes even daily—not just to act, but to reflect. This is not idleness; it's mental labor of the highest kind. Take Jeff Bezos, for instance—he famously scheduled time to think deeply about Amazon's long-term strategy, often making decisions that wouldn't bear fruit for years but transformed the company's trajectory. Similarly, Satya Nadella's thoughtful approach at Microsoft involved reimagining company culture and future priorities before implementing sweeping changes.

This principle applies to entrepreneurs, managers, and anyone navigating complexity. When you sit quietly and ask yourself, "What truly matters right now?" or "What is the root of this challenge?" you create space for insight to emerge. One hour of clear thinking can save weeks of misdirected effort. So, treat thinking time as sacred. Put it on your calendar like a board meeting. Disconnect from devices. Step back from the noise. In the stillness, you'll often find the clarity that action alone cannot deliver.

47. Review Your Digital Footprint

Where does your time go online? It's a confronting question, but a necessary one for anyone striving for excellence. Many people wake up energized but end the day drained—without having done any meaningful work. The hidden culprit? Mindless digital consumption. Scrolls, reels, random clicks, autoplay videos, endless notifications—all engineered to hijack attention and fragment focus. You think you're "just checking something quickly," but that 5-minute scroll often turns into 45 minutes of lost intention.

To reclaim your time and mental clarity, you must first **measure** your digital behavior. Use tools like **Screen Time** on iPhone, **Digital Wellbeing** on Android, or apps like **Rescue Time** and **Freedom** to audit your habits. What apps are consuming the bulk of your day? Are you consuming more than you're creating? Awareness is the first step toward discipline.

Once you have the data, **prune your inputs ruthlessly**. Unfollow accounts that don't uplift or educate. Mute distractions. Disable non-essential notifications. Curate your feed like your mind depends on it—because it does. Imagine your brain as fertile soil; if you keep feeding it junk content, don't expect clarity, creativity, or calm to grow. But when you nourish it with thoughtful, high-quality material—books, podcasts, insightful videos—you elevate your energy and sharpen your focus.

Leaders and high performers treat their attention like a sacred resource. They know that **what you feed your brain daily shapes your decisions, mood, energy, and ultimately, your future.** So take control. Be ruthless in cutting out the noise and intentional in what you let in.

48. Work from Vision, Not from Task List

In today's fast-paced world, it's easy to become a productivity machine—checking off tasks, answering messages, attending meetings. But true fulfilment and long-term success don't come from just being busy; they come from being *aligned*. Before diving into your to-do list, pause and zoom out. Ask yourself: *Are these tasks serving my larger purpose? Is this list moving me toward my vision, or just keeping me in motion?*

Imagine someone climbing a ladder furiously, only to realize it's leaning against the wrong wall. That's what happens when you chase tasks without checking direction. A salesperson might work tirelessly following up with cold leads, but if their bigger goal is to build a referral-based network, they're missing the strategic shift they need. An entrepreneur might keep updating their website endlessly, while their true breakthrough lies in reaching out to mentors or exploring partnerships.

Vision is your internal compass. It defines *why* you're doing what you're doing and helps you discern between noise and necessity. When you work from vision, your tasks aren't just activities—they're stepping stones. You stop reacting and start *creating*.

Steve Jobs once said, "Deciding what *not* to do is as important as deciding what *to* do." This wisdom comes alive when you're anchored in vision. Suddenly, you realize that saying *no* to ten good things may be necessary to say *yes* to one great thing.

So, before you start your day, don't just ask, *what do I need to do?* Ask, *what am I building? Who am I becoming?* Let your task list be the servant of your vision—not the other way around.

49. Keep One Day Light and Free

In a culture that glorifies hustle and back-to-back schedules, keeping a day light and spacious may feel like a luxury—but in reality, it's a *strategic necessity*. When every hour of your week is packed with meetings, calls, and tasks, your brain stays in reactive mode. You're constantly responding, solving, and delivering. But creativity, insight, and visionary thinking don't come from pressure—they emerge from *space*.

That's why the most effective leaders, thinkers, and creators deliberately **protect one day each week**—keeping it free from meetings, heavy decisions, or tightly packed obligations. This doesn't mean it's a "day off" (though it can be); it means it's a **day with freedom**. You might use it to think deeply, catch up on reading, plan your next move, or just take a walk to let your mind wander. It's a day to get *off the treadmill* and onto the balcony—to see the bigger picture of your work and life.

Bill Gates famously had "Think Weeks," where he'd go off-grid with a pile of books and a notepad. While we may not have the luxury of an entire week, **one uncluttered day a week** can offer similar clarity. It's often in this white space that game-changing ideas appear, difficult decisions become obvious, and the fog lifts from your strategy.

In network marketing or leadership roles, where the pace is intense and energy is everything, this day can also be used for **rejuvenation**—resting your body, reconnecting with loved ones, or simply being still. Remember: rest is not a reward for work done; it's fuel for the work ahead.

So, block off that one day. Guard it like gold. It might just become the most valuable day of your week—not because of what you *do*, but because of the space it gives you to *see*, *create*, and *be*.

50. Easy Does it

The concept of "Easy Does It" in time management revolves around the idea of working smarter, not harder. It's about pacing yourself and avoiding the trap of rushing through tasks in a frantic attempt to check things off a list. Instead, this principle encourages a balanced, measured approach, where you focus on steady, sustainable progress. In practice, this means prioritizing tasks that align with your larger goals and giving yourself the space to execute them thoughtfully. By breaking down larger projects into manageable steps, you can avoid feeling overwhelmed and reduce the risk of burnout. It's not about avoiding work, but about working with intention and focus—one task at a time—so that each action brings value without causing unnecessary stress. When you slow down, you also create room for creativity and clarity, allowing your mind to think critically and solve problems more effectively. This approach ensures that your energy is directed toward meaningful work, not just filling your schedule with tasks that may not contribute to your bigger vision. Ultimately, "Easy Does It" teaches that consistent, thoughtful progress often leads to more successful and sustainable outcomes than rushing through the process.

Topic 3
OUR RELATIONS

Relationships, both personal and professional, are fundamental to our growth, well-being, and success. For years, I found myself focusing on changing others, believing that if I could just influence their actions, attitudes, or behaviours, things would be better. However, I soon realized that this approach was not only frustrating but ineffective. The truth is, true change begins with oneself. Relationships are mirrors that reflect our own beliefs, behaviours, and attitudes. When we shift our focus from trying to change others to examining our own role in the dynamic, we unlock the power to foster healthier, more authentic connections. Personal growth, self-awareness, and emotional intelligence play pivotal roles in improving our interactions with others. By taking responsibility for our reactions, behaviours, and expectations, we create a space where mutual respect and understanding can thrive. This shift in perspective not only enhances our personal relationships but also leads to greater success in the professional realm. Strong, positive relationships are the foundation of trust, collaboration, and influence—essential components of any successful career. Ultimately, when we invest in changing ourselves, we transform our relationships and create environments where growth, connection, and success can flourish for everyone involved.

I. CONFLICT MANAGEMENT

Conflict management is crucial in building and maintaining strong relationships, whether personal or professional. When conflicts arise, how they are handled can significantly impact the strength and longevity of the relationship. Effective conflict management involves addressing issues calmly and respectfully, listening to differing perspectives, and finding mutually beneficial solutions. By resolving conflicts in a constructive manner, trust and understanding are strengthened, and individuals or teams can move forward with greater clarity and cohesion. In contrast, unresolved conflicts can lead to resentment, miscommunication, and a breakdown in relationships. Therefore, mastering conflict management fosters a culture of respect and collaboration, which is essential for nurturing lasting and positive relationships.

1. Conflict Is Natural and Healthy

Conflict is a natural and inevitable part of human interaction. It's not something to be avoided, but rather something to be navigated with care. Conflict arises because of differing opinions, beliefs, or approaches, and its presence often signals engagement rather than dysfunction. A healthy amount of conflict can spark creativity and innovation. For example, in Pixar's creative process, they encourage "brainstorming with conflict" because it leads to better ideas. Aristotle's quote, "*It is the mark of an educated mind to be able to entertain a thought without accepting it,*" reminds us that conflict fosters critical thinking and forces individuals to broaden their perspectives.

2. Why Conflict Arises

Conflict can arise from a variety of sources: differing values, motivations, goals, or perceptions. For instance, a manager may value efficiency and speed, while an employee may value thoroughness and quality. These opposing priorities are not inherently bad, but unless managed properly, they can lead to tension. Understanding why conflict arises is key to resolving it effectively. As an example, two team members might have different communication styles—one prefers concise, direct exchanges, while the other thrives on detailed discussions. By recognizing these differences early, the conflict can be pre-emptively managed and channeled productively.

3. Challenging Ideas Respectfully

Conflict often arises when people challenge each other's ideas, but it's crucial to approach disagreements with respect. In Pixar's creative process, they use a technique called "plussing," which involves not just pointing out flaws in ideas, but also offering improvements. This is a form of constructive conflict that invites creativity and keeps discussions positive. Instead of saying "That won't work," try, "What if we took a different approach?" By phrasing disagreements constructively, you encourage collaboration rather than confrontation.

4. Know Your Conflict Style

Understanding your default conflict style is essential to managing disagreements effectively. The Thomas-Kilmann Conflict Mode Instrument outlines five main styles: Competing (assertive and uncooperative), Collaborating (assertive and cooperative), Compromising (moderately assertive and cooperative), Avoiding (unassertive and uncooperative), and Accommodating (unassertive and cooperative). For example, if you typically avoid conflict, it may be necessary to push yourself to engage when the situation demands it. Conversely, if you tend to dominate discussions, learning to collaborate or compromise can help reach better resolutions. Knowing your conflict style helps you understand where your default reactions might lead and how to adjust them in varying situations.

5. Avoid the 'Win-at-All-Costs' Mindset

In conflict resolution, it's easy to fall into the trap of wanting to win. However, a win-at-all-costs approach damages relationships and limits collaboration. Rather than focusing solely on "winning" the argument, strive to understand the needs and perspectives of everyone involved. As Marshall Rosenberg, the founder of Nonviolent Communication, suggests, "*Behind intimidating messages are simply people appealing to meet their needs.*" Shifting from a mindset of winning to a mindset of understanding promotes healthier, long-term solutions. Think about conflicts in teams where focusing on the outcome (such as meeting deadlines) rather than the individual process (such as how members interact) could lead to burnout.

6. Focus on the Present, Not the Past

Many conflicts get sidetracked when past issues are dragged into current discussions. Bringing up old grievances can cloud the focus and escalate the situation unnecessarily. For example, if two colleagues are arguing over a missed deadline, referring to past mistakes only serves to prolong the conversation and turn it personal. Instead, focus on solving the present issue— "*How can we address the current delay and avoid it in the future?*" Sticking to the issue at hand creates a space for resolution, prevents unnecessary emotional escalation, and promotes a solution-oriented approach.

7. Know When to Let Go

Not every conflict needs to be resolved. Sometimes, the best course of action is to let things go. If a conflict is no longer productive and the resolution would require more emotional or cognitive energy than it's worth, it might be best to walk away. This doesn't mean avoiding issues, but rather recognizing when to disengage and allow emotions to cool down. As Epictetus, a Stoic philosopher, said, "*It's not what happens to you, but how you react to it that matters.*" If you're facing a situation where resolution seems impossible or counterproductive, it's okay to step back, reflect, and allow time for perspective.

8. Remain Calm

When conflict escalates, emotions often override logic, making it hard to think clearly or communicate effectively. The first step in managing conflict is to remain calm. When you're calm, you make better decisions, and you're more likely to listen and empathize with others. Neurobiologists have found that when people are angry, their brain's amygdala takes over, clouding judgment. A simple technique like counting to ten or taking deep breaths can help reset your emotional state. Maintaining calmness signals maturity and respect for the other person's perspective, and it sets the stage for a more productive discussion.

9. Use "I" Statements

Using "I" statements instead of ""You're" statements can drastically shift the tone of a conflict. ""You" statements often sound accusatory and can cause the other person to become defensive. For example, saying, "You always interrupt me!" will likely trigger defensiveness. Instead, saying, "I feel frustrated when I don't get a chance to finish my thoughts" focuses on your experience, rather than blaming the other person. This shift makes it easier for both sides to stay focused on resolving the issue, rather than engaging in a blame game.

10. Address One Issue at a Time

When multiple issues are brought up at once, the conflict becomes overwhelming and resolution becomes harder to achieve. Instead of tackling everything in one conversation, address one issue at a time. For instance, if two team members are arguing about both deadlines and quality of work, focus first on resolving the deadline issue, and then move to the quality issue. This sequential approach makes it easier to reach a resolution on each topic without getting tangled in multiple concerns. It also keeps the conversation structured and focused, preventing the conversation from spiraling out of control.

11. Avoid Personal Attacks

It's essential to separate the person from the issue at hand. When conflicts get personal, they escalate quickly and make it difficult to resolve anything. For example, rather than saying, "You're always so disorganized," say, "I feel that the lack of organization affects our team's productivity." This subtle shift keeps the focus on the behavior or the situation, rather than attacking someone's character. Personal attacks not only hurt the other person but also undermine the trust and respect necessary for healthy conflict resolution.

12. Don't Stockpile Complaints

It's tempting to let small grievances accumulate, but addressing issues as they arise is much more effective. Holding onto complaints can cause resentment to build up, making it harder to resolve issues later on. For example, if a colleague is late to meetings regularly, mentioning it right away in a calm and constructive manner can prevent resentment from building up. When people bring up issues early, it gives both parties a chance to correct course before negative emotions intensify.

13. Be a Better Listener

Good communication in conflict begins with active listening. Listening attentively shows that you value the other person's perspective. Active listening involves more than hearing words; it requires fully engaging with the speaker, reflecting their message, and asking clarifying questions. Stephen Covey's principle of "*Seek first to understand, then to be understood*" emphasizes that in any conflict, your first role should be to listen with empathy. By truly understanding the other person's position, you can respond more thoughtfully and reduce the chances of further escalation.

14. Don't Interrupt

Interrupting signals a lack of respect. It's essential to let the other person finish speaking before you respond. Interruptions disrupt the flow of communication and can create defensiveness. In some situations, a simple pause after the other person speaks gives both parties time to process what's been said before responding. By actively avoiding interruptions, you show that you value the other person's voice, which can lead to more productive conflict resolution.

15. Use Empathic Prompts

Empathic prompts such as, "*What would make you feel better?*" or "*I'm hearing that you're upset about this—could you explain a little more?*" invite the other person to share their feelings and concerns. These questions help to foster understanding and open up dialogue, rather than just placing blame. Instead of saying, "*You're wrong,*" try asking, "*Can you explain your side of this? I want to understand.*" This approach makes the other person feel heard and respected, setting the stage for more collaborative conflict resolution.

16. Acknowledge Emotions

Emotions are a fundamental part of conflict. Whether it's frustration, anger, or sadness, they influence how we behave and how we perceive the situation. Ignoring or dismissing emotions can worsen the conflict. Acknowledging emotions, both yours and the other person's, is an important step in resolution. For example, if a colleague is visibly upset, acknowledging their feelings with a statement like, "*I can see that this situation is frustrating for you*" can diffuse tension. This act of empathy shows that you're not just focusing on the issue but also on the emotional aspect of the conflict, which helps foster understanding and openness.

17. Separate Facts from Interpretations

In many conflicts, the facts of the situation get clouded by interpretations. For example, if one colleague misses a deadline, the fact is that the task was late, but the interpretation might be, "*He's always careless.*" The interpretation might be biased, based on assumptions or emotions. To avoid escalating the situation, separate the facts from your interpretations. By focusing on the specific issue at hand—like the missed deadline—rather than making assumptions about the person's character, you reduce the chances of unnecessary conflict. This approach helps both parties see the issue more clearly and resolve it effectively.

18. Look for Common Ground

In every conflict, there is usually some shared interest or goal, even if it seems difficult to identify. Focusing on these commonalities can help turn the conflict into a collaborative effort. For instance, if two departments are fighting over resources, both may want the success of the organization as their primary goal. By recognizing that they both want the same outcome (organization success), they can shift the conversation from confrontation to cooperation. Finding common ground builds rapport and reminds both parties that they are working towards the same objective, reducing the tension.

19. Stay Solution-Focused

Instead of getting bogged down in the details of the problem, focus on finding a solution. In most conflicts, when individuals remain fixated on blaming or discussing the issue, they miss the opportunity to resolve it. A solution-focused approach keeps the conversation forward-thinking. For example, in a workplace conflict over resource allocation, instead of focusing on who's at fault for the current shortage, the conversation could shift to how the resources can be better distributed in the future. As Albert Einstein said, "*We cannot solve our problems with the same thinking we used when we created them.*" A solution-oriented mindset leads to better outcomes and reduces prolonged tension.

20. Take Responsibility for Your Part

Conflicts are rarely one-sided. Each party often has a role to play in the escalation. Taking responsibility for your part in the conflict—whether it's in communication, actions, or misunderstandings—helps de-escalate tension. Acknowledging, "*I understand that I may have contributed to this by not communicating clearly*" shows accountability and maturity. This willingness to own your part can encourage the other person to do the same, creating an environment where both parties can work together towards a resolution. It fosters mutual respect and reduces defensiveness.

21. Don't Let Ego Drive the Conflict

Ego can often prevent conflict resolution because individuals feel the need to protect their self-image or be "right." When ego takes over, it leads to prideful responses that prevent progress. To manage conflict successfully, it's essential to put aside ego and focus on the issue at hand. When you're fixated on being "right," it can cloud judgment and keep you from seeing solutions. A useful way to counteract ego is to approach conflicts with humility and openness, asking yourself, "*What can I learn from this situation?*" This attitude can defuse tension and encourage a more constructive dialogue.

22. Choose the Right Time and Place

Timing and environment are crucial when dealing with conflict. Addressing an issue when emotions are high or in front of others can escalate the situation. To foster a productive conversation, choose a neutral, calm space and a time when both parties are more likely to be receptive. For instance, having a private discussion with a colleague after a meeting might be more effective than raising the issue during the meeting itself. Creating a comfortable, private environment allows both parties to speak openly and focus on resolving the issue without outside pressures.

23. Use Humor Wisely

Humor, when used appropriately, can diffuse tension and create a lighter atmosphere. However, it's essential to be sensitive to the situation and the other person's emotions. A well-timed, non-derogatory joke can provide relief in a tense situation, helping both parties to relax. For example, if two team members are caught in a heated discussion, lightening the mood with a neutral joke might ease the tension. However, humor should never be used to belittle the other person or avoid the issue. As long as it's used with respect and consideration, humor can promote a sense of camaraderie and ease.

24. Stay Open to Feedback

Sometimes, when conflict arises, it's easy to become defensive and shut down others' viewpoints. However, staying open to feedback, even if it's uncomfortable, is key to resolving conflict. For example, if a colleague points out that you've overlooked a crucial detail in a project, rather than defensively explaining yourself, take a moment to listen, evaluate, and consider their input. Constructive feedback can help you grow, improve your communication, and prevent similar conflicts in the future. Being open to feedback signals maturity and a willingness to improve, both of which are essential in conflict resolution.

25. Use Neutral Language

Language is a powerful tool in conflict resolution. Words can either escalate or defuse tension. Using neutral, non-inflammatory language helps prevent the conflict from becoming more emotionally charged. For example, instead of saying, "*You never help with this,*" try saying, "*I'd appreciate it if we could share the responsibilities more equally.*" Neutral language fosters a more collaborative environment and encourages both parties to focus on the issue, rather than each other. This helps build mutual respect and makes the conflict easier to resolve.

26. Know When to Seek Mediation

Sometimes, despite best efforts, conflicts can become too complicated or entrenched to resolve without outside help. In such cases, seeking mediation can provide a neutral, objective perspective. A mediator can help both parties articulate their concerns and guide the conversation towards finding a resolution. For example, if two departments are locked in a long-standing dispute, bringing in a neutral HR professional as a mediator can help facilitate a more productive conversation. Mediation often leads to faster resolution and helps preserve relationships by preventing escalation.

27. Be Willing to Compromise

Compromise is often a necessary element of conflict resolution. Rarely will both sides get everything they want, so being willing to find a middle ground can help both parties feel heard and valued. For example, if two employees are fighting over a particular project role, a compromise could involve splitting the responsibilities in a way that aligns with both their strengths. When both parties give something up in the interest of resolution, it can help build mutual trust and show that collaboration is valued over individual gain.

28. Maintain Boundaries

While it's essential to engage in conflict resolution, it's also important to maintain personal boundaries. Some conflicts may touch on sensitive topics, and it's crucial to ensure that discussions remain respectful and do not cross into personal attacks. For example, if a colleague brings up personal grievances that you're uncomfortable with, calmly set a boundary by saying, *"I think we should focus on the professional aspects of this situation."* Maintaining boundaries ensures that the conversation remains productive and prevents further emotional harm.

29. De-escalate the Situation

When conflict begins to escalate, it's crucial to take steps to de-escalate before things get out of control. This might involve using calming body language, speaking in a softer tone, or taking a break from the conversation. A simple statement like, "*I think we both need to take a moment to cool down and revisit this*" can prevent an argument from spiraling. De-escalation techniques help to reduce the emotional intensity of the situation and create space for rational discussion. It's a way of taking control of the situation and guiding it back toward resolution.

30. Recognize the Importance of Apologizing

An apology can be a powerful tool in conflict resolution, especially if it's heartfelt and sincere. When you acknowledge your mistakes and take responsibility for them, it can mend relationships and help build trust. For example, if you've spoken harshly to someone during a disagreement, offering a genuine apology can clear the air and demonstrate maturity. As Dr. Marshall Rosenberg says, "*An apology is not about admitting fault, it's about showing empathy for the pain caused.*" A well-timed, sincere apology can often be the key to resolving a conflict and restoring the relationship.

II. RELATIONS WITH CUSTOMERS-

1. Customer Experience Drives Loyalty and Revenue

Customer experience is one of the most powerful drivers of both loyalty and revenue in any organization. When companies focus on improving customer service and enhancing the overall experience, they often see a direct and significant increase in their bottom line. In fact, research shows that 84% of companies that prioritize customer experience report positive revenue growth. This statistic alone underscores the critical importance of delivering exceptional service and support. The impact of great customer experience is even more pronounced when you look at customer retention. A mere 5% increase in retention can lead to a profit boost of up to 25%, proving that holding onto existing customers is far more cost-effective and rewarding than constantly acquiring new ones.

Beyond just retention, the quality of a customer's experience can directly influence their purchasing Behaviour. Studies show that 50% of customers are likely to increase their purchases after a positive experience, demonstrating that a great interaction can lead to more revenue from existing customers. But perhaps most telling is the fact that a positive experience not only strengthens loyalty but also generates word-of-mouth referrals. Around 69% of customers are likely to recommend a company after a positive experience, effectively turning them into brand ambassadors who help bring in new business.

Creating exceptional customer experiences goes beyond simply meeting expectations. It's about consistently exceeding them—offering unexpected value, going the extra mile, and making customers feel valued at every touchpoint. By doing so, organizations can boost customer lifetime value, which refers to the total revenue a customer will generate for a company over the course of their relationship. As customer loyalty strengthens, so does the company's reputation, ultimately creating a powerful cycle of growth. Stronger brand loyalty and an increase in customer retention are key drivers of sustainable success, leading to higher profits, improved market position, and long-term viability.

2. Treat Customers Like Guests in Your Home

The way you treat your customers has a direct and lasting impact on your business's reputation. Just as you would treat guests in your home with warmth, respect, and care, the same principle should apply to how you interact with your customers. If they feel valued and appreciated, they're more likely to return, recommend your business to others, and remain loyal long-term. For example, brands like Zappos have built a loyal following by treating their customers as if they were personal guests, offering free returns and going above and beyond in resolving any issues, no questions asked. This level of care has earned them a stellar reputation, not just in retail but as a beacon of excellent customer service.

However, a negative experience can undermine even the best marketing efforts. No number of flashy ads or promotions can erase the memory of a customer feeling mistreated or ignored. Take the example of United Airlines, which faced significant backlash after a passenger was forcibly removed from a flight. Despite their marketing campaigns, the damage to their reputation was significant because they failed to handle the situation with empathy and prompt resolution. This highlights the fact that customer service should always prioritize solving problems quickly and effectively. In contrast, when companies respond to customer complaints with genuine concern and urgency, they have an opportunity to turn a negative situation into a positive one.

A real-life example of this is when Starbucks faced criticism for an incident at one of their stores, where two African American men were arrested for not making a purchase. Instead of ignoring the issue or issuing a generic apology, Starbucks responded swiftly by closing thousands of stores for a day of racial-bias training for employees. This sincere and personal response not only addressed the immediate issue but also demonstrated their commitment to customer care and inclusivity. It helped restore trust and ultimately strengthened their relationship with their customers.

A personal and swift acknowledgment of any inconvenience ensures the customer feels heard and valued. When you make an effort to address their concerns personally, it sends a message that you genuinely care about their experience and that their business is important to you. For instance, if a customer complains about a delayed product delivery, a simple, personalized message such as, “We understand how frustrating this must be, and we’re doing everything we can to ensure it arrives as quickly as possible. Thank you for your patience,” can go a long way in calming their frustrations and retaining their loyalty. Personalizing the response, by remembering their past interactions or addressing their specific concerns, makes a world of difference in fostering trust and a lasting relationship with your customers. When customers feel personally valued, they’re more likely to forgive mistakes and continue doing business with you.

3. Focus on Customer Success Over Product Selling

The primary focus of a business should not be merely on how effectively it can sell a product, but on how well it can help customers succeed in their own endeavors. When businesses center their efforts around serving the customer's best interests, they naturally foster relationships built on trust, loyalty, and mutual benefit. This approach goes beyond the transactional nature of a typical sale, creating an environment where the success of the customer is as important, if not more, than the immediate revenue generated from the sale. When customers feel that a company is genuinely invested in helping them achieve their goals, they are more likely to stay loyal, returning not only for the products or services but for the support and partnership the company offers.

A prime example of this philosophy can be seen in the way Salesforce, a leading CRM software provider, operates. Instead of just selling a product, Salesforce focuses on understanding its clients' specific needs and challenges. They work with businesses to tailor solutions that drive success and create long-term value. Salesforce's success is deeply tied to the success of its customers, which is why they provide extensive support, training, and consulting services to ensure their clients can maximize the use of their products. Their commitment to helping businesses succeed, rather than just pushing a sale, has made them a trusted partner to many companies, fostering deep loyalty and continued business relationships.

This approach is not limited to large companies. Even smaller businesses can adopt this mindset. For instance, a local fitness trainer who takes the time to understand the fitness goals and challenges of their clients—not just selling them a series of sessions—will see clients who feel genuinely cared for and supported. These clients are more likely to keep coming back because they feel the trainer's interest in their progress, rather than just a one-time transaction. Similarly, this customer-first philosophy can be seen in companies like Amazon, which is known for obsessing over customer satisfaction. By continuously striving to improve the customer experience, Amazon has built not just a shopping platform, but a service that aligns with the personal and professional needs of its users.

To create such deep connections, businesses must take the time to truly understand the customer's needs, desires, and pain points. This means asking the right questions, listening actively, and being ready to adapt. By focusing on building a partnership, where both sides benefit, the relationship moves beyond a simple transaction and evolves into a long-term collaboration. The goal isn't just to make a sale; it's to provide value, ensure success, and nurture the kind of customer loyalty that can withstand market changes. When customers succeed, the business succeeds, and that mutual success is the foundation of sustainable growth and long-term profitability.

4. Create Value and Stand Out in the Marketplace

In today's crowded marketplace, where businesses often offer similar products and services, the ability to create real value for your customers becomes the critical differentiator that sets you apart from your competitors. It's no longer enough to simply sell a product or service; to stand out, businesses must focus on creating solutions that directly address the unique needs and challenges of their customers. Value creation selling is all about deeply understanding your customers' goals and providing tailored solutions that not only meet their needs but go beyond their expectations, creating an experience that delights and adds meaningful benefits to their lives or businesses.

For example, consider Apple's approach to its products and services. While many tech companies offer smartphones and laptops, Apple has consistently differentiated itself by focusing on creating seamless, user-friendly, and high-quality experiences. Their focus isn't just on the hardware itself but on the ecosystem, they build—where the iPhone, Mac, Apple Watch, and other products work together in harmony. This commitment to quality and user experience allows Apple to charge a premium for their products. Customers are not just buying a device; they're buying into a lifestyle that promises ease of use, innovation, and reliability. By consistently delivering exceptional value, Apple has cultivated an incredibly loyal customer base, willing to pay a higher price for the perceived benefits that Apple products offer.

The idea of value creation selling also applies to other industries. For instance, in the service sector, companies like Ritz-Carlton have mastered the art of creating value. By deeply understanding their customers' needs and preferences—whether it's remembering a returning guest's room preferences or providing personalized recommendations for activities—they provide an experience that exceeds what is expected. The Ritz-Carlton doesn't compete on price but on providing a level of luxury and attention to detail that customers are willing to pay for, thus justifying their premium prices.

In contrast, businesses that focus solely on competing through lower prices or offering discounts often find themselves in a race to the bottom, struggling to maintain profitability and customer loyalty. While discounts can bring short-term sales, they often don't build the kind of lasting relationships that create long-term success. When a business shifts the focus from simply cutting costs to creating value that aligns with what the customer truly cares about, it can command higher prices and avoid the trap of price-based competition. For example, Tesla has positioned itself as a leader in electric vehicles not just by offering an alternative to traditional cars, but by delivering superior technology, sustainability, and performance. Customers are willing to pay more for a Tesla because they perceive the value they are receiving goes beyond just transportation—it aligns with their environmental values, technological expectations, and desire for innovation.

Ultimately, the key to differentiation in any market is understanding what truly matters to the customer and delivering it consistently. This means continuously engaging with customers, gathering feedback, and evolving your offerings to meet their changing needs. Businesses that prioritize value creation over cost-cutting not only build stronger customer loyalty but also establish a sustainable competitive advantage, enabling them to charge higher prices for better products and services. By focusing on creating exceptional, personalized experiences, companies can transform transactional relationships into long-term partnerships that benefit both the customer and the business.

5. Post-Sales Service is Crucial for Long-Lasting Relationships

The idea that post-sales experience plays a critical role in fostering long-term, profitable relationships is reinforced by several leading business thinkers. In his book *The Loyalty Effect*, author Frederick Reichheld emphasizes that retaining customers is far more profitable than acquiring new ones. Reichheld argues that increasing customer retention rates by just 5% can lead to profit increases of up to 25%, highlighting the importance of the post-sale experience in maintaining customer loyalty and driving long-term profitability.

Additionally, in *Delivering Happiness*, Tony Hsieh, the CEO of Zappos, discusses the significance of exceptional customer service, both during and after the sale. Hsieh built Zappos into a billion-dollar company by ensuring that the post-sales experience was just as remarkable as the sales process itself. Zappos offers free returns and a customer service model that goes above and beyond to meet customer needs, resulting in high levels of customer satisfaction and loyalty.

The concept of creating tailored value propositions for customers, as mentioned in the creation of a Value Account Plan (VAP), can also be seen in the teachings of Clayton Christensen in his book *The Innovator's Solution*. Christensen discusses how companies can create long-term customer relationships by focusing on providing continuous value and adapting to customers' evolving needs, rather than just pushing products.

All of these examples illustrate the importance of a strong post-sales experience and how it drives customer retention, loyalty, and profitability. By integrating these practices into a company's overall customer relationship strategy, businesses can cultivate lasting connections that go beyond the initial transaction.

III. BUILDING RELATIONSHIPS FOR PERSONAL AND PROFESSIONAL GROWTH

Relationship building within a team is essential for creating a collaborative, productive, and positive work environment. Strong relationships among team members foster trust, open communication, and mutual respect, which are critical for effective collaboration. When individuals feel valued and understood, they are more likely to contribute their ideas, share feedback, and work towards common goals. Trust is the foundation of any high-performing team, and without it, members may hesitate to take risks, voice concerns, or fully support one another. Relationship building also helps in resolving conflicts efficiently, as team members who have established positive connections are more likely to approach disagreements constructively and with empathy. Furthermore, strong interpersonal relationships enhance morale, leading to higher levels of engagement and job satisfaction. In teams with a healthy, supportive atmosphere, members feel a sense of belonging, which increases their motivation and commitment to the team's success. Ultimately, when relationships within a team are nurtured, the overall productivity, creativity, and problem-solving capabilities of the team are significantly strengthened, leading to greater achievements and a more harmonious work environment.

1. The Power of Respectful Disagreement

Practicing empathy in communication involves not necessarily agreeing with someone's opinion, but respecting it. This creates an environment where all voices feel valued, even if their views differ.

It's essential to remind yourself and others that disagreement doesn't equate to disrespect. By acknowledging differing perspectives with empathy, we create healthier, more open communication channels. For example, a manager may not agree with an employee's approach but can still express appreciation for the effort, which fosters trust and mutual respect.

A great example of this is Howard Schultz, the former CEO of Starbucks. Schultz has often emphasized the importance of listening to employees and valuing their input, even when he doesn't agree with every idea. During a tough period for the company, Schultz would regularly meet with baristas and staff to hear their concerns, even if their views were critical of management. This practice helped build strong relationships, increase employee engagement, and ultimately contributed to the company's recovery. Similarly, when an employee at a mid-sized company suggested a new marketing campaign that seemed risky, the CEO didn't immediately dismiss the idea. Instead, they said, "I understand your vision, and while we may need to adjust a few things, I appreciate your bold approach. Let's refine it and see how we can make it work." This kind of empathetic communication helps maintain trust and creates an environment where everyone feels comfortable contributing their ideas, even if they challenge the status quo.

2. The Role of Ego in Communication

Communication breakdowns often stem not from a lack of clarity but from egos clashing. When we fail to listen or empathize, it's not a communication issue but an ego problem. Practicing humility and empathy can defuse many potential conflicts. A great example would be during team meetings where a leader listens first, acknowledging each person's perspective before responding. This approach opens up constructive dialogue and leads to more fruitful discussions. Here are some of the ways to keep our ego in check during any conversation-

a. **Practice Active Listening**: Make a conscious effort to listen without interrupting. Focus on understanding the speaker's perspective rather than preparing your own response. This shows respect and allows for a more productive conversation.

b. **Acknowledge Others' Perspectives**: Before responding, validate the viewpoints of others. This helps shift the focus from asserting your own opinion to fostering mutual understanding. For example, a leader can say, "I hear what you're saying, and that's a valuable point."

c. **Cultivate Humility**: Recognize that no one has all the answers, including yourself. Humility allows for openness to new ideas and prevents your ego from overshadowing others' contributions. It's important to acknowledge that there is always room for growth and improvement.

d. **Separate Self-Worth from Opinions**: Don't take disagreements personally. When your opinion is challenged, it's not a reflection of your value as a person but a difference of perspective. This mindset reduces defensiveness and promotes a more open and respectful dialogue.

e. **Seek Feedback Regularly**: Actively request feedback from others, showing that you value their input. This not only helps you grow but also demonstrates that you're not above others' opinions, which can help keep ego in check.

f. **Empathize with Others**: Practice empathy by putting yourself in the shoes of others. When you empathize with their experiences and viewpoints, you're less likely to let your ego control the conversation and more likely to engage constructively.

g. **Lead by Example**: As a leader, demonstrating humility and empathy can encourage others to do the same. If you set the tone by listening and respecting others' opinions, it fosters a collaborative, ego-free environment where everyone feels valued.

3. Taking a Step Back When Emotions Run High

If emotions are running high during a discussion, it's better to take a pause rather than forcing a resolution. Stepping back allows both parties to cool down and approach the issue calmly. It's not about avoiding the conflict; it's about ensuring that the conversation is constructive when both sides are in a better emotional state. A personal story could be when a manager feels frustrated with a team member's performance but chooses to step away from the situation until the emotions settle, leading to a more productive and solution-oriented conversation later.

Here are some practical tips for taking a step back when emotions run high:

a. **Recognize the Emotional Trigger**: Be aware of your emotional state and the emotions of others. If you feel yourself getting angry or frustrated, acknowledge it to yourself before reacting. This self-awareness is the first step toward managing emotions effectively.

b. **Use a Pause or Timeout**: Politely request a short break if things are getting heated. You can say, "I think we both need a moment to think things over. Let's reconvene in 10 minutes." This pause can help both parties cool down and gain perspective.

c. **Practice Deep Breathing**: If you feel overwhelmed by emotion, try deep breathing exercises. Breathing deeply for a few seconds can help reduce the physiological symptoms of stress, making it easier to think clearly and respond thoughtfully.

d. **Suggest a Future Conversation**: If the discussion isn't progressing, propose to continue the conversation later. For instance, "I think it would be more effective if we revisit this topic after we've had some time to reflect." This keeps the door open for resolution without forcing a decision in the heat of the moment.

e. **Set a Clear Time to Reconnect**: Agree on a specific time to return to the discussion, whether it's after an hour, the next day, or a few days later. This ensures that the conversation is not avoided but is given the time it needs for a more productive outcome.

f. **Acknowledge Emotions Calmly**: When you reconvene, acknowledge the emotions felt during the initial discussion. You can say, "I realize we were both frustrated earlier, but now we're in a better space to talk about this."

g. **Focus on the Issue, Not the Emotion**: When you resume the conversation, keep the focus on resolving the issue rather than rehashing past emotions. Stay solution-oriented by saying things like, "Let's look at ways we can move forward together."

h. **Set Ground Rules for Emotional Conversations**: Before intense discussions, agree on guidelines to manage emotions. For example, no interrupting, using "I" statements instead of blaming, and allowing each person to speak without judgment. This can prevent the conversation from escalating in the first place.

When confronted with difficult Behaviour, it's important to approach the situation with compassion. Understanding that the person may be dealing with external factors that influence their Behaviour can lead to a more effective resolution. For example, if an employee is overly defensive during a review, rather than assuming they are simply being difficult, a leader might consider whether personal stress or dissatisfaction is contributing to the Behaviour and approach the situation with understanding.

4. Understanding Through Active Listening

Empathy starts with listening. It's not just about hearing the words but also understanding how the other person feels. When someone expresses frustration, saying "I understand how you feel" can make a big difference in making them feel heard. This builds rapport and trust. An example would be a customer service representative acknowledging a frustrated customer's concerns by saying, "I can see how this situation has been inconvenient for you, let's see how we can resolve it together."

You can practice the following tips for listening actively -

a. **Give Full Attention**: When someone is speaking, make sure you're fully present. Put away distractions like your phone or computer and focus on the person speaking. This signals that you value their input.

b. **Maintain Eye Contact**: Appropriate eye contact shows that you are engaged in the conversation and are paying attention. It also helps the speaker feel understood and respected.

c. **Use Non-Verbal Cues**: Nod, lean slightly forward, and use facial expressions to demonstrate that you're actively listening and processing what the other person is saying.

d. **Reflect and Paraphrase**: After hearing what someone has said, paraphrase or summarize it back to them to ensure understanding. For example, "So what I'm hearing is that you feel frustrated because the issue wasn't resolved in the time frame promised."

e. **Ask Clarifying Questions**: If something is unclear, ask questions to gain a deeper understanding, like "Can you help me understand what you meant by...?" This shows genuine interest and helps avoid misunderstandings.

f. **Avoid Interrupting**: Let the other person finish their thoughts before responding. Interrupting can make them feel disrespected and undermine effective communication.

g. **Be Non-Judgmental**: Approach the conversation with an open mind and refrain from jumping to conclusions. Active listening requires you to withhold judgment and let the speaker express themselves fully.

h. **Acknowledge Emotions**: Show empathy by acknowledging not just the words, but also the feelings behind them. For example, "It sounds like you're feeling really upset about this situation." This can go a long way in building trust.

Non-judgmental listening is key to building strong interpersonal relationships. When we listen without judgment, we allow others to speak freely and honestly, which fosters trust. For example, when a team member shares a mistake, a manager who listens attentively without immediately passing judgment creates an environment where the employee feels safe to admit mistakes and learn from them.

5. Practicing Empathy

Empathy is the cornerstone of healthy workplace dynamics and effective team collaboration. It's the ability to understand and share the feelings of others, creating a bond of trust and respect. In the workplace, empathy goes beyond just being kind; it involves genuinely understanding your colleagues' perspectives, recognizing their emotions, and responding thoughtfully. Empathy fosters an environment where people feel valued and heard, which in turn, nurtures open communication, enhances collaboration, and drives collective success. For example, a manager who takes the time to listen to a team member's concerns during a stressful project can help alleviate anxiety, build rapport, and keep the team motivated. Practicing empathy doesn't mean always agreeing with others but acknowledging their emotions and being sensitive to their needs. A simple act of active listening—where you give your full attention and validate what others are saying—can make a world of difference. Furthermore, showing empathy in challenging situations, like resolving conflicts or offering constructive feedback, encourages problem-solving with mutual respect. By practicing empathy, we create a supportive work environment where collaboration thrives, people feel emotionally safe, and teams achieve higher levels of performance and satisfaction. Empathy isn't just a skill to develop; it's a mindset that strengthens relationships, motivates individuals, and ensures long-term success for both people and organizations.

Few questions we can ask to know another person's point of view-

a. "Can you tell me more about what happened?"
b. "What's been the most challenging part of this for you?"
c. "How can I best support you in this situation?"
d. "What would make this situation easier for you?"
e. "I can see this has been frustrating for you. What would you like to see happen next?"
f. "What can I do to help resolve this for you?"

g. "Is there anything else you'd like to share about this?"
h. "I can't imagine how difficult this must be for you. How have you been coping with it?"
i. "How would you like to move forward with this?"

Phrases to Show Empathy

a. "I understand how you feel."
b. "That sounds really tough. I'm so sorry you're going through this."
c. "I can imagine how frustrating that must be."
d. "Thank you for sharing that with me. It helps me understand where you're coming from."
e. "I see this has been really challenging for you. Let's work together to find a solution."
f. "I'm really sorry you're dealing with this. How can we make it right?"
g. "I hear you. Let's see how we can address this together."
h. "That must have been a really difficult situation. Thank you for being patient with me."
i. "I'm grateful you're sharing this with me. Let's make sure we figure this out."

6. Mastering the Art Giving & Receiving Feedback

a. Giving feedback effectively is a skill that involves balancing honesty with care. To give feedback that leads to improvement, focus on specific actions and outcomes rather than making general comments. Use positive reinforcement to show where the person is excelling. A well-balanced feedback conversation allows the individual to feel valued while also being provided with clear guidance on how to improve.

b. Receiving feedback, whether positive or negative, is an essential part of personal and professional development. However, it's important to assess the **legitimacy of the feedback** before reacting. Is the feedback coming from a place of genuine concern, or is it influenced by personal bias or misunderstanding? For instance, if a colleague critiques your presentation style, take time to reflect on whether their feedback is based on constructive criticism or simply personal preference. This discernment ensures that you focus on feedback that will truly help you grow.

Negative feedback, when approached correctly, can be a powerful tool for strengthening relationships. By approaching feedback with the intent to help rather than criticize, you foster trust and respect. An employee who receives constructive feedback on how to improve their work performance, paired with support, is more likely to see their relationship with their manager as a partnership.

Great Organizations encourages direct, open, and honest feedback while maintaining a foundation of care and respect. This approach leads to faster growth and trust within teams. For example, a manager who regularly offers constructive feedback while showing care for the employee's personal development can create an environment where feedback is seen as an opportunity for growth, not a threat.

7. Understanding and Overcoming Biases in Communication

Biases can significantly affect how we perceive others and communicate with them.

For example, **Bandwagon Bias** can lead us to agree with the majority opinion, even when it might not align with our true beliefs. Similarly,

Confirmation Bias may cause us to seek information that supports our pre-existing views, potentially overlooking valuable input from others.

Recognizing these biases helps avoid assumptions and enables more objective decision-making. To **avoid biases** in communication, it is essential to **assess the legitimacy of feedback** objectively—distinguishing between genuine input and personal preferences.

For instance, when receiving feedback from team members or peers, resist the urge to filter it through your own biases and consider its merit based on facts rather than preconceived notions. Leaders should also be mindful of how their biases affect team dynamics. Instead of focusing only on information that confirms their opinions, they must **evaluate the impact of feedback** and understand its relevance to the team's goals and performance.

Additionally, approaching feedback with **positive intent**, even when it's negative, fosters an open-minded and solution-focused environment. By stepping back, assessing the impact of feedback, and prioritizing objective evaluation, leaders and team members alike can communicate more effectively, avoid biased decision-making, and create a more inclusive and productive environment.

Perception Bias happens when we make assumptions about others based on their group membership. This can result in unfair treatment and poor team dynamics. Recognizing and challenging these biases allows for a more inclusive and supportive environment. A team leader who dismisses a new member's ideas because they are from a different department could unintentionally harm team cohesion. Acknowledging such biases helps ensure that everyone's voice is heard and valued.

IV TEAM WORK

Once upon a time, in a small village nestled between mountains, there was a group of farmers who lived and worked independently. Each farmer had their own plot of land, and they believed that success was a personal achievement. One year, a particularly harsh storm hit the village, washing away fences, damaging crops, and leaving behind destruction.

The farmers struggled to rebuild on their own. They each tried to repair their land in isolation, but the damage was overwhelming. The resources were limited, and every attempt seemed futile. One farmer, an elderly man named Tomas, observed his neighbours' struggles. He called for a meeting of all the farmers, suggesting that they work together to rebuild. At first, many were hesitant—each had their own ways of doing things and weren't sure how cooperation could help.

Tomas, however, shared a story from his youth: "There was a time, long ago, when our ancestors faced an even greater storm. They too worked alone at first, but then they realized that together, they could rebuild faster, share resources, and use each other's strengths to overcome what seemed impossible."

Reluctantly, the farmers agreed to try working together. They decided to combine their efforts: one farmer with strong hands worked on the damaged fences, another with a keen eye for irrigation focused on water systems, and others shared seeds, tools, and advice. They pooled their resources and quickly set to work. Over time, the village was rebuilt—stronger and more resilient than before.

The moral of the story is that teamwork is not just about dividing tasks, but about sharing strengths, ideas, and support. When individuals come together with a common goal, they can achieve far more than they could alone. The farmers learned that by combining their efforts, they didn't just rebuild their land, they also built trust, camaraderie, and a sense of unity. Working together, they not only overcame the storm's damage but also set a foundation for stronger, more prosperous years ahead.

1. Empathy as a Bridge

Empathy in teams is not just about being kind; it's about genuinely trying to understand others' perspectives. It's the ability to put yourself in someone else's shoes and see the world through their eyes. When conflict arises, it's easy to assume we know the other person's feelings or motivations. However, without taking the time to listen and understand, we risk misunderstanding and miscommunication. For example, a team member might seem uncooperative or distant, but instead of making assumptions, a manager could ask open-ended questions like, "I noticed you seem frustrated with this task. Can you help me understand what's going on?" By actively listening and responding with empathy, the situation can be addressed without escalating tensions.

In a team, empathy is the glue that binds people together. It fosters trust, makes people feel heard, and builds deeper connections. When team members practice empathy, they are more likely to collaborate effectively, share ideas, and work towards a common goal. An example of this can be seen in a well-known story from the tech world—Google's Project Aristotle. The project found that the most successful teams had one common trait: psychological safety, which is rooted in empathy. Team members felt safe to express their thoughts, share mistakes, and offer feedback without fear of judgment.

Plato's words, "Be kind, for everyone you meet is fighting a hard battle," remind us that every team member may have unseen struggles—personal or professional—that can impact their work. Empathy can help bridge those gaps, creating an environment where every individual feels understood, valued, and supported. This in turn not only helps in resolving conflicts but also strengthens team cohesion, productivity, and long-term success. By cultivating empathy within teams, we create spaces where people thrive and work together more effectively.

2. Focus on Solutions, Not Blame

In moments of failure, shifting the focus from "Whose fault, is it?" to "What can we do to solve this?" ensures that the energy in the team is focused on growth and improvement. For instance, during a product launch that didn't meet expectations, rather than blaming the marketing or development teams, a team leader could guide the group to focus on analyzing what went wrong and how they can refine their strategy moving forward. Blame creates division, while solutions promote collaboration. A team becomes stronger when everyone rallies around fixing the issue rather than pointing fingers. The words of the famous philosopher Epictetus, "It's not what happens to you, but how you react to it that matters," capture the essence of this mindset. When each team member takes ownership of finding a solution, it fosters a sense of shared responsibility and collective accountability, making the team more resilient in future challenges.

3. Understand Team Members' Strengths and Weaknesses

Each team member brings unique strengths and challenges to the table. Recognizing these differences helps in forming a well-rounded team. For instance, in a marketing team, one person may excel in creative thinking, coming up with innovative campaign ideas, while another might shine in execution, ensuring the plans are implemented efficiently and effectively. Acknowledging and celebrating these strengths prevents frustration and creates mutual respect. When a leader encourages cross-functional collaboration, they can leverage each person's talents. For example, a project manager might pair the idea generator with the implementer, ensuring both strengths are maximized in a complementary manner. This not only drives team success but also fosters an environment where everyone feels valued for their contributions. As Voltaire wisely stated, "Appreciation is a wonderful thing: It makes what is excellent in others belong to us as well." When a team truly values and appreciates the diverse skills within it, the collective output becomes greater than the sum of its parts, leading to more innovative solutions and a more harmonious work environment.

4. Perfection Is Not the Goal

While striving for excellence is essential, expecting perfection from your teammates or yourself is a fast track to disappointment. For example, in a product development team, if the focus is solely on achieving a flawless product from the start, it can lead to delays and frustration, as the team may struggle to meet unattainable standards. Perfection often leads to burnout and missed opportunities. Instead, focus on continuous improvement. A team that celebrates small wins, like refining a feature or improving customer feedback, rather than expecting perfection, will maintain motivation and momentum. Celebrate progress, not flawless execution. As Vincent Van Gogh said, "Great things are not done by impulse, but by a series of small things brought together." A perfect outcome may not always be possible, but incremental steps can lead to significant progress. For example, a sales team that gradually improves its conversion rates over time by focusing on refining their approach each month will eventually surpass their original goals, achieving sustained success.

5. The Power of a Shared Vision

A clear, shared vision helps align the team's efforts. For instance, in a marketing team working on a product launch, when every team member understands that the ultimate goal is not just to sell but to introduce an innovative solution to customers, motivation naturally increases. Each member's role, whether it's designing visuals, managing social media, or crafting compelling copy, is tied to the larger purpose. A team without a vision can easily drift or lose focus. A customer service team, for example, that doesn't have a clear understanding of how they contribute to overall company success may struggle with morale and customer satisfaction. But when each member sees how their efforts contribute to a collective goal, engagement soars. For example, if the team knows that improving customer satisfaction by even a small percentage directly impacts the company's reputation and bottom line, they're more likely to be committed. Helen Keller beautifully put it, "Alone we can do so little; together we can do so much." This emphasizes that a united purpose amplifies the efforts of individual team members, as seen in collaborative projects where teams often exceed expectations by pooling their diverse skills and resources.

6. Alignment with the Bigger Picture

It's crucial for every team member to understand how their work contributes to the broader company or societal goals. For example, a software developer working on a product might not only see their role as writing code, but as helping provide a solution that improves the customer's day-to-day life. This alignment fosters a sense of purpose and direction. When each person understands the why behind their tasks, the how becomes more meaningful. For instance, a marketing team member working on an ad campaign may feel more motivated when they see how their creative effort will drive sales and support the company's mission. In Peter Drucker's words, "The best way to predict the future is to create it." Each contribution, no matter how small, is a building block towards creating a better future, as seen when all departments of a company unite to launch a new product successfully, each adding their expertise towards the common goal.

7. Effective Goal Setting

For example, let's say a sales team is tasked with increasing revenue by 20% over the next quarter. To make this goal SMART, they could break it down into smaller, measurable actions:

- **Increase the number of client meetings by 15%** (Specific, Measurable, Achievable, Relevant, Time-bound)
- **Improve the close rate by 10%** (Specific, Measurable, Achievable, Relevant, Time-bound)
- **Upsell additional services to existing clients by 20%** (Specific, Measurable, Achievable, Relevant, Time-bound)

By assigning specific team members to each task, setting deadlines, and tracking progress along the way, everyone understands their contribution toward the larger goal. Regular check-ins and celebrating milestones—like hitting 10% of the target—keep the team engaged and motivated. By focusing on these smaller, achievable goals, the overall vision of increasing revenue becomes clearer and more attainable. This structure helps the team stay focused and aligned, ensuring that progress is made every step of the way.

8. Team Role Clarity

Without clear roles, teams can quickly become disorganized. Assigning roles based on strengths and expertise ensures that everyone knows their responsibilities. For instance, in a marketing team, one member might be skilled in graphic design, while another is great with copywriting, allowing them to focus on what they do best. But it's also important to remain flexible—roles can evolve as the team grows. In a startup, for example, team members may take on multiple roles initially, but as the company scales, the roles become more specialized. A lack of role clarity leads to duplicated efforts, missed opportunities, and conflict. Take the case of a tech development team where two programmers were unknowingly working on the same task due to unclear role allocation, leading to wasted time. Aristotle's quote, "The whole is greater than the sum of its parts," highlights the importance of each member's contribution to the team's success. When everyone is aligned with their strengths, the team becomes more efficient and productive.**10. The Five Stages of Team Tasks**

Every team task can be divided into five stages: direction-setting, planning, briefing, action, and review. Direction-setting helps clarify the goal, while planning and briefing ensure everyone knows their role. Action brings the plan to life, and reviewing the outcome allows for reflection and learning. As Lao Tzu said, "*A journey of a thousand miles begins with a single step.*" It's essential to break tasks down into manageable phases to keep progress on track.

9. Fostering the Right Environment

A team thrives in an environment that encourages creativity, openness, and collaboration. Foster a culture of openness, where team members feel safe to express their ideas without fear of judgment. For instance, a leader might set up regular brainstorming sessions where everyone's input is valued and where no idea is dismissed prematurely. This could be something as simple as a weekly "idea hour" where team members are encouraged to share any new thoughts, challenges, or concepts they are exploring. By creating spaces, both physically and mentally, that promote the free flow of thoughts and ideas, the team feels empowered and valued. As Walt Disney said, "The way to get started is to quit talking and begin doing." In one real-world example, Google's "20% time" encourages employees to dedicate a portion of their work hours to projects they are passionate about, which has led to the creation of products like Gmail and Google News. The right environment, where individuals feel supported and trusted, can ignite productivity and innovation.

10. Speak Up for Team Success

In any team, clear and open communication is vital. If something doesn't sit right, or if there's room for improvement, speaking up can prevent small issues from snowballing into bigger ones. For example, during a project, if a team member notices a potential flaw in the process but doesn't speak up, the issue might go unnoticed until it becomes a major setback later. A good example can be seen in the software development industry, where early communication about bugs or concerns can save countless hours of work in the long run. It's crucial to create an environment where everyone feels comfortable expressing their thoughts. At Google, for instance, they promote a culture where all team members, regardless of hierarchy, are encouraged to share their ideas and concerns openly. "Silence is a source of great strength," said Lao Tzu, but in a team setting, speaking up is often the key to progress. When a member speaks up, it opens the floor for others to address issues collaboratively, leading to better outcomes and stronger teamwork.

11. Handling Team Size

In a real-world scenario, a project management team at a tech company may find that when their team size exceeds 8 members, communication becomes fragmented. This is often seen when important updates or feedback are lost in long email threads or team meetings. For example, when the team grew beyond 8 members, a manager noticed that some team members started feeling overlooked, which led to disengagement. Conversely, when they reduced the team size to 5, every team member felt more connected, and feedback could be shared more efficiently. The smaller size allowed for quicker decision-making and clearer accountability, creating a more cohesive and productive environment. This example shows that the ideal team size should not only match the task at hand but also ensure that each team member's contributions are valued and communicated clearly.

12. Managing Group Dynamics

To illustrate, in a marketing team, one member may naturally take the lead in brainstorming ideas, but this can unintentionally silence others who have valuable contributions to make. By establishing a team rule where each person has a turn to speak, the group ensures that everyone's voice is heard, leading to more diverse ideas. For example, during a product launch, a project manager might organize brainstorming sessions where everyone is given time to present their ideas, which can help balance the contributions of both dominant and quieter members. Moreover, in larger teams, breaking down tasks into smaller sub-teams can improve efficiency. A team working on a new software development project might split into sub-teams focused on different aspects, such as UI design, backend development, and testing, allowing each group to concentrate on their specialized tasks. This structure not only boosts productivity but also ensures clearer accountability, as each sub-team can report back with specific outcomes.

13. Setting Measurable Accountability

Accountability keeps teams focused and on track. Define clear roles and deadlines, and ensure that each team member is held responsible for their part of the task. Regular check-ins and updates help maintain momentum. "Accountability breeds responsibility," said Stephen Covey. In the food industry, this is especially important for ensuring smooth operations. For example, in a food production facility, the team responsible for quality control must be accountable for inspecting every batch of ingredients or products. If there is a delay in the packaging process, the team members involved in that step must address it immediately to avoid further setbacks. When each person knows their role and how it impacts the final product, there's less chance of errors, and the workflow remains steady. Regular updates during shifts or team huddles ensure that everyone is aligned, which boosts performance and helps deliver consistent results.

14. Addressing Dominance in Teams

Some team members may have strong personalities that dominate discussions. While these individuals often have valuable insights, it's important to ensure that others have the chance to share their thoughts as well. For instance, in a marketing team, one member may be particularly vocal and assertive during brainstorming sessions. To avoid one person taking over, the team leader can implement strategies like round-robin discussions or "silent brainstorming" sessions, where everyone writes down their ideas before sharing them aloud. This ensures that quieter team members are encouraged to contribute. In fact, a team leader could also implement time limits on speaking to maintain balance, allowing everyone an equal opportunity to share. As Ken Blanchard's words, "The key to successful leadership today is influence, not authority," remind us, leadership isn't about controlling the conversation but creating a space where everyone feels valued and heard. By encouraging diverse input and managing dominant voices, the team can build a more inclusive and effective decision-making process.

15. Using Disagreements to Improve Plans

Disagreements within a team should be seen as opportunities to refine ideas. When team members challenge each other's opinions, they can identify flaws, strengthen arguments, and create better solutions. For example, in a product development team, two designers may have differing opinions on the user interface. By discussing their views and providing feedback, they can come to a design that blends the best of both approaches. Disagreement should never be seen as personal but as a constructive process for improving the team's work. One tip for navigating disagreements is to foster an environment where differing opinions are welcomed, such as using a "debate-and-contribute" format where everyone gets a turn to voice their perspective without interruption. Additionally, keeping the focus on the issue at hand rather than making it personal is crucial. As Abraham Lincoln said, "The best way to predict the future is to create it." By addressing disagreements constructively, teams create better outcomes for the future.

16. Turning Slower Progress into Strength

If one team member struggles with a task, rather than rushing to complete it for them, take the time to support them. This ensures better overall results and strengthens the collaborative spirit within the team. For instance, in a marketing team, if a member is struggling with creating an ad copy, instead of taking over the task, a more helpful approach could be to guide them through brainstorming ideas, offer feedback, or suggest resources. By involving them in the process, you not only help them improve but also ensure that they gain the confidence to handle similar tasks in the future. Slower progress may expose areas that need improvement, preventing bigger issues down the road. In a project management scenario, one team member might take longer to grasp a new software tool. Instead of doing it for them, the team can collectively have training sessions or assign a mentor to help them learn. Robert Collier's quote, "Success is the sum of small efforts, repeated day in and day out," emphasizes the importance of patience and steady work for long-term success. By being patient and offering support, you're investing in the growth of both the individual and the team as a whole.

17. Avoiding Risky Shift

In group decision-making, a phenomenon known as the "risky shift" often occurs, where groups tend to make riskier decisions than individuals would on their own. This happens because group members may feel a sense of shared responsibility, which can lead to decisions that they might avoid if they were acting alone. The presence of others can create an environment where individuals feel less accountable for the outcomes, thus increasing the likelihood of taking risks.

For example, a marketing team might decide to invest in an unproven advertising campaign that carries a high risk, believing that the collective decision of the team will somehow lessen the individual accountability if it fails. This decision might not have been made if the decision rested with just one person, who might have been more cautious.

To prevent the risky shift, teams should implement structured decision-making processes. For example, using a "pre-mortem" approach, where the team envisions potential failures before making a decision, can help mitigate rash choices. Additionally, having a designated person to play "devil's advocate" ensures that all angles are thoroughly considered, reducing the chances of overly risky decisions.

The quote by Ryunosuke Satoro, "Individually, we are one drop. Together, we are an ocean," reminds us that while collaboration can bring strength, it's essential to ensure that the collective power of the group doesn't lead to decisions made in haste or without proper caution.

18. Celebrate Collective Wins

Celebrating the team's achievements, no matter how small, fosters a sense of belonging and reinforces the value of teamwork. Acknowledging every success creates a culture of appreciation, motivating the team to continue striving for excellence. This could be as simple as a congratulatory email or a small team gathering. For example, a sales team that hits a milestone might receive a team lunch, or an office team could be recognized in a monthly meeting for completing a project ahead of schedule. "Success is best when it's shared," said Howard Schultz, reminding us that collective victories inspire future collaboration and strengthen bonds within the team. These moments of recognition, no matter how small, remind everyone that their contribution is valued, fostering a positive and productive work environment.

19. Diversity is Strength

A diverse team brings a variety of perspectives that can lead to more innovative solutions. Diverse teams—whether in terms of gender, age, ethnicity, or professional backgrounds—are better equipped to approach problems from multiple angles. For example, a tech startup might benefit from having team members with backgrounds in both computer science and design, as their collaboration can result in products that are not only technically robust but also user-friendly. "Strength lies in differences, not in similarities," said Stephen R. Covey. Embrace the diversity within your team, as it enhances creativity and problem-solving ability, fostering a richer environment for growth. To maximize the benefits of diversity, encourage open dialogue and provide platforms for everyone's voice to be heard. This can include regular team meetings where ideas are shared openly, or brainstorming sessions where everyone is encouraged to contribute, ensuring that diverse viewpoints are valued and considered in the decision-making process.

20. Transparency in Communication

Transparency is essential for building trust and fostering an environment where team members feel valued and informed. For example, in a tech company, when leaders share the progress of a project, including the challenges and potential roadblocks, the team is better prepared to adapt and contribute. In contrast, if a team leader withholds this information, rumors can spread, and team members may feel left out or disconnected from the project's goals.

Some tips to enhance transparency include holding regular team meetings to update everyone on the project's status, sharing success stories and challenges openly, and encouraging open dialogue where everyone feels comfortable sharing their thoughts. Additionally, tools like project management software can help everyone stay on the same page by providing clear visibility into tasks, deadlines, and individual contributions.

As Brene Brown aptly says, "Clear is kind. Unclear is unkind." This reinforces the importance of clarity and honesty in communication to avoid unnecessary confusion and foster an environment of mutual respect and collaboration.

21. Encourage Risk-Taking in a Safe Environment

Teams that operate in an environment where taking risks is encouraged (and not punished) are more likely to innovate and excel. When employees are not afraid of failure, they feel free to share bold ideas and creative solutions. This fosters a culture of growth and innovation. "The greatest risk is not taking any risk," says Mark Zuckerberg. Encourage your team to step out of their comfort zones while knowing that failure is simply part of the learning process.

- **Create a Safe Space for Experimentation:** One example is Google's famous "20% time," where employees were encouraged to spend 20% of their workweek on personal projects or new ideas. This led to the creation of successful products like Gmail and Google News.
- **Celebrate Learning from Failures:** At Pixar, post-mortem meetings after a project—whether successful or not—are held to discuss what worked, what didn't, and how they can improve next time. This creates a culture of learning from mistakes rather than hiding them.
- **Encourage Small Risks:** In a startup environment, encourage your team to test new strategies or products on a small scale before committing to full execution. For instance, launching a beta version of a product to gauge customer feedback can provide invaluable insights before the full launch.
- **Provide Positive Reinforcement:** Celebrate small wins and learning moments from risk-taking. Instead of focusing on the failed aspects, highlight the value gained from the attempt, such as new knowledge, skills, or insights that can improve future projects.

22. Trust and Accountability Go Hand in Hand

For a team to function effectively, trust and accountability must coexist. Team members must trust one another to fulfil their responsibilities, while holding themselves accountable to the group. Establishing clear expectations and responsibilities from the beginning ensures that everyone understands their role in the team's success. For example, in a product development team, if one member is responsible for conducting market research, the rest of the team must trust that they will deliver valuable insights on time. Similarly, that team member must hold themselves accountable for meeting deadlines and ensuring their findings are accurate.

One helpful tip is to set regular check-ins or progress updates to foster accountability. For instance, a weekly meeting where each member shares their progress helps ensure that the team stays aligned and issues are addressed early. This practice reinforces the sense of responsibility while maintaining transparency.

As author Stephen M.R. Covey says, "Trust is the highest form of human motivation." When trust is present, accountability becomes a natural byproduct. Consider Google's practice of allowing employees to dedicate 20% of their time to personal projects. This trust in their employees' judgment fosters innovation, while the accountability to deliver results ensures the projects align with the company's goals.

23. Value Constructive Feedback

Feedback is a critical element in personal and professional growth. Encouraging constructive criticism helps team members learn from their mistakes and refine their skills. However, it's essential that feedback is given respectfully and with the intention to help others improve. As Ken Blanchard puts it, "*Feedback is the breakfast of champions.*" When used correctly, feedback can be a powerful tool for continuous improvement.

Tips for Giving Constructive Feedback:

a. **Be Specific:** Instead of general statements like "Good job," or "You need to improve," be specific. For example, "Your presentation was clear, but next time, consider slowing down to give your audience more time to absorb the information."

b. **Balance Positive and Negative Feedback:** Start with positive feedback to encourage the person, then gently share areas of improvement. For example, "I love how well you organized the report, but next time, we should ensure all the data is updated to avoid confusion."

c. **Focus on Behaviour, Not Personality:** Critique actions and behaviours, not the individual. For instance, "I noticed that some of the tasks were delayed last week. Let's discuss what happened and how we can prevent that in the future," instead of, "You are always late with tasks."

d. **Use "I" Statements:** This reduces defensiveness and helps the person receiving the feedback to feel that it's a shared experience. For example, "I felt a bit confused when the report didn't include all the details we discussed. Could you ensure this next time?" instead of, "You didn't follow through."

e. **Provide Actionable Suggestions:** Feedback should be followed by suggestions on how to improve. Instead of just pointing out what went wrong, offer ideas for improvement. "Maybe we could implement a checklist to make sure we're not missing any steps in future projects."

24. Effective Delegation Drives Results

Delegating tasks effectively within the team ensures that everyone is working at their highest potential. Understanding your teammates' strengths allows you to delegate tasks that suit their expertise, helping them thrive. Overloading one person with work can lead to burnout and missed opportunities. *"Delegation is not a sign of weakness; it's a sign of strength,"* said John C. Maxwell. A good leader understands the importance of empowering others through trust and responsibility.

Here are some tips to enhance the effectiveness of delegation-

a. **Know Your Team's Strengths:** Understand what each team member excels at. Delegate tasks based on skills and experience to ensure that the right person is handling the right task. For example, if a team member is great with data analysis, delegate tasks that require this skill to them.

b. **Provide Clear Instructions:** When delegating, make sure the task is clearly outlined. Set expectations and deadlines, and ensure that the person you're delegating to knows what success looks like for that task.

c. **Empower and Trust:** While it's essential to provide guidance, allow team members the autonomy to execute the task their way. This builds confidence and promotes ownership.

d. **Follow Up, Don't Micromanage:** Check in periodically to ensure progress, but avoid hovering over your team members. This shows you trust them to get the job done while providing support when needed.

e. **Encourage Open Communication:** Ensure that team members feel comfortable asking questions or seeking clarification. This creates a collaborative environment, even as tasks are delegated.

For example, In a marketing team, a manager might delegate content creation to the most creative team member, while delegating data analysis to someone who excels in numbers. When a product launch is coming up, the manager may delegate the outreach campaign to someone with strong communication skills and leadership qualities. By knowing the strengths of each team member, the manager maximizes the team's potential, ensuring that the tasks are completed effectively without overburdening anyone.

25. Avoid Groupthink

Groupthink is a psychological phenomenon that occurs when a group of people strives for consensus and harmony over making the best possible decision. In this situation, the desire for group cohesion and the avoidance of conflict leads individuals to suppress their own opinions, ignore alternative solutions, and overlook risks, ultimately resulting in poor or flawed decision-making.

Groupthink occurs when the desire for harmony within the group leads to poor decision-making. To avoid groupthink, encourage diverse opinions, constructive dissent, and debate.

Ensure that all viewpoints are considered before making important decisions.

As Irving Janis, who coined the term, said, "*Groupthink is the process of avoiding real conflict in order to keep the group together.*" A healthy level of conflict can be productive, pushing the team to create better solutions and more effective strategies.

26. Create a Feedback Loop for Improvement

A feedback loop is a continuous process of receiving feedback and using it to improve. Encourage your team to not only receive feedback but to act on it. For instance, in a software development team, after every sprint, developers might hold a retrospective meeting where they discuss what went well and what can be improved for the next sprint. By incorporating feedback into the next cycle, the team can constantly refine their methods and achieve better results. This cycle leads to a constant evolution of processes and results. As Andy Grove, co-founder of Intel, said, "Success breeds complacency. Complacency breeds failure. Only the paranoid survive." In the context of teamwork, consistent feedback loops ensure that teams stay on their toes and continuously improve. A company that encourages feedback from its customers and employees is more likely to identify areas of improvement quickly, staying ahead of competitors and improving product quality.

27. Build Psychological Safety

For a team to thrive, every member must feel that it is safe to take risks, make mistakes, and share ideas without fear of judgment. Psychological safety is the foundation for innovation and creativity. When people feel safe, they're more likely to speak up and share valuable insights. Amy Edmondson, who researched this concept, states, "Psychological safety is a belief that one will not be penalized or humiliated for speaking up with ideas, questions, concerns, or mistakes." Cultivating this safety leads to a more engaged, productive, and innovative team.

In a software development team, when team members felt psychologically safe, they were encouraged to share ideas and raise concerns without fear of being judged. One developer suggested an unconventional solution to a recurring bug, which led to a breakthrough and improved the system's efficiency. Without the safe environment for open discussion, this idea might have been dismissed too quickly.

At a manufacturing company, a team faced consistent delays in the production process. One worker, who initially feared the repercussions of speaking up, finally shared that the issue stemmed from a misalignment in the workflow. His input led to a restructuring of the production line, which improved efficiency and reduced delays significantly.

Tip 1: Encourage open dialogue by actively asking team members for their opinions and concerns. Create regular opportunities for feedback and ensure that responses are constructive and supportive, not punitive.

Tip 2: Celebrate mistakes as learning opportunities. When a mistake is made, discuss it openly without blame, and explore how the team can prevent it in the future. This approach builds trust and reinforces the idea that mistakes are part of the learning process.

28. Adaptability to Change

Change is inevitable, and teams must be able to adapt to it quickly. Whether it's a shift in team roles, project requirements, or company priorities, the ability to pivot without losing momentum is crucial for long-term success. For example, when a software development team suddenly needs to switch from one tech stack to another due to evolving client demands, their openness to learning and adjusting quickly can determine the project's success or failure.

Encourage your team to embrace change as an opportunity for growth rather than as an obstacle. Consider a situation where a marketing team faces a last-minute campaign direction change due to market feedback. Instead of resisting, a high-performing team would brainstorm fresh strategies, reassign tasks, and execute swiftly—turning potential disruption into innovation.

"It is not the strongest of the species that survive, nor the most intelligent, but the one most responsive to change," said Charles Darwin. Adaptability ensures that your team stays relevant and resilient in the face of challenges. Just like companies that successfully navigated the COVID-19 pandemic by quickly transitioning to remote work and digital-first models, teams that adapt can not only survive—but thrive.

29. Celebrate Individual Contributions

While teamwork is about collective effort, recognizing individual contributions ensures that each person feels valued. Publicly acknowledge the unique skills and hard work each member brings to the team. For instance, during a product launch, while the entire team might be applauded for the success, highlighting that Priya led the user experience design or that Arjun resolved a last-minute technical glitch makes their efforts visible and appreciated.

This recognition boosts morale and fosters a culture of appreciation. As Maya Angelou said, "You can't use up creativity. The more you use, the more you have." Encouraging individual growth and acknowledging it reinforces a culture where both individual and collective success is celebrated. Just like in a successful orchestra, the harmony is beautiful, but the excellence of each solo performance enriches the whole.

30. Patience is Key to Team Success

Achieving team goals takes time, and the journey often requires patience. Not every task or objective will be completed immediately, and it's essential to manage expectations. For example, a sales team entering a new market might not see immediate conversions despite consistent effort. It could take months of outreach, trust-building, and brand visibility before results start to show. Leaders must remind the team that early struggles are part of the process and that perseverance will pay off.

Encourage your team to remain patient and persistent, knowing that success is built over time. "Patience is not the ability to wait, but the ability to keep a good attitude while waiting," said Joyce Meyer. Maintaining a positive attitude while waiting for results is essential in building a resilient, long-term team dynamic. Just like farmers who sow seeds knowing harvest comes later, teams must nurture their goals with consistent effort and belief.

31. Continuous Learning for Team Growth

Teams must always be in a state of learning to stay competitive. Encourage ongoing education, whether through formal training, mentoring, or learning from past experiences. For example, a customer support team that regularly attends workshops on empathy, conflict resolution, and new product updates will be far more effective in handling complex client issues compared to one that relies only on outdated knowledge.

A team that embraces continuous learning is more likely to stay innovative and adaptable to change. "An investment in knowledge pays the best interest," said Benjamin Franklin. Knowledge-sharing within the team helps everyone grow and elevates the team's overall performance. A tech company, for instance, might hold weekly 'knowledge-sharing huddles' where one member teaches the rest about a tool or insight they've recently mastered—turning individual growth into collective progress.

32. Support Each Other's Growth

A strong team supports not only the goals of the group but also the individual aspirations of its members. By helping each other grow, both professionally and personally, the team strengthens its overall cohesion. For example, in a marketing team, if one member expresses a desire to learn graphic design, a colleague with design experience might offer to mentor them during lunch breaks or after work. This not only helps the individual grow but also adds new skills to the team's collective toolkit.

"A rising tide lifts all boats," said John F. Kennedy. Team members who help each other succeed create a positive environment where collaboration is natural and productive. Over time, such mutual investment fosters trust, loyalty, and a shared sense of achievement that goes beyond just meeting targets.

33. Encourage Innovation Through Collaboration

Innovation often happens when diverse minds come together to solve problems. Encourage team members to collaborate across different functions, sharing unique perspectives. For instance, a product development team might work closely with the marketing department to ensure that new features align with customer needs, while also considering feedback from customer support about pain points. By combining insights from different areas, the team can create a product that is both technically advanced and user-friendly.

The best ideas often emerge through this cross-pollination of thoughts and skills. "Innovation is the ability to see change as an opportunity – not a threat," said Steve Jobs. Teams that collaborate effectively can turn challenges into opportunities for creative solutions. A great example is how Apple's design and engineering teams work together, fusing creativity with functionality to launch revolutionary products like the iPhone, which emerged from the collaboration of designers, engineers, and marketers sharing insights and perspectives.

34. Recognize and Leverage Team Synergy

Synergy occurs when the collective output of the team is greater than the sum of individual contributions. By aligning goals, talents, and efforts, teams can achieve remarkable outcomes. For example, in a software development project, a group of developers, designers, and testers each plays a critical role. While each individual's contribution is valuable, the team's collective effort, where everyone's skills complement each other, results in the successful release of a user-friendly and bug-free application that no single person could have achieved alone.

Recognizing this synergy helps teams understand that their combined efforts have exponential power. "Alone we can do so little; together we can do so much," said Helen Keller. A great example is the Apollo 11 mission, where engineers, astronauts, scientists, and support staff all worked together towards one goal—landing a man on the moon. Their collective efforts achieved something far greater than what any individual could have accomplished.

Encouraging this unity strengthens team morale and accelerates progress. When teams see the powerful impact of their combined efforts, it inspires them to collaborate more effectively and pursue even greater achievements.

35. Encourage Accountability Through Ownership

When team members take ownership of their roles, they are more motivated to ensure the success of the team. Ownership means taking responsibility for tasks, results, and continuous improvement. For example, in a sales team, when a member takes full ownership of their pipeline—tracking leads, following up, and ensuring timely communication—they not only contribute to the team's target but also improve the process by suggesting new ways to streamline communication or increase conversion rates.

It builds trust and commitment within the team. As Patrick Lencioni wrote, "The true measure of a team is not how well it performs when things are going well, but how well it responds when things are difficult." A great example of this is a product development team that, during a tight deadline, rallies together to fix an unexpected bug just before a product launch. Each team member steps up—whether it's a developer troubleshooting the issue, a designer adjusting the interface, or a project manager coordinating the efforts—showing how ownership leads to collective resilience during challenging times.

Encouraging ownership leads to a culture where every member is invested in the team's success. When individuals feel responsible for their tasks, they are more likely to go above and beyond, ensuring that the team thrives even in the face of adversity.

36. Foster Open Dialogue

Open dialogue is the foundation of effective communication within a team. Encourage honest, respectful conversations where every team member feels free to express their thoughts, concerns, and ideas. For example, during a project debrief, if a team member feels that a deadline was unrealistic but fears speaking up, it can lead to frustration and burnout. However, when the team has established a culture of open dialogue, the member feels comfortable voicing concerns early, which allows for adjustments and ensures the team avoids avoidable pitfalls.

By fostering an open-dialogue culture, you reduce misunderstandings and increase collaboration. A practical instance is in a design team where a member expresses dissatisfaction with the current design direction. Instead of silently accepting it, the team engages in a respectful discussion, incorporating different viewpoints to refine the project. This leads to a stronger final product and a more engaged team.

As Peter Drucker said, "The most important thing in communication is hearing what isn't said." Listening actively to what is not being said is just as crucial as speaking openly. For example, if a team member isn't speaking up about their workload concerns, a manager who actively listens to body language or detects signs of stress can step in to provide support, preventing potential issues before they escalate.

37. Promote a Work-Life Balance

A team that values work-life balance ensures that team members remain productive and motivated. Overworking leads to burnout and reduced creativity. For example, a marketing team that pushes through long hours to meet a tight deadline may initially see high output, but over time, their creativity and energy levels will drop. On the other hand, a team that takes regular breaks and disconnects when needed can come back to their tasks with fresh ideas and renewed enthusiasm. A team member who leaves work at a reasonable hour to pursue a hobby, like painting or cycling, may return the next day with new perspectives that contribute to a more innovative approach to their projects.

Encourage your team to take breaks, disconnect, and make time for personal growth. A case in point is Google's policy of allowing employees to spend 20% of their work time on personal projects. This has led to some of the company's most successful innovations, such as Gmail and AdSense. Encouraging your team to disconnect from their routine tasks and explore new interests not only prevents burnout but also fosters innovation.

"Time is what we want most, but what we use worst," said William Penn. Respecting personal time promotes long-term success and ensures that team members can maintain energy and creativity over time. For example, a team in a tech startup may set clear boundaries for after-hours work, ensuring that employees aren't overwhelmed by constant notifications or the pressure to be always "on." This respect for personal time helps prevent exhaustion and creates an environment where employees are eager to bring their best selves to work each day.

38. Build Resilience Through Challenges

Teams often face obstacles that can either break or strengthen them. Resilience is crucial for overcoming setbacks, and it comes from learning how to handle adversity together. For instance, during a product launch, a tech team might face unexpected technical difficulties that delay the release. Instead of blaming one another or panicking, the team comes together to troubleshoot, reassign tasks, and adjust timelines. By pooling their resources and focusing on solutions, they manage to release the product with enhanced features that customers appreciate.

When challenges arise, instead of pointing fingers, teams should unite and find solutions collaboratively. A great example is how the Japanese automaker Toyota responded to the 2011 tsunami. Despite the destruction, Toyota's resilient team was able to recover and rebuild quickly, ensuring that production was back on track sooner than expected. They did so by focusing on collective problem-solving and sticking together through adversity.

As Winston Churchill said, "Success is not final, failure is not fatal: It is the courage to continue that counts." Building resilience strengthens the team's character and equips them to handle future challenges with confidence. Resilience becomes a key asset, especially when teams face more pressure or uncertainty in future projects.

39. Maintain a Shared Vision

A team without a shared vision can struggle to stay aligned and motivated. It's important that every team member understands the common goal and the "why" behind it. For example, a product development team at a tech company might have a vision of creating an app that makes mental health resources accessible to everyone. If each team member understands the larger purpose behind this vision—helping individuals lead healthier, happier lives—they are more likely to remain motivated and focused on achieving the same goal, whether they're working on coding, design, or marketing.

This collective sense of purpose drives every decision and action. **"Vision is the art of seeing what is invisible to others,"** said Jonathan Swift. A shared vision gives the team direction and ensures that all efforts are focused on achieving a common objective. For instance, when NASA's Apollo 11 team set out to land a man on the moon, every member understood how their work contributed to this audacious goal, from engineers to astronauts. This unified vision allowed them to overcome numerous challenges, culminating in one of humanity's greatest achievements.

40. Invest in Team Development

Teams that invest in their development—whether through skill-building, team-building exercises, or regular training—are better equipped to succeed in the long term. For example, a sales team at a growing company might attend quarterly workshops that enhance their negotiation skills, learn about new tools for prospecting, and engage in team-building exercises to strengthen their communication. These regular investments in their development help them stay competitive, improve their performance, and maintain a high level of motivation.

Continuous development creates a culture of growth and adaptation, which keeps the team at the cutting edge of performance. A great example of this is how IBM has invested in its employees for decades by providing continuous learning opportunities and leadership development programs. This commitment to development has helped them stay relevant in the tech industry, continually adapting to new technologies and market trends.

"The only way to do great work is to love what you do," said Steve Jobs. By investing in people and fostering their development, you can unlock their full potential and contribute to the team's ongoing success. When employees feel supported in their growth, they are more likely to be engaged, contributing ideas that lead to innovation and long-term achievement.

41. Create a Culture of Respect

Mutual respect is the bedrock of any effective team. Team members must treat one another with dignity, even when they disagree. For example, in a marketing team brainstorming ideas for a new campaign, team members may have differing opinions on the direction the campaign should take. If each individual is respectful of others' viewpoints and willing to listen without judgment, the team can come to a consensus that combines the best ideas from all perspectives, fostering a sense of collaboration and unity.

Disrespectful Behaviour can tear a team apart, whereas respect creates trust and collaboration. A great example is how Southwest Airlines has built its culture on mutual respect, where employees are encouraged to voice their opinions and contribute openly, regardless of their rank. This culture has led to a loyal, highly engaged workforce that works together to deliver excellent customer service, even in challenging situations.

As Maya Angelou wisely noted, "We all should know that diversity makes for a rich tapestry, and we must understand that all the threads of the tapestry are equal in value no matter their colour." In a team setting, this respect for diversity means embracing the unique contributions of each member—whether they bring a different skill set, background, or way of thinking. When every voice is respected, the team thrives.

42. Foster Healthy Competition

Competition within a team can drive individuals to perform at their best, as long as it is healthy and supportive. For example, in a sales team, setting up friendly competitions where each team member tracks their own progress toward meeting sales targets can encourage them to push themselves to achieve more. However, when the competition is framed as an opportunity to learn from one another, such as sharing best practices and celebrating each other's wins, it fosters a collaborative atmosphere rather than creating division.

When competition is framed as a way to push each other to grow, rather than to tear others down, it strengthens the team's performance. A great example of this is the approach used by companies like Zappos, where team members are encouraged to compete in a way that aligns with the company's core values, such as exceptional customer service. This type of competition encourages employees to perform at their highest level while still supporting one another, knowing that the success of one person contributes to the success of the entire team.

"Competition brings out the best in products and the worst in people," says David Sarnoff. While competition can spur innovation and performance, it's essential to ensure that competition is rooted in mutual respect and shared goals, so it motivates the team without creating division. For instance, a software development team might compete to create the most efficient algorithm, but they do so with the understanding that collaboration and sharing insights will lead to the best overall outcome for the project, strengthening the team's unity rather than fostering resentment.

43. Align Team Roles with Strengths

When team members are aligned with tasks that match their strengths, they are more likely to be engaged, motivated, and productive. For instance, in a design team, assigning a team member who excels at user interface design to work on the visual aspects of a new website project allows them to shine in an area where they are most skilled. Meanwhile, another team member who is great at coding might be focused on the technical aspects. When each person works in their area of strength, the project progresses smoothly, and the team is more likely to meet its goals efficiently.

Understanding the unique abilities of each member and ensuring they work on tasks suited to their skills boosts both individual and team performance. A great example is when Google formed a team to work on artificial intelligence. By carefully matching team members to the roles that best suited their expertise—such as data scientists working on algorithms and engineers handling the coding—Google was able to create highly successful products like Google Assistant and DeepMind.

"Do what you do best and outsource the rest," advised Peter Drucker. A strong team leverages each individual's strengths, creating a more harmonious and effective work environment. For example, in a small startup, a leader might focus on business strategy and client relations, while a talented technical expert handles product development. This division of labor allows the team to operate at peak efficiency, maximizing its collective potential.

44. Encourage Cross-Functional Collaboration

Encouraging collaboration across different functions—marketing, finance, product development, etc.—can unlock new perspectives and innovative solutions. For example, when a tech company develops a new product, bringing together product designers, engineers, marketing experts, and finance professionals can lead to a more well-rounded approach. The product team may design something innovative, while marketing can help position it to meet consumer needs, and finance ensures it is profitable. This collaboration often results in a better product with a stronger market fit.

Cross-functional teams are more likely to understand the big picture and align their efforts for the overall success of the organization. A great example of this is when Apple's design and engineering teams collaborate closely during product development. The seamless coordination between functions ensures that the product is not only aesthetically appealing but also functional, with a cost structure that meets the business model, leading to the company's consistent market success.

"If everyone is moving forward together, then success takes care of itself," said Henry Ford. By bringing together diverse skill sets, teams can tackle complex problems from multiple angles and create holistic solutions. For example, at a global consulting firm, cross-functional teams might work together to solve a client's complex issue—where marketing strategists, data analysts, and legal experts each bring a unique perspective. The result is a solution that is more comprehensive and impactful, leveraging the strengths of each department to ensure success.

45. The Power of Saying "No" in Team Dynamics

In a team, setting healthy boundaries is just as important as collaboration. Knowing how to say "No" is a crucial skill that ensures your emotional well-being and preserves the integrity of your relationships. Too often, we say "Yes" out of a desire to please others or avoid conflict, only to feel overwhelmed, resentful, or burnt out. By saying "No" in a respectful and thoughtful way, you can maintain your authenticity and focus on what truly matters for the team's success.

1. **The Curious No** – "I'm not sure how I'm going to do that." This approach gives you the space to step back and assess the request more carefully. It helps you acknowledge that you're unsure about taking on another responsibility, while signaling that you're open to understanding the task more deeply before committing.
2. **The Helpful No** – "I love that you thought of me, but I'm unable to participate. Let me help you find someone who can do that." This response focuses on offering support without taking on the task. You're not only refusing but also contributing to the solution, which maintains positive team dynamics and shows that you're still invested in the team's success.
3. **The Appreciative No** – "Your idea is fabulous, and I'm not able to participate at this time." This response communicates gratitude and recognition of the team member's idea, but sets a clear boundary on your availability. It shows respect for the other person's initiative while standing firm in your limitations.
4. **The No with a Future Yes** – "I'd love to participate, but at a later date. Can you ask me again next month?" This form of saying "No" keeps the door open for future opportunities. It shows that while you cannot commit right now, you remain interested and available in the future, fostering goodwill without overextending yourself.

In team relationships, it's essential to understand that saying "No" is not a rejection of the other person but an affirmation of your priorities and well-being. A healthy team should be able to accept "No" without resentment. If "No" is not tolerated, it's a sign that the team dynamic is unhealthy or that the team members are not respecting each other's boundaries.

Sacrifices within a team should come from genuine willingness, not from guilt or manipulation. When we feel obligated to say "Yes" because of fear or expectation, it undermines trust and creates transactional relationships rather than authentic connections. As we develop emotionally, we must learn to find stability within ourselves, rather than relying on the approval or needs of others to define our worth.

By mastering the art of saying "No," you set the tone for healthy communication, respect, and mutual understanding within your team. It strengthens the foundation of trust and ensures that every team member can contribute meaningfully, without the burden of unnecessary stress or resentment.

Topic 4
COMMUNICATION SKILLS

Effective communication goes beyond simply speaking—it requires a combination of good judgment, timing, courage, and prudence. A skilled communicator is one who can convey their message clearly and listen attentively to others. Ralph Waldo Emerson's quote, "What you are shouts so loudly in my ears I cannot hear what you say," emphasizes that actions often speak louder than words. A person's Behaviour, demeanor, and body language can convey far more about their intentions and values than the words they speak.

Communication is not just about speaking; it is primarily about listening. Active listening forms the foundation of any successful interaction. According to the Carnegie Institute, 85% of job success comes from soft skills, while only 15% is attributed to hard skills and technical knowledge. In fact, 94% of recruiters believe that hiring is based on soft skills, and 93% of employers consider them to be important. These statistics highlight the power of communication in professional success.

1. ELEMENTS OF COMMUNICATION

I. Visual Communication (55%)

Visual communication refers to the non-verbal cues we use to express ourselves, including body language, facial expressions, and gestures. These visual elements often carry more weight than the spoken word itself, shaping how our message is perceived by others. In fact, non-verbal communication makes up a significant portion of human interactions, with research suggesting that over half of what we communicate is visual.

- **Body Language:** The way we carry ourselves speaks volumes about our feelings, attitudes, and openness. For example, a manager who crosses their arms while speaking with a team member might unintentionally signal defensiveness or disinterest, even if their words are encouraging. Conversely, an open posture and leaning slightly forward in a conversation typically signal engagement and interest.
- **Facial Expressions:** A smile can indicate warmth and approachability, while a furrowed brow may convey confusion or concern. Our face often reveals emotions that we may not even consciously express with words, making it a powerful tool in communication.
- **Gestures:** Hand movements and nods can complement verbal communication, helping to emphasize or clarify points. Think of Steve Jobs' presentations, which were not only praised for their content but also for his purposeful body language. His gestures and deliberate use of eye contact kept the audience engaged and reinforced the messages he was delivering.

Non-verbal communication, often referred to as visual communication, plays a critical role in conveying messages without using words. While speech can articulate our thoughts, non-verbal cues frequently reveal our true feelings, thoughts, and attitudes, often before we even speak.

Understanding these subtle yet powerful signals can significantly enhance our interactions, as they offer immediate insight into how someone may be feeling or what they may be thinking.

Key Components of Non-Verbal Communication

Non-verbal communication encompasses various elements that influence how our messages are received. Below are key components that form the foundation of non-verbal communication:

- **Clothing**

The way one dresses can speak volumes about their professionalism, personality, or level of commitment to a given situation. For instance, a lawyer attending a courtroom session dressed in formal attire not only conveys professionalism but also shows respect for the court's authority. In contrast, casual clothing might give off the impression that the individual lacks seriousness or reverence for the proceedings.

- **Grooming**

Personal grooming goes beyond appearance; it represents an individual's attention to detail, self-respect, and awareness of their surroundings. Good personal hygiene and appropriate grooming are vital in creating a positive, lasting impression. Consider the impact of a well-groomed individual during an interview versus someone with messy hair and untidy clothes. The former tends to communicate confidence, organization, and professionalism, whereas the latter may unconsciously signal carelessness or lack of preparation.

- **Body Language**

How we carry ourselves speaks louder than words. Body language involves posture, gestures, facial expressions, and movements, which convey confidence, openness, or defensiveness. For example, an individual who sits up straight in a meeting with open body language and makes regular eye contact demonstrates engagement and a willingness to collaborate. Conversely, someone who avoids eye contact or slouches may unintentionally suggest disinterest or insecurity.

- **Etiquette**

Etiquette includes the small gestures and manners that contribute to the atmosphere of respect and trust in interactions. Simple acts, like offering a firm handshake or nodding politely, can foster positive relationships and enhance communication. A colleague who greets you with a warm handshake and a genuine smile will likely create a more welcoming and cooperative environment than one who avoids eye contact or fails to acknowledge your presence.

Powerful Body Language Tips

Non-Verbal Communication: Enhancing Your Message through Body Language

Non-verbal communication plays a crucial role in how your message is received and how others perceive you. Understanding and mastering body language can significantly improve your communication effectiveness. Below are some practical tips to help you enhance your interactions through non-verbal cues:

I. Power Pose

Confidence through Posture

Standing tall with shoulders back conveys confidence and self-assurance. This simple posture change can dramatically improve how others view you and help manage anxiety, especially in high-pressure situations.

- Before delivering a presentation, adopting a power pose—such as standing with your hands on your hips—can help reduce stress and boost your confidence, allowing you to present with greater ease.

II. Look Like You Are Listening

Attentiveness through Eye Contact and Nodding

Non-verbal cues such as maintaining eye contact and nodding in agreement convey attentiveness and respect, making the other person feel heard and valued.

- During a conversation with a client, maintaining eye contact and nodding intermittently shows that you are engaged, fostering rapport and trust.

III. Remove Physical Barriers

Open Posture for Better Connection

Physical barriers—like crossing arms or sitting too far from the speaker—can create a disconnect and hinder communication. Instead, adopting an open posture fosters engagement and encourages a collaborative atmosphere.

- In a team meeting, sitting with an open posture (rather than crossing your arms) encourages open dialogue and helps foster a more inclusive environment.

IV. Mirror Expressions and Postures

Subtle Mimicry for Empathy and Connection

Mirroring the body language of the person you are conversing with can strengthen your bond and increase empathy. This technique creates a sense of shared understanding and rapport.

- If your conversation partner is smiling and leaning forward, subtly mirroring these actions can signal your empathy and make the interaction feel more harmonious.

V. Use Your Hands to Improve Speech

Gestures as Enhancers of Meaning

Using hand gestures to emphasize points during a conversation can make your message clearer and more impactful. Gestures help convey enthusiasm and draw attention to important ideas.

- When explaining a complex idea, using your hands to describe the size, shape, or movement of the concept can make it more relatable and memorable for your audience.

VI. Uncross Your Arms and Legs

Inviting Openness and Reducing Defensiveness

Uncrossing your arms and legs signals openness and receptiveness. This simple adjustment can help reduce defensiveness and foster more collaborative, productive interactions.

During a negotiation, uncrossing your arms can communicate that you are open to discussion, reducing tension and encouraging a more solution-oriented conversation.

Body Language Components

Understanding the Nuances of Body Language in Communication

Effective communication goes beyond words; it involves subtle cues that convey meaning. Understanding body language is crucial to enhancing communication, as it often reveals more than verbal exchanges. Below are the key aspects of body language that influence how we are perceived:

I. Paralinguistics

Paralinguistics refers to the tone, pitch, and speed of your speech. These elements can significantly impact how your message is received. For instance:

- A leader who speaks in a calm and steady tone is often perceived as more competent, reliable, and in control. On the other hand, speaking too quickly or with a fluctuating pitch may suggest uncertainty or lack of confidence.

II. Kinesics

Kinesics is the study of movement, including hand gestures, facial expressions, and posture. These non-verbal cues can significantly enhance or diminish the clarity of your message.

- A teacher who uses hand gestures while explaining a concept is more likely to engage students and make the material easier to understand. Gestures add emphasis and help to visually demonstrate what is being discussed, fostering a deeper connection with the audience.

III. Postures

Posture conveys messages about confidence, attentiveness, and openness. How you position your body sends non-verbal signals to others.

- A team member who sits up straight during a meeting is perceived as engaged and attentive. In contrast, someone who slumps or slouches may appear disengaged, disinterested, or lacking confidence.

IV. Proxemics

Proxemics involves the use of space in communication, especially how physical proximity can affect interactions. Personal space varies across cultures, but understanding its role is critical to respectful communication.

- In a business setting, standing too close to someone in an elevator may make them uncomfortable, while maintaining an appropriate distance respects personal space and fosters a sense of security.

V. Haptics

Haptics is the use of touch in communication, which can carry significant meaning depending on the context. A well-timed touch can enhance rapport, while the lack of touch or an inappropriate touch may create discomfort.

- A firm handshake after an interview conveys confidence, professionalism, and sincerity. Conversely, a weak handshake may be interpreted as insecurity or a lack of commitment.

II. Verbal Communication (7%)

Words have the power to influence emotions and build clarity. Understanding how to ask questions and use assertive language can greatly enhance conversations.

I. Questions You Ask

The way you phrase a question can have a significant impact on the direction and tone of a conversation. A well-posed question can encourage reflection, openness, and problem-solving, while poorly chosen ones can create defensiveness or hinder effective dialogue.

Imagine you're working with a team member who missed a deadline. Instead of asking, "Why didn't you finish the task?"—which may come across as accusatory or critical—try asking, "What challenges did you face in completing the task?" This shift in phrasing helps to move the conversation away from blame and toward understanding. It signals to the other person that you're interested in uncovering obstacles and offering support, rather than simply pointing out failure.

This approach fosters a collaborative environment where both parties are more likely to contribute openly to problem-solving. It also opens the door for the team member to share any issues they might have faced, whether related to workload, resources, or understanding the task itself. By asking insightful and empathetic questions, you're creating a space for learning and growth, which is essential for fostering a productive and positive team culture.

In a workplace meeting, rather than reprimanding an employee for missing a deadline, a manager could ask, "What could we do to better support you in meeting your deadlines in the future?" This question not only avoids a confrontational tone but also encourages proactive solutions and team collaboration.

II. Conversational Clout

Assertive language reflects strength, confidence, and clarity, while maintaining respect for others. It's about expressing your views and needs clearly without undermining others or being overly aggressive. Assertive communication is an essential skill for leaders, as it fosters respect, trust, and an atmosphere of transparency.

For instance, an assertive leader might say, "I believe this is the best approach, but I'm open to hearing your thoughts." This statement demonstrates confidence in the leader's own opinion, while also signaling respect for others' perspectives. It invites collaboration and shows a willingness to listen, which makes others feel valued and included in the decision-making process.

When leaders use assertive language, they are less likely to be perceived as passive (indecisive or unsure) or aggressive (overbearing or dismissive). Instead, they come across as clear, confident, and willing to engage in productive dialogue. Assertiveness is key to effective leadership because it helps to set boundaries, express needs, and resolve conflicts in a manner that supports both individual and group needs.

Consider a scenario where a manager is leading a project meeting. Instead of saying, "I think this idea might work, but I'm not sure," the manager could assert, "I believe this approach is the most effective, but I'm interested in hearing everyone's thoughts." By confidently expressing their belief while being open to feedback, the manager conveys authority without closing the door on others' input. This creates an environment where team members feel their contributions are both needed and respected.

By mastering the art of asking thoughtful questions and using assertive language, you can enhance communication within any setting. These techniques lead to greater clarity, deeper understanding, and stronger relationships, fostering a more collaborative and effective work environment.

III. Vocal Communication (38%)

Effective vocal communication is essential to delivering a message with impact. The tone, volume, pitch, speed, and resonance of your voice can elevate your message, making it memorable and emotionally compelling. These elements work together to capture attention, convey emotions, and ensure understanding.

I. Rate of Speech

The pace at which you speak can either enhance or hinder your communication. Speaking too quickly may confuse the listener, while speaking too slowly can lead to boredom and disengagement. The ideal rate of speech is one that allows your audience to follow along comfortably while keeping their attention.

- A politician delivering a speech at a comfortable pace ensures their audience remains engaged and comprehends the message, rather than losing focus due to a rushed or slow delivery. A balanced pace creates a natural flow that invites active listening and retention.

II. Modulation

Modulating your pitch is a key aspect of maintaining the listener's interest. By varying the pitch of your voice, you add emotional depth to your words. A monotone delivery may come across as dull and disengaging, whereas strategic changes in pitch can convey enthusiasm, seriousness, or excitement, depending on the context.

- A public speaker who changes their pitch to reflect excitement, sadness, or seriousness is far more captivating than one who speaks in a flat, monotone voice. This variation in pitch not only enhances the message but also helps convey emotion, which can drive the point home more effectively.

III. Tone

The tone of your voice reflects the underlying emotional message behind your words. Whether you're conveying urgency, respect, kindness, or authority, your tone plays a pivotal role in how your message is received. A well-chosen tone can foster connection, build trust, and influence the listener's perception.

- A customer service representative who uses a calm, empathetic, and reassuring tone when handling an upset customer can de-escalate the situation more effectively than one who speaks with frustration or defensiveness. The right tone promotes positive interactions and helps manage emotions in delicate situations.

IV. Volume

Speaking at the appropriate volume ensures that your message is heard clearly without straining the listener's ability to understand. Adjusting your volume based on the environment and context is crucial for maintaining the effectiveness of your speech. Too loud or too soft can cause misunderstandings or disengagement.

- A manager who adjusts their volume to match the setting—speaking softly in a one-on-one meeting and louder in a team briefing—creates a more comfortable communication environment. The ability to vary volume based on the situation enhances clarity and maintains focus.

V. Usage of Pause

Pauses are a powerful tool in communication. They allow listeners to process what has been said, emphasize key points, and create a sense of anticipation. Pauses also give the speaker time to think and collect their thoughts, promoting a more thoughtful and deliberate response.

- In a high-stakes negotiation, strategically pausing before responding can demonstrate confidence and give the impression that you are thoughtfully considering the situation. The pause not only emphasizes the importance of your response but also encourages others to reflect on what has been said.

VI. Resonance

The resonance of your voice plays a critical role in making your message memorable and impactful. A voice that resonates with the listener's values, struggles, or aspirations establishes a deeper connection. This connection leads to greater engagement, empathy, and an increased likelihood that your message will have a lasting effect.

- A motivational speaker whose words resonate with the audience's struggles and aspirations can inspire action and empathy. The speaker's message, aligned with the audience's experiences, creates a stronger bond, resulting in a more impactful and memorable communication experience.

By mastering the components of vocal communication, you can transform your delivery and ensure that your message is received not only with clarity but also with emotional depth, ensuring that it resonates with your audience.

2. LISTENING AND COMMUNICATION SKILLS: ENHANCING UNDERSTANDING

Effective communication involves more than just speaking; it's about understanding how messages are crafted, received, and interpreted. In this chapter, we delve into the core pillars of communication, explore common barriers to effective listening, and offer practical strategies to improve your listening skills for deeper, more meaningful interactions.

Listening is not a passive activity—it is a powerful leadership tool that often speaks louder than words. True listening is the act of being fully present, not just hearing words but understanding emotions, intentions, and unspoken cues. In today's fast-paced world, where everyone is eager to talk and be heard, the ability to genuinely listen has become a rare and precious quality. Great leaders are not those who dominate conversations, but those who create a space where others feel heard, valued, and respected. Take the example of Mahatma Gandhi, who was known for his attentive listening during meetings with the masses. He made people feel that their voices mattered, and that alone inspired loyalty and trust. In the corporate world, Satya Nadella, CEO of Microsoft, transformed the company's culture by shifting from a "know-it-all" to a "learn-it-all" approach—an ethos grounded in active listening. His empathetic leadership style emphasized listening to employees, customers, and even critics, fostering innovation and inclusivity. Another powerful example comes from the world of coaching: John Wooden, the legendary basketball coach, once said, "Listen if you want to be heard." He would observe his players keenly, listening not just to their words but to their body language, fatigue, and morale, adjusting his training accordingly. Effective listening also means resisting the urge to interrupt or mentally prepare a response while the other person is still speaking. It requires humility, patience, and the discipline to silence the ego. When a team member shares a concern and the leader listens without judgment or rushing to fix things, it builds psychological safety and trust—core elements of a high-performing culture. Listening, therefore, is not just a soft skill—it is a strategic strength that can heal conflicts, unlock creativity, strengthen relationships, and drive collective progress. When you truly listen, you lead with compassion and clarity—and in that moment, you become the kind of leader people are willing to follow.

II. Blocks to Listening

Several factors can hinder effective listening, leading to poor understanding and communication. Recognizing and addressing these barriers is crucial for becoming an active and empathetic listener.

1. External Distractions

   Noises, phone calls, or interruptions can pull attention away from the speaker, preventing full engagement in the conversation.

2. Internal Distractions

   Mental fatigue, stress, hunger, or preoccupation with personal concerns can cloud focus, making it difficult to listen attentively.

3. Response Rehearsal

   Often, while the other person is speaking, we begin planning our response. This premature focus on our reply causes us to miss important points of the conversation.

4. Being Judgmental

   Jumping to conclusions or forming opinions too early shuts off the flow of understanding and can create an atmosphere of defensiveness.

5. Problem-Solving Mode

   Trying to immediately fix a problem instead of fully listening can hinder understanding. This often leads to missing the emotional or contextual aspects of the issue.

6. Being Selective

   Selectively listening to only the parts of the conversation that align with your interests or preferences leads to an incomplete understanding of the message.

3. DEALING WITH DIFFERENT PERSONALITIES AND BEHAVIOURS IN COMMUNICATION

Communication is at the heart of every successful relationship, whether in personal or professional life. Understanding and managing different personalities and behaviours can create an environment of mutual respect, growth, and collaboration. Each personality brings its own unique set of communication challenges and opportunities, and responding effectively to these requires skill, patience, and adaptability.

In this section, we will explore how to recognize various personality types, effectively manage difficult Behaviour, and proactively prevent such issues by building a positive communication culture.

I. Understanding Different Personalities

Every personality type brings distinct communication challenges, yet understanding these differences can unlock opportunities for productive dialogue.

a. Aggressive People

Aggressive individuals tend to dominate conversations and assert their opinions forcefully. This type of communication often leads to conflict, making it important to approach them calmly and with confidence.

- **Response:** Respond with calm confidence. Redirect conversations toward solutions rather than engaging in confrontations. Keeping your composure will not only de-escalate the situation but can also model appropriate behavior for others.

b. Passive People

Passive individuals tend to avoid expressing their opinions or desires, often leaving conversations unresolved or unclear. They may hesitate to share their true thoughts for fear of conflict or criticism.

- **Response:** Encourage participation through open-ended questions and reassurance. Creating a safe space for passive communicators to express themselves will help them feel heard and valued. It's important to gently coax them into sharing their thoughts without pressuring them.

c. Passive-Aggressive People

Passive-aggressive individuals express their frustrations in indirect or covert ways, often through sarcasm or procrastination. This behaviour can be difficult to address as it is not overtly confrontational but undermines effective communication.

- **Response:** Stay calm and avoid getting drawn into the subtle conflict. Clarify intentions and focus on promoting open discussion. Address the issue directly but in a respectful manner to ensure transparency and to resolve underlying tensions.

d. Manipulative People

Manipulative individuals may use tactics to achieve their personal or professional agendas, often bypassing transparency or fairness. Their Behaviour can be both subtle and persistent.

- **Response**: Respond factually, maintain composure, and assertively set clear boundaries. Recognize their tactics and don't be swayed by emotional manipulation. Encourage openness and fairness in communication, but don't let them control the narrative.

e. Assertive People

Assertive communicators are direct, clear, and respectful in their communication. They express their needs and desires while respecting others' viewpoints.

- **Response:** Engage respectfully with assertive individuals, leveraging their strengths for solution-focused dialogue. Collaboration with assertive people can be highly effective, as their clarity and confidence often lead to productive outcomes.

II. Responding to Difficult Behaviour

When faced with difficult behaviours, it is essential to adapt your approach. The key to managing these situations effectively is understanding the emotional and behavioral patterns involved.

a. Indirect Hostility

Sometimes individuals may express their dissatisfaction through passive-aggressive behaviours like sarcasm or backhanded compliments.

- Response: Do not mirror their Behaviour. Seek to understand the root cause of their hostility and address the matter privately. Use active listening to ensure they feel heard, and provide a safe space for them to express their true feelings without judgment.

b. Narcissistic Behaviour

Individuals with narcissistic tendencies often have an inflated sense of self-importance and a need for constant validation.

- Response: Praise their achievements publicly but reserve any constructive criticism for private conversations. Set clear boundaries to avoid being manipulated, and ensure that any feedback remains objective and respectful.

c. Aggressive Behaviour

Aggressive Behaviour can escalate conflicts and create tension within teams or personal relationships.

- Response: Protect your space by clearly defining acceptable Behaviour. Limit exposure to overly aggressive individuals if needed while maintaining empathy and seeking peaceful resolutions. Stand your ground, but remain composed.

d. Micro-Managing Behaviour

Micro-managers exhibit an excessive need to control every aspect of a process, often undermining the autonomy of others.

- Response: Assume positive intent by assuming they may be struggling with trust issues. Propose systems for updates to keep them informed, and assert your capability to perform the task independently. Offering regular progress reports and demonstrating trustworthiness can reduce their need to control.

III. Preventing Difficult Behaviour

Creating an environment that fosters positive communication and reduces the likelihood of difficult behaviours can be achieved through proactive measures. Building trust, encouraging open dialogue, and practicing empathy are key to creating a supportive atmosphere

a. Focus on Your Own Work

Lead by example. Being productive and maintaining a positive attitude can influence others to mirror your Behaviour. When you show commitment to your work, you inspire those around you to do the same, fostering a culture of respect and responsibility.

b. Build Trust and Rapport

Action: Establish relationships built on consistency, integrity, and support. People are more likely to communicate openly and cooperatively when they trust you. Regularly engage in supportive actions, and provide help or encouragement when needed.

c. Give the Benefit of the Doubt

Avoid jumping to conclusions or assuming bad intentions. People may have struggles you are unaware of, and understanding their context can help prevent unnecessary conflict. Approach situations with kindness and seek to understand before judging.

d. Regular Social Interactions

Encourage casual social interactions outside of work to humanize your relationships. These informal conversations can help you build deeper trust and foster a sense of camaraderie, making it easier to navigate difficult situations when they arise.

e. Seek Feedback Respectfully

Make yourself approachable by inviting feedback from others. Show that you value their input and are open to making improvements. Feedback fosters continuous improvement and helps create an atmosphere of mutual respect.

IV. Flow Chart for Responding to Difficult Behaviour

A reflective, step-by-step approach can help you manage difficult behaviours thoughtfully. The following decision-making process guides you on how to assess and address problematic behaviours in a calm, structured manner.

a. Separate Person from Behaviour

Critique actions, not the character of the individual. This approach preserves respect and maintains open channels for dialogue. A Behaviour-focused critique is more likely to lead to productive conversations without damaging relationships.

b. Evaluate the Issue

Consider whether the Behaviour is a one-time slip-up or a recurring pattern. Is this issue worth addressing, or can it be overlooked for the sake of harmony? The severity of the Behaviour will dictate the appropriate response.

c. Practice Empathy

Try to understand the underlying triggers or context behind the behavior. This will help you avoid knee-jerk reactions and allow you to respond with compassion, which can diffuse tension and encourage understanding.

d. Reflect on Whether You're the Right Person

Assess whether you are the best person to address the issue, or if another person would be better suited to resolve it. Sometimes, having the right person handle a sensitive matter can make all the difference in how the issue is received and resolved.

e. Wait Until Calm

Emotional reactions often cloud judgment. It's important to allow time for composure before addressing any issue. When you approach difficult behavior with a calm demeanor, your responses will be more measured and constructive.

By understanding and responding to different personalities and behaviors effectively, you not only enhance communication but also create a work and social environment where respect, empathy, and collaboration thrive. Developing these skills takes time and practice, but the payoff in stronger, more effective relationships is well worth the effort.

4. MASTERING PRESENTATION SKILLS – A POWERFUL TOOL FOR EFFECTIVE COMMUNICATION

Presentation skills are vital in both personal and professional life. Whether you are a leader delivering a keynote speech, a manager presenting to your team, or a sales professional pitching to clients, the ability to communicate effectively can make or break your success. This chapter will explore the art of crafting a compelling presentation, ensuring that your message resonates with the audience and achieves the desired impact.

I. The Importance of Presentation Skills

In the world we live in today, clear and confident communication is essential. Presentation skills are not just about speaking well; they're about engaging your audience, conveying your message with impact, and leaving a lasting impression. It is the difference between delivering just information and creating an experience that motivates, informs, and inspires. A well-crafted presentation can shape perceptions, influence decisions, and drive change.

II. Structuring Your Presentation

Every great presentation starts with a well-organized structure. Without a clear flow, even the most interesting content can be lost. Here are the essential building blocks:

a. Define Your Purpose:

   The first step in any presentation is to define your purpose. What is the core message you want to deliver? Whether it's to educate, inform, inspire, or persuade, having a clear goal sets the direction for the entire presentation. Always ask yourself: *What do I want my audience to walk away with?*

b. Start with a Hook:

   The opening of your presentation is crucial for capturing attention. You have a few seconds to engage your audience. Start with a hook—an intriguing question, a shocking statistic, or a personal story. This will immediately draw the audience in and set the tone for the rest of your talk.

   Example: "Did you know that 70% of people give up on their New Year's resolutions by the end of January? What makes the difference between success and failure?"

c. Create a Logical Sequence:

   Organize your presentation in a clear and logical order. A good structure is the backbone of a successful presentation. Break your content into key sections that build upon each other. This could be problem-solution, cause-effect, or a simple chronological order. Each part should transition smoothly to the next, allowing your audience to follow along without confusion.

d. Maintain Engagement:

   A presentation should never feel like a monologue. It should be a conversation, even if you're the only one speaking. Keep your audience engaged by asking questions, offering opportunities for reflection, and encouraging participation. This ensures your message is not only heard but internalized.

Example: "Let's take a quick poll—how many of you struggle with time management? Raise your hands!"

III. Using Visual Aids Effectively

Visual aids can elevate your presentation and help illustrate your points in ways words alone cannot. But they should complement your speech, not distract from it.

a. Keep It Simple:

   Avoid cluttering your slides with too much information. Use images, graphs, and charts to simplify complex ideas and enhance understanding. Each visual should be clean, clear, and purposeful. Remember, less is more.

b. Support with Data Visualizations:

   Data is often a powerful part of any presentation. Use graphs and charts to present key statistics or trends in a way that is visually engaging. This not only keeps the audience's attention but also helps them absorb and retain the information better.

   Example: "Here is a graph that shows how improved time management led to increased productivity in multiple industries."

c. Use High-Quality Images:

   The quality of the visuals you use speaks volumes about the professionalism of your presentation. Avoid low-resolution or stock images that feel impersonal. Choose high-quality, relevant images that resonate with your message and audience.

IV. Timing Your Presentation

Managing your time during a presentation is as crucial as managing the content. You don't want to rush through your material, but you also don't want to overrun your allotted time.

a. Time Management for Yourself:

   Practice the timing of each segment of your presentation before you go live. Allocate specific times for each section and stick to them. This will help ensure you cover all key points without rushing through or dragging out any one section.

b. Be Flexible with Time:

   While timing is important, flexibility is also key. Sometimes, audience questions or the need for deeper discussion will require you to adjust. Be ready to adapt while maintaining control over the session.

c. Practice for Timing:

   Rehearse your presentation several times, both alone and in front of others. Doing so will allow you to adjust your pacing, ensuring that each point is delivered thoughtfully without feeling rushed.

V. Engaging the Audience

Effective presenters are not just speakers—they are storytellers and facilitators of dialogue. Engage your audience to make the experience more dynamic and memorable.

a. Ask Open-Ended Questions:

   Start by asking thought-provoking questions that invite reflection. Open-ended questions encourage your audience to think critically about the topic and share their perspectives.

   Example: "What are some of the biggest time management challenges you face? Let's discuss."

b. Incorporate Audience Polls or Surveys:

   Utilize real-time polling tools to encourage participation. Polling not only engages the audience but also provides insight into their opinions and needs, making the presentation more interactive and relevant.

   Example: "I'd like to know where everyone stands on this issue. Please take a moment to answer this poll."

c. Use Humor and Relatable Stories:

   Humor can help break the ice and make the presentation feel less formal. It also builds rapport with your audience. Relatable personal stories will humanize your message and make the content more memorable.

VI. Handling Difficult Situations

Not every presentation will go smoothly, and it's important to be prepared for challenges. Whether it's a tough question, a disruptive audience, or technical issues, handling such situations gracefully is a sign of a skilled presenter.

a. Dealing with Difficult Questions:

   Difficult questions can be challenging, but they are an opportunity to show your expertise. If you don't know the answer, admit it honestly, and offer to follow up. This builds credibility and trust.

   Example: "That's a great question, but I'll need to look into it further and get back to you with a comprehensive answer."

b. Managing Distractions or Interruptions:

   Stay calm if there are interruptions or distractions. Politely acknowledge the disruption, address it if needed, and continue with your presentation. Maintaining composure during difficult situations reflects your professionalism.

c. Stay Confident and Adaptable:

   Things won't always go according to plan. Stay confident and adaptable. If the projector malfunctions or the audience seems disengaged, adjust your approach without fluster. Your poise will ensure that your message still shines through.

VII. Closing the Presentation

The way you close your presentation is just as important as how you open it. The final impression you leave on your audience should reinforce your message and leave them with something to take away.

a. End with a Strong Message:

   Conclude your presentation by summarizing your key points and delivering a strong, memorable closing statement.

   Example: "Remember, time is your most valuable asset—spend it wisely, and it will reward you exponentially."

b. Offer to Answer Questions:

   Allow time for questions. This shows that you value the audience's input and are open to further discussion. Answer questions thoughtfully and confidently.

c. Provide a Follow-up Resource:

   Offer the audience additional resources, such as a handout, link to your slides, or follow-up reading. This ensures that your presentation extends beyond the meeting room.

Conclusion

Mastering the art of presentation skills is not just about delivering information—it's about creating an experience that engages, educates, and inspires your audience. By structuring your presentation thoughtfully, using visuals effectively, engaging your audience, and handling challenges with confidence, you can become a powerful and persuasive communicator. Remember, every presentation is an opportunity to share your message and leave a lasting impact.

Topic 5

BE STRESS FREE AND LIVE A HAPPY LIFE

The words of Buddha, "*Success is not the key to happiness, happiness is the key to success,*" offer profound wisdom for navigating life and achieving personal fulfilment. In a world that often equates success with external achievements—wealth, status, and accolades—it's easy to overlook the true source of lasting contentment: happiness. When we prioritize inner peace and contentment, success becomes a natural byproduct of our mindset, not the ultimate goal. In this chapter, we will explore how embracing happiness and well-being first can unlock a more meaningful and sustainable version of success.

1. The Power of Progression Over Perfection

One of the biggest myths about happiness is that it is the result of achieving perfection—perfect grades, a flawless relationship, a dream physique, or an ideal career. But true happiness doesn't bloom in the sterile soil of perfectionism; it flourishes in the rich, messy terrain of progression.

Perfectionism is often a silent thief. It whispers that unless everything is done exactly right, it's not worth celebrating. It convinces us that "almost" is a failure and "good enough" is never enough. This mindset creates a constant sense of inadequacy, even in the midst of progress. People stuck in the perfection trap often suffer from anxiety, burnout, or chronic dissatisfaction because they set standards that are not only high—but often unattainable.

Now, contrast that with the mindset of progression. Progression is rooted in the belief that growth happens step by step. It doesn't demand flawlessness; it values effort and learning. When you shift your focus from the finish line to the footsteps, you begin to appreciate the journey, not just the destination.

Take the example of someone learning to play the guitar. A perfectionist might quit after a few frustrating practice sessions because their fingers can't move fast enough or their chords don't sound clean. But someone who values progression finds joy in strumming a single chord right for the first time. They find motivation in being slightly better than yesterday. Over weeks and months, those small wins accumulate—and eventually, the beginner becomes a skilled musician.

Or think of someone trying to lose weight and get fit. A perfectionist mindset might insist on strict diets, flawless workout routines, and visible results in weeks. The moment they skip a workout or eat something "unhealthy," guilt and self-criticism flood in, often leading to a complete breakdown of their plan. But someone focused on progression might start with a 10-minute walk, then build up to a consistent routine. They might enjoy the energy they feel after working out, even if the scale doesn't move quickly. Their joy comes not from instant transformation, but from seeing progress over time.

Consider professional life too. A new entrepreneur who believes they must get everything perfect on Day One might delay launching their business endlessly, paralyzed by fear of failure. Meanwhile, another entrepreneur launches with an imperfect product, learns from feedback, adapts, and grows. The latter embraces imperfection as part of the journey, and in doing so, stays happier, more resilient, and ultimately more successful.

This principle applies to emotional and personal growth as well. Letting go of perfection allows us to be kinder to ourselves. It gives us the emotional space to make mistakes, learn from them, and grow stronger. When you recognize that every small improvement—every new habit, every book you read, every effort to be more patient or disciplined—is a step forward, you start to feel more fulfilled. This mindset builds sustainable happiness rooted in self-respect and internal progress.

Remember, the pursuit of perfection can become a form of self-punishment. The pursuit of progress, on the other hand, is a path to self-love.

So give yourself permission to be a work in progress. Celebrate the small victories. Be proud of your imperfect efforts. Life is not a performance to be perfected—it's a process to be embraced.

2. Restraint: The Silent Strength Behind Inner Peace

In a world that often glorifies instant reactions and loud expressions, restraint is a quiet but mighty virtue. It is not weakness; it is willpower. It is not suppression; it is intentional preservation. Restraint is one of the most powerful tools we have to maintain our inner peace and protect the harmony of our relationships.

When emotions run high—anger, frustration, jealousy, or irritation—it's easy to be swept away by the impulse to speak or act. But what we often forget is that these impulsive moments, though brief, can leave long-lasting damage. A sharp word, a sarcastic reply, or a hasty decision can burn bridges we've spent years building. Restraint acts as a pause button. It allows us to respond with wisdom instead of reacting with emotion.

Consider a simple scenario: you're in a meeting and someone criticizes your idea publicly. Your instinct might be to snap back or defend yourself aggressively. But choosing to take a deep breath, acknowledging their viewpoint, and responding calmly—even if it's hard—can completely change the atmosphere. You not only keep your dignity intact, but also demonstrate emotional maturity and earn respect. Later, in a private conversation, you can address the issue more constructively.

Or think about a parent dealing with a disobedient child. Shouting might bring momentary control, but it often creates fear or resentment. Choosing instead to step away, calm down, and return to the conversation with empathy can build trust and long-term understanding. This is restraint in action—not as suppression, but as strategic emotional intelligence.

Even in digital spaces, where quick replies and emotional outbursts are common, restraint is gold. That urge to respond to a critical comment online, or to vent on social media about a coworker or friend, can feel irresistible. But often, after just a few moments—or hours—those emotions fade. And if we acted on impulse, we are left with regret, embarrassment, or broken connections. Restraint is not about being passive; it's about being powerfully selective in how we use our energy and words.

Mahatma Gandhi once said, "*The weak can never forgive. Forgiveness is the attribute of the strong.*" The same could be said for restraint. It takes strength to pause, to choose silence over sarcasm, patience over provocation, or grace over revenge. Restraint creates space—for reflection, for empathy, and for better decisions.

When we practice restraint, we stay anchored. We stop ourselves from being dragged by every emotion, every opinion, every external trigger. And in doing so, we protect our peace—not by avoiding conflict, but by choosing how and when to engage with it.

In leadership, restraint allows you to listen before reacting. In friendships, it helps you forgive rather than hold grudges. In marriage, it lets you pause before saying something you'll regret. In parenting, it helps you teach through love instead of fear.

To cultivate restraint:

- **Pause before reacting**—even a few seconds can shift your response.
- **Breathe deeply**—this regulates your emotional state.
- **Ask yourself**— "Will I regret this later?"
- **Practice silence**—not everything needs a response.

Ultimately, restraint is about honoring your peace more than your pride. It is choosing the long-term well-being of your relationships and your emotional health over temporary gratification.

3. Embracing Impermanence: The Gift of the Present Moment

Life is in constant motion. Seasons shift, relationships evolve, emotions rise and fall, and circumstances change without warning. One of the most grounding truths we can accept is this: *nothing lasts forever.* And while this truth might initially seem unsettling, it is also profoundly liberating.

Much of our stress, anxiety, and inner turmoil come not from what is happening now—but from what *has* happened or what *might* happen. We replay past mistakes in our minds, hoping somehow, we'll rewrite history. Or we project ourselves into the future, imagining worst-case scenarios, trying to control outcomes that haven't yet occurred. In doing so, we abandon the only moment we truly possess: the present.

Take the example of someone who made a costly mistake in their business. They may carry the weight of guilt, constantly asking, "What if I had chosen differently?" But no amount of rumination will alter the past. By choosing instead to focus on what they can learn from that mistake *today*, they can grow, adapt, and eventually build something stronger.

Or consider someone awaiting the results of a medical test. Their mind may spiral with "what ifs," imagining every worst-case scenario. But in truth, the results are not in their control at this moment. What is within their control is how they spend *this* day—perhaps taking a walk, connecting with a friend, reading something inspiring, or simply sitting with a cup of tea and noticing the quiet stillness around them.

When we focus on the present, we relieve ourselves from the exhausting burden of what we cannot change or predict. Mindfulness practices, like conscious breathing, walking slowly without distraction, or observing nature, can gently anchor us back to the now. Imagine standing outside and simply noticing the gentle rustle of leaves, the way light filters through the trees, or the coolness of the breeze on your skin. These moments may seem small, but they contain the profound truth that *life is only ever lived in the present.*

Spiritual traditions across the world have echoed this wisdom for centuries. The Buddha taught impermanence (*anicca*) as one of the core truths of existence. The Bhagavad Gita reminds us to act with full presence and surrender the outcome. Even Stoic philosophers like Marcus Aurelius encouraged acceptance of change and the discipline of staying grounded in the present moment.

When we truly internalize the impermanence of life, we stop taking things for granted. We begin to cherish ordinary moments—a conversation with a loved one, the laughter of a child, the taste of food, or the silence between two thoughts. We develop an inner steadiness that is not shaken by every shift of circumstance.

To live well, we must live *now*. Not yesterday, not tomorrow, but *here*. This is not about ignoring the past or abandoning future goals—it's about refusing to let them rob us of the richness of the present. It's about finding stillness in a constantly changing world by choosing to be fully awake to what is in front of us.

Let this moment be enough. Let it be sacred. Because in truth, it's all we ever really have.

4. The Power of Purpose: IKIGAI and the Fulfilment in Every Moment

Having a sense of purpose is like having a compass in life—it guides you through even the most uncertain or slow periods. Without purpose, we can easily feel adrift, waiting for external events to bring meaning to our days. But when we are anchored in purpose, we can weather the quiet times with peace, knowing that every day is a chance to align with something meaningful.

The Japanese concept of *IKIGAI* beautifully illustrates this principle. Translated roughly as "a reason for being," *IKIGAI* represents the intersection of four key elements: what you love, what you're good at, what the world needs, and what you can be paid for. It's the sweet spot where passion, talent, contribution, and reward align, providing not only a sense of meaning but also long-term fulfilment.

Imagine someone who is passionate about teaching. They may love helping others learn, and they're good at explaining complex concepts simply. But they might also feel fulfilled by teaching not just because they enjoy it, but because there is a growing demand for accessible education in their community or industry. And if they're also compensated for their work, their purpose is further validated. This alignment between passion, skill, societal need, and reward creates a powerful sense of fulfilment, even when external circumstances seem stagnant.

But *IKIGAI* isn't just about finding a career or a vocation. It's a holistic approach to life. Consider an artist who may not have immediate commercial success but continues to create because they love expressing themselves through their art. Even if their artwork doesn't yet sell, the act of creating provides them with a deep sense of purpose. They stay motivated, engaged, and calm, regardless of external validation, because they are connected to something greater than fleeting success.

In times of uncertainty or when progress seems slow, having a purpose grounded in *IKIGAI* can help you stay resilient. If you love writing, for example, you might start by writing a blog or recording a podcast. Even if there's no immediate income or widespread recognition, the act of creation—of doing something you love and are good at—will continue to give you meaning. This process of engaging with your purpose, without the pressure of immediate outcomes, fosters inner peace and keeps you on track with your personal growth.

A real-world example is the story of Steve Jobs. When he was ousted from Apple, the company he co-founded, he didn't give up. Instead, he found new purpose through his work with Pixar and the development of Next. Even though the immediate external circumstances seemed bleak—losing control of his company—Jobs stayed aligned with his passion for innovation and creation. His *IKIGAI*—the love for technology and design, the skill he had developed, the societal needs of innovation, and the financial reward that followed—continued to propel him forward. This alignment of purpose helped him navigate the rough patches and ultimately led to his return to Apple, where he revolutionized the industry once again.

What makes *IKIGAI* so powerful is that it encourages us to look within ourselves to find fulfilment, rather than relying on external events. It reminds us that happiness doesn't always need to come from immediate results or achievements. When we align with our purpose—whether through hobbies, work, or personal endeavors—we can experience a deep, lasting peace. Even during quiet moments, when the world seems to move slowly, we are anchored in the present, knowing that we are contributing to something meaningful, no matter how small it may seem at the time.

By tapping into *IKIGAI*, we create a life that's driven by purpose, not just by circumstances. And in doing so, we open ourselves to a profound sense of fulfilment that transcends external validation. This internal peace becomes our greatest ally in times of uncertainty, keeping us calm and engaged no matter what the world outside may bring.

5. The Art of Slowing Down: Finding Joy in the Present Moment

In today's fast-paced world, there's a constant pressure to hurry—to rush through tasks, achieve results quickly, and juggle multiple responsibilities at once. The prevailing culture often encourages us to move swiftly from one thing to the next, believing that faster is always better. Yet, in our pursuit of speed, we may overlook one of the most important elements of well-being: slowing down.

The phrase "Easy does it" offers a refreshing counterpoint to this high-speed lifestyle. It encourages us to approach life with mindfulness, intentionality, and a focus on quality over quantity. Rather than racing through life, it suggests that we pause, breathe, and savor the present moment. In fact, taking the time to slow down and engage more deeply with our experiences can significantly reduce stress and enhance the richness of our daily lives.

For instance, imagine you're having dinner with your family. In many households today, it's common for everyone to be distracted by their phones, responding to messages or scrolling through social media. While multitasking may seem productive, it often takes away from the essence of the moment. Instead, if you choose to leave your phone aside, you create space to be fully present. You can engage in deeper conversation, truly listen to each other, and appreciate the food and company around you. In this slower, more mindful approach, the meal becomes more than just sustenance; it becomes an experience to cherish.

The benefits of slowing down are not confined to family dinners. Consider the example of someone at work, constantly juggling tasks, meetings, and emails, trying to respond to everything at once. The result? Overwhelm, exhaustion, and a sense of burnout. By consciously slowing down and focusing on one task at a time, they can improve the quality of their work and, paradoxically, complete it more efficiently.

This shift not only reduces stress but also fosters a sense of satisfaction and accomplishment, knowing that each task was done with care and attention.

Another example can be found in the simple act of enjoying nature. If you're on a walk through the park, it's tempting to rush to your destination or to be distracted by thoughts and technology. However, by intentionally slowing down and observing your surroundings—watching the leaves sway in the breeze, listening to the birds sing, or feeling the warmth of the sun—you can transform a routine walk into a grounding, peaceful experience. This mindful approach helps you reconnect with your environment and your inner calm.

Slowing down doesn't mean being lazy or unproductive—it means prioritizing intentionality over haste. By reducing the constant pressure to rush, we create more space for creativity, joy, and meaningful connections. This slower pace allows us to live more fully, savoring each experience instead of merely completing tasks for the sake of completion.

Living at a pace that suits your needs, one that feels authentic and sustainable, brings a deeper sense of fulfilment. It frees you from the endless cycle of busyness that leads to burnout and dissatisfaction. Instead, you create room for true enjoyment, where each moment is appreciated for what it is, not for how quickly you can get through it.

In a world that often values speed, *Easy does it* is a reminder that sometimes the best way to move forward is to slow down and embrace the present moment. By taking time to focus on what really matters, you'll find that life becomes not only more enjoyable, but also far more meaningful.

6. Anxiety Is Just a Feeling, not a State of Being

Anxiety is a common emotional reaction to stress, but it is important to remember that anxiety itself is not permanent. It's simply a feeling that will pass, just like joy or sadness. For instance, if you're anxious about an upcoming presentation, remind yourself that these feelings are temporary. Focus on the steps you can take to prepare and then trust yourself. Recognizing that anxiety is not who you are allows you to detach from it, manage it better, and ultimately not let it rule your life.

7. The Harm of Anger and How to Manage It

Holding onto anger can cause more harm than the original reason for the anger itself. Imagine you have a disagreement with a friend or colleague, and instead of letting it go, you stew over it for days. This prolonged anger can affect your mental health, cause sleepless nights, and even damage the relationship. To break this cycle, use distractions to cool off, like going for a walk or listening to calming music. Avoid confronting the person immediately, as you're more likely to say things you don't mean. Instead, take time to reflect on what made you angry, challenge your thoughts, and address the issue later in a calm, respectful manner.

Managing Anger: Three Key Steps

Anger is a natural emotion, but how we handle it can make all the difference.

a. **Use distractions**: When you feel anger rising, engage in an activity that helps you calm down, like listening to soothing music, journaling, or even a short exercise session.

b. **Avoid confrontation**: It's important not to confront someone when you're emotionally charged. Wait for a time when you can approach the situation rationally.

c. **Challenge your thoughts**: Sometimes, anger stems from misunderstandings or assumptions. Writing down what you're angry about can help you view the situation more objectively and see whether your anger is justified.

d. This method helps you maintain control over your reactions and preserve relationships.

Let Go of Anger, Let God Handle Others

People will always act in ways that may frustrate you, but it's essential to remember that you can't control others' actions, only your response. By letting go and trusting that everything will unfold as it's meant to, you protect your peace. For example, if a colleague regularly interrupts you during meetings, instead of harbouring resentment, choose to pray or meditate for peace. Focus on your own actions and reactions, letting go of the need to change others, which will ultimately bring you a greater sense of calm and happiness.

The 3-Day Rule for Anger Management

When you're in the heat of anger, it's easy to say or do things that you might regret later. Take a 3-day rule before reacting. If you feel anger bubbling up, commit to waiting for three days to think through the situation. For example, if a friend cancel plans at the last minute, instead of confronting them immediately, take time to reflect. After three days, you'll often find that your anger has dissipated, and you can approach the issue more calmly, keeping the relationship intact.

8. Don't Carry Yesterday's Baggage into Today

Stress doesn't always arise from external circumstances—often, it's the emotional residue from the past that lingers and compounds over time. When we carry unresolved emotions from one day into the next, it's like adding layers of unnecessary weight to our mental and emotional state. Each new day becomes more challenging as we allow yesterday's frustrations, disappointments, or conflicts to influence our thoughts and actions.

For example, imagine you had a heated discussion with a family member the evening before. Maybe words were said that you regret, or perhaps a disagreement left you feeling unsettled. If you wake up the next morning still holding onto that negative energy, it can easily carry over into your interactions with others. You might be more irritable, less patient, or find yourself snapping at people who have nothing to do with yesterday's conflict. This accumulation of unresolved emotions only adds stress to your life and disturbs your peace of mind.

But the good news is that you have the power to choose how to start your day and how to let go of the past. One of the simplest yet most effective ways to reset your emotional state is by creating a morning ritual that allows you to leave yesterday's baggage behind. This can help clear your mind, refresh your perspective, and set a positive tone for the rest of the day.

For instance, upon waking up, try taking a few deep breaths—breathing in slowly through your nose and exhaling through your mouth. This simple practice helps activate the parasympathetic nervous system, calming your body and mind. It's an opportunity to center yourself and release any tension that may have carried over from the night before.

Alternatively, you could start your day with a gratitude journal. Take a moment to jot down three things you're thankful for, whether big or small. This act of focusing on the positive can shift your mindset from one of stress or negativity to one of appreciation and calm. Even something as simple as being grateful for the opportunity to start a new day or the comfort of a warm bed can ground you in the present and prevent yesterday's emotional baggage from clouding your thoughts.

Consider the example of someone who had a difficult conversation with a coworker the day before. They may have left the conversation feeling frustrated or upset, and if they carry that frustration into the next day, it may negatively affect their work and relationships. However, if they take a few moments in the morning to focus on what they can control—such as taking a deep breath or visualizing a productive day—the emotional charge from yesterday's encounter can dissipate. This practice of emotional reset not only helps reduce stress but also prevents past experiences from dictating your present Behaviour.

Another example could be a parent who had an argument with their teenager the previous evening. Instead of allowing that tension to linger, they could use the morning as a fresh start. Perhaps they take time to reflect on what they value in their relationship with their child and decide to approach the day with understanding and patience. In doing so, they open the door for healthier interactions moving forward, free from the emotional residue of the past.

These small yet powerful rituals—breathing deeply, journaling, or simply deciding to start fresh—help you release yesterday's emotions and create mental and emotional space for the present moment. When you practice this daily, it becomes easier to leave behind negative energy and start each day with a clean slate. By not allowing past stressors to influence your current interactions, you foster healthier relationships and reduce the impact of accumulated emotional tension over time.

The key takeaway here is that stress often comes from holding onto unresolved emotions. By consciously letting go of yesterday's baggage, you set the stage for a calmer, more peaceful day. Over time, these small habits of emotional reset can make a significant difference in your overall stress levels, helping you to live with greater mindfulness, peace, and presence.

9. The Shadows on the Wall: Seeing Beyond Appearances- Plato's Cave

Plato's allegory of the cave is a powerful metaphor for how limited perspectives shape our understanding of the world. In this allegory, prisoners are chained to a wall, unable to see anything except the shadows cast on the wall by objects behind them. These shadows represent a distorted version of reality—the prisoners only see a fragment of the whole truth. They make assumptions about the world based on these partial shadows, unaware that there is more to the story just beyond their limited view.

In much the same way, our perspectives are often confined by the boundaries of our own experiences, biases, and assumptions. When we encounter a situation, we can easily make judgments based on a narrow view, without considering the full scope of what's happening or the motivations behind people's actions. This tendency to judge based on incomplete information can create misunderstandings and unnecessary stress, especially in our relationships and work environments.

For instance, consider a scenario where a colleague's actions upset you. Maybe they didn't respond to your email right away, or they seemed distant during a meeting. It's easy to assume the worst—that they're ignoring you, being uncooperative, or even harboring resentment. These assumptions can lead to frustration and stress, potentially even escalating into conflict if left unchecked. However, by expanding your perspective, you can approach the situation with more understanding.

Rather than jumping to conclusions, take a step back and try to see things from their point of view. Perhaps your colleague is overwhelmed with their own workload or dealing with personal challenges that are affecting their Behaviour. When you take the time to understand their situation, you realize that their actions weren't a personal attack but rather a reflection of their own stress or circumstances.

This shift in perspective doesn't just reduce stress—it also prevents unnecessary conflict. Instead of reacting impulsively or defensively, you can respond with empathy and patience. For example, instead of confronting your colleague angrily about their delayed response, you might ask, "I noticed you didn't get a chance to reply to my email—everything okay on your end?" This approach opens the door for a constructive conversation and a better understanding of each other's circumstances.

The same principle applies in other areas of life. Imagine you're dealing with a family member who seems to be short-tempered or distant. It's easy to assume they're upset with you or that they're being difficult on purpose. However, by broadening your perspective and considering the external factors they might be facing—stress at work, health issues, or emotional challenges—you can approach them with more compassion. Instead of reacting to their Behaviour, you respond with understanding, which helps maintain harmony and reduces the likelihood of conflict.

Expanding your perspective is not just about understanding others—it's also about challenging your own assumptions. We all have biases and preconceived notions that shape the way we interpret situations. By actively questioning these assumptions and seeking a more complete picture, we can break free from the limitations of our own perspective.

For example, in a team meeting, if you find yourself becoming frustrated with someone's ideas or contributions, ask yourself: "Am I missing something here?" Sometimes, a small shift in perspective—like considering the person's background or experience—can reveal insights that were previously overlooked. When you open yourself up to new viewpoints, you're better equipped to handle differences in opinion, reducing stress and promoting collaboration.

In relationships, whether personal or professional, expanding your perspective allows you to navigate misunderstandings with greater ease. By choosing to view situations through a lens of curiosity rather than judgment, you invite more open, compassionate dialogue. Instead of assuming the worst about someone's intentions, you embrace the opportunity to learn more about their experience, which fosters deeper connection and lessens the stress of miscommunication.

Ultimately, by challenging the shadows on the wall and striving to see beyond your limited perspective, you can break free from the stress caused by assumptions and misunderstandings. This expanded view allows you to approach life with greater empathy, patience, and clarity, leading to more harmonious relationships and a more peaceful mind.

10. The Two Faces of Stress: Turning Pressure into Growth

Not all stress is created equal. While the word "stress" often carries a negative connotation, it's important to understand that some stress is actually good for you. The key lies in distinguishing between **eustress** and **distress**—two very different forms of stress with dramatically different impacts on your body, mind, and performance.

Eustress is the positive, motivating kind of stress. It energizes you, sharpens your focus, and pushes you toward meaningful challenges. Think of it as a burst of adrenaline before a big moment—a tool that can help you rise to the occasion. For instance, consider the nervous excitement you feel before giving a public speech or taking on a new leadership role. That tension can drive you to rehearse more, stay alert, and perform at your best. Athletes often experience this kind of stress before a competition, and it's what helps them tap into their full potential.

Imagine you're working on an important project with a tight deadline. Eustress helps you prioritize, concentrate better, and avoid procrastination. It creates a sense of urgency without overwhelming you. You may feel the pressure, but it's accompanied by a sense of capability and purpose. When managed well, this kind of stress leads to **personal growth**, **resilience**, and a **sense of accomplishment**.

On the flip side is **distress**, the harmful type of stress that wears you down. This is the kind that triggers anxiety, burnout, and emotional fatigue. If you find yourself constantly worrying about outcomes, losing sleep, or feeling physically unwell due to stress, that's a clear sign of distress. It's like a pressure cooker without a release valve—sooner or later, something will explode.

Take the same example of giving a presentation. A bit of nervousness (eustress) is healthy—it shows you care. But if that nervousness turns into panic, if your mind goes blank or your heart races uncontrollably, you're moving into the territory of distress. You may start to doubt yourself, avoid challenges, or shut down completely, which leads to missed opportunities and declining well-being.

The trick is not to eliminate stress entirely—because doing so would also remove the fuel that drives motivation and achievement. Instead, the goal is to **recognize the difference between eustress and distress** and learn how to manage both. This awareness can help you **use stress as a tool** instead of letting it become a threat.

Here are some ways to harness eustress and avoid distress:

a. **Reframe the challenge** – When you feel pressure, tell yourself, "This is an opportunity to grow," instead of "I can't handle this." Your mindset determines whether the stress will energize or paralyze you.

b. **Prepare, don't panic** – Nervous before an exam or presentation? Channel that energy into preparation. Use your stress as a signal to focus, not to freeze.

c. **Take mindful breaks** – Even good stress needs balance. Make time to breathe, stretch, and step away to recharge. Avoiding burnout is essential to maintaining sustainable eustress.

d. **Talk about it** – Sometimes, just sharing your stress with a trusted friend or mentor can help transform it into a manageable form. Verbalizing worries helps you gain perspective.

e. **Practice recovery** – Just like muscles need rest after a workout, your mind needs rest after mental exertion. Meditation, sleep, journaling, or spending time in nature can help reset your system.

Recognizing when you're operating in a state of **constructive tension** versus **destructive overload** allows you to stay in control. You become the driver of your growth, not a victim of your circumstances.

Stress, when channeled properly, is not the enemy—it can be a powerful ally. Eustress pushes you to stretch your limits and reach new heights. Distress, if left unchecked, pulls you down. The wisdom lies in knowing the difference, listening to your body, and responding with self-awareness.

11. Gratitude: A Daily Ritual for Inner Peace

Gratitude is one of the most powerful yet underrated tools for reducing stress and enhancing emotional well-being. In a world that constantly urges us to chase more—more success, more possessions, more recognition—gratitude gently brings us back to the present and reminds us that we already have enough to feel content.

Start each day with a moment of intentional reflection. Before reaching for your phone or diving into your to-do list, pause. Take a deep breath and ask yourself: *What am I thankful for right now?* It could be something as simple as the warmth of your blanket, the smile of a loved one, or the aroma of freshly brewed tea.

Even on challenging days, there is always something to appreciate. For instance, if you're going through a difficult period at work, you might still be grateful for the support of your family, your resilience, or the lessons the struggle is teaching you. Gratitude does not mean ignoring pain; it means choosing not to let that pain define your entire experience.

Try this simple practice each morning:

- **Write down three things you're grateful for.** They don't need to be profound. "I'm grateful for my breath." "I'm grateful for the quiet morning." "I'm grateful for my child's laughter."
- **Add a few affirmations to anchor your mindset.** Phrases like:
- *"I am calm."*
- *"I am capable."*
- *"I am open to joy today."*
- *"I am grateful for all that I have and all that is to come."*

Affirmations are not about denying reality; they are about choosing the lens through which you see it. Just like physical exercise builds your body, gratitude and affirmations strengthen your emotional resilience.

This practice is especially helpful during moments of stress. For example, if you're stuck in traffic and feeling irritated, instead of spiralling into frustration, take a deep breath and think: "*I'm grateful I have a car. I'm grateful I'm safe. I'm grateful I have somewhere to go.*" It sounds simple, but this mental pivot can completely change your emotional state.

The key is to **live one day at a time**. As the saying goes: "*Just for today, I will be grateful.*" When we focus on managing the present moment with gratitude, the future feels less overwhelming and the past less burdensome.

Gratitude softens the edges of life's difficulties. It trains the mind to seek beauty even in imperfection. Over time, it rewires your mental patterns, reduces stress hormones, and makes space for more joy, empathy, and peace.

Remember, gratitude is not about waiting for everything to be perfect. It's about appreciating the small blessings that are already part of your journey. Just for today, slow down, breathe in, and give thanks.

12. Create a Digital Detox Zone

In our hyper-connected world, smartphones and digital devices have become extensions of ourselves. They keep us informed, entertained, and accessible—but they also compete for our attention, drain our focus, and subtly elevate our stress levels. Notifications buzz, messages pour in, and before we realize it, hours slip by scrolling aimlessly.

While technology is a powerful tool, its misuse can lead to mental clutter, reduced productivity, and disconnection from what truly matters.

One of the most effective ways to regain control over your time and inner peace is to set boundaries with your digital life. This doesn't mean abandoning your phone completely, but rather becoming more intentional about **when, how, and why** you use it.

Consider this simple strategy

Designate certain hours of the day as "tech-free zones." For instance, you might choose to avoid screens during your first hour in the morning and your last hour before bed. During these times, focus on activities that nourish your body and mind—reading, journaling, walking in nature, or having an uninterrupted conversation with a loved one.

Take inspiration from Arianna Huffington, founder of Thrive Global, who experienced burnout firsthand and radically changed her relationship with technology. She now advocates for digital detox practices, especially in the evenings. Arianna even keeps her phone outside the bedroom, treating her rest space as sacred. Her philosophy is simple: just like we charge our devices, we must give our minds and bodies the chance to recharge.

Try this challenge

Put your phone on airplane mode for one hour a day and use that time for deep work or deep rest. You'll be surprised at how much more focused and creative you become. Or, create a family rule—no phones at the dinner table—to cultivate real conversations and eye contact.

These small changes can lead to profound benefits. Less screen time means more mental space. Fewer distractions lead to better quality work. And by disconnecting from the digital world, you reconnect with your inner world.

Technology should serve your goals, not sabotage them. By consciously stepping away from screens, even briefly, you allow space for clarity, presence, and peace.

13. Riding the Emotional Waves: Let the Train Pass

Emotions, like weather patterns, are ever-changing. Some days are sunny and bright, filled with joy and ease. Others are cloudy with anxiety, or stormy with frustration, grief, or anger. But just as no weather lasts forever, no emotional state is permanent. Understanding this truth can bring tremendous relief during difficult moments.

Imagine yourself standing on a train platform. A train approaches—it's loud, chaotic, and unsettling. This train is your anger, sadness, or fear. You have two choices: you can either get on the train and let it take you wherever it's going, or you can let it pass, observing it as a temporary visitor. The wise choice is to acknowledge the emotion—observe it, name it—but not become it.

When you feel overwhelmed by sadness, say to yourself, "*This is sadness. It is here now, but it won't stay forever.*" This simple act of naming the emotion creates space between you and the feeling. You are not your sadness. You are the observer of it.

Here's a real-life example

Suppose you receive criticism at work and feel a wave of anger rising. Instead of reacting instantly—perhaps by snapping at a colleague or sending a sharp email—pause and take a breath. Recognize that your anger is valid but fleeting. You might step outside, go for a short walk, or write down your thoughts in a journal. By doing this, you allow the emotional train to pass without derailing your day.

This principle is echoed in many spiritual and psychological traditions. In mindfulness practices, for instance, emotions are treated like clouds in the sky—floating by, constantly moving. Even the darkest clouds eventually give way to blue skies.

Try this simple exercise

When you're overwhelmed, place your hand on your heart and say, "*This is temporary. I am safe. I can wait for this to pass.*" You'd be surprised at how this gentle self-talk diffuses intense emotions.

By learning to ride the waves of emotion without being drowned by them, you develop emotional resilience. You become more grounded, more present, and more peaceful—even when storms roll in.

Let the trains pass. The station is yours.

14. Gossip: The Poison of Relationships

Gossip might seem harmless, even entertaining at times—but it quietly erodes trust, weakens relationships, and undermines your own integrity. Words are powerful. When misused, especially behind someone's back, they can sow seeds of doubt, jealousy, and division that are hard to undo.

It starts subtly. A colleague whispers, "Did you hear what he did?" or a friend casually remarks, "She always acts like she's better than us." Before you know it, you are part of a cycle of criticism and judgment that adds no value—but takes so much away. Gossip gives the illusion of connection, but it's built on tearing someone else down, not lifting anyone up.

Think about this: If someone is comfortable gossiping with you, chances are they are also gossiping about you.

Let's take an example from the workplace. Imagine a team member who constantly complains about others when they're not around. Initially, it may feel like you're bonding over shared frustrations. But over time, you'll start to question if they're saying similar things about you. Trust deteriorates. Team unity suffers. And worse, the person spreading gossip becomes known not for their work, but for their words.

Now imagine the opposite. Someone who, when the opportunity arises to gossip, gracefully changes the subject or says something positive instead. That kind of person becomes a safe space—a trusted, respected presence. Their words build, not break. People naturally gravitate toward them, knowing they're grounded in character and integrity.

Here's a powerful practice

Before speaking about someone, ask yourself:

- Is it true?
- Is it necessary?
- Is it kind?

These three filters—often attributed to ancient wisdom—can prevent countless conflicts and regrets.

Gossip can't survive in the presence of empathy. When you try to understand someone's struggle or perspective, judgment fades. Instead of criticizing, you find yourself wondering, "*What might they be going through?*" This mindset not only protects your relationships—it protects your peace.

Use your words to uplift. Praise someone's effort. Speak well of someone even when they're not around. If you're hurt or have an issue, have the courage to address it directly rather than behind someone's back.

In a world that thrives on drama and whisper networks, be the person whose voice spreads light, not shadows. Let your silence in gossip and your strength in kindness speak volumes.

15. The Tranquility of Acceptance: The Stoic Path to Happiness

Stoicism, one of the ancient Greek philosophies, teaches us a profound yet simple lesson: true happiness is not about chasing pleasure or avoiding discomfort, but rather cultivating a state of inner peace and tranquility. According to Stoic teachings, it is not the absence of pleasure that we should seek, but the absence of negative emotions like fear, anger, and anxiety, which often arise when we allow external events to control our inner world.

In the modern world, we are constantly seeking pleasure—whether it's in material possessions, social validation, or fleeting experiences. Yet, in our pursuit of these pleasures, we often fall victim to their control over us. The joy we find from external sources is temporary, and when those sources are gone or unavailable, we are left feeling anxious, frustrated, or dissatisfied. Stoicism offers a different perspective: rather than clinging to pleasure or avoiding discomfort, we should seek peace by mastering our reactions to life's events.

Here's an example to illustrate this principle

Imagine you're at a family gathering, and someone makes a comment that irritates you. In that moment, your natural reaction might be to feel anger or frustration. However, a Stoic would pause and reflect before reacting. By recognizing that the comment is outside of your control, and that your response is within your control, you can choose to let go of that anger. Rather than allowing that negative emotion to dictate your mood, you can maintain your composure, enjoy the rest of the gathering, and remind yourself that peace of mind is more valuable than any fleeting emotion.

A Stoic's approach to pleasure

Pleasure, in the Stoic sense, is not to be rejected. Life's joys—whether it's a delicious meal, a beautiful sunset, or a satisfying conversation—are to be enjoyed, but not clung to. Stoics believe in experiencing pleasure without allowing it to control you. For instance, if you're enjoying a nice cup of coffee in the morning, instead of becoming obsessed with how good it tastes or trying to chase that feeling, you can simply appreciate the moment for what it is. When you finish, you don't feel deprived or empty—you simply move on, knowing that peace comes not from possession but from acceptance.

Epictetus, a Stoic philosopher, once said, "Wealth consists not in having great possessions, but in having few wants."

This concept is key to understanding the Stoic approach to happiness. Happiness is not about accumulating more, but about learning to be content with less. It's about finding freedom in the acceptance of what is, and relinquishing the emotional attachment to outcomes.

Consider this scenario: You've planned an exciting vacation, but at the last minute, your plans are disrupted by unforeseen circumstances—a cancelled flight, bad weather, or an illness. A person who clings to the expectation of pleasure might become upset, frustrated, and angry. A Stoic, on the other hand, would accept the situation as it is. They would focus on what they can control—perhaps finding a new way to enjoy the day, or even appreciating the unexpected downtime. By accepting life's unpredictability and remaining cantered, you protect your inner peace.

A practical Stoic exercise

At the beginning or end of each day, take a moment to reflect on your experiences. Ask yourself:

- Did I let fear or anger take control today?
- Did I allow external events to disturb my inner peace?
- How can I cultivate more tranquility in my reactions?

By practicing this daily reflection, you begin to strengthen your ability to maintain equanimity, regardless of what life throws your way.

Ultimately, the Stoic path to happiness is about acceptance and mastery of self. By focusing on controlling our responses rather than our circumstances, we can live with a deeper sense of peace, free from the tyranny of negative emotions. In the end, tranquility is not the absence of challenges, but the ability to navigate them with calm, clarity, and composure.

16. The Cost of Always Being Right: Embracing Collaboration Over Conflict

The relentless pursuit of being right—often driven by ego, pride, or insecurity—can lead to unnecessary frustration, tension, and conflict. While it's natural to want to prove your point or defend your beliefs, constantly striving to be right can create barriers to genuine connection, growth, and mutual understanding. In fact, the need to always be right often results in winning an argument but losing the relationship in the process.

Consider a situation where two people are having a disagreement. One person insists on proving their perspective with every piece of evidence they can muster. The other, feeling cornered and misunderstood, becomes defensive. The conversation quickly escalates into a power struggle, where both parties are more focused on "winning" than understanding each other. In the end, neither person feels heard or respected, and the relationship suffers. The need to be right, in this case, does more harm than good.

A Workplace Conflict

Imagine a scenario at work where a team is brainstorming ideas for a new project. One team member, let's call him Jack, feels very strongly about a particular approach and argues relentlessly that his way is the best. Despite others offering their ideas, Jack insists that his solution is superior. His focus is on winning the argument rather than collaborating with his colleagues to find the best solution. This leads to frustration among the team, and the group dynamic begins to falter.

If Jack had let go of the need to be right and embraced the idea of collective input, he would have opened himself up to the possibility that the best solution might come from someone else's perspective. Collaboration thrives when individuals listen to one another, respect different viewpoints, and work together toward a common goal. In the long run, this not only leads to better outcomes but also fosters an environment of trust and mutual respect.

Personal Relationships

In a personal relationship, constantly needing to be right can have similar consequences. Let's say Sarah and her partner, Ben, are in the midst of a disagreement about household responsibilities. Sarah feels strongly that Ben should take on more of the chores, but instead of approaching the conversation with openness, she focuses on being "right"—proving that her perspective is valid, and his is wrong. Ben, feeling cornered and defensive, shuts down, leading to heightened tension and a lack of resolution.

On the other hand, if Sarah were to approach the conversation with a willingness to listen and understand Ben's point of view, it would lead to a much more constructive discussion. For example, she could say, "I understand that you're really busy at work, but I feel overwhelmed by the chores at home. Can we find a way to share the responsibility that works for both of us?" By letting go of the need to "win" the argument, Sarah opens the door to collaboration and understanding, which leads to a healthier, more balanced relationship.

The Power of Letting Go of the Need to Be Right

When we let go of the need to always have the last word or prove our correctness, we shift our focus from personal victory to mutual understanding. It's a shift from individualism to collaboration. This doesn't mean that we should abandon our principles or stop advocating for our ideas. Rather, it means recognizing that the ultimate goal isn't to "win" but to learn, grow, and strengthen our relationships with others.

For instance, in a meeting or a family discussion, instead of fighting to be right, try asking questions to understand the other person's point of view. For example, "Can you help me understand why you feel that way?" or "What do you think would work best for everyone?" These open-ended questions demonstrate humility and a willingness to collaborate, which can defuse potential conflict and lead to more productive and peaceful conversations.

Personal Growth Through Collaboration

Personal growth often comes from being open to new ideas, not from holding tightly to our existing beliefs. A good example of this is a mentor-mentee relationship. A mentor who always feels the need to be right can hinder the growth of the mentee by not allowing them to explore their own perspectives or make mistakes. Conversely, a mentor who listens actively, encourages questions, and embraces different viewpoints fosters an environment of learning and development.

For example, imagine a mentor named John who is guiding his mentee, Lisa, through a project. John could simply dictate how everything should be done, but this would limit Lisa's ability to develop critical thinking skills. Instead, John asks Lisa, "What do you think is the best approach?" and, after listening to her response, suggests ways to refine her ideas. By letting go of the need to always be right and giving Lisa the space to contribute, John creates a learning opportunity that leads to Lisa's growth and, ultimately, her success.

A Simple Shift for Lasting Change

It may be difficult at first to let go of the need to always be right. However, it's important to remind ourselves that being "right" in every situation isn't the ultimate goal. The real goal is connection, understanding, and growth. When we focus on collaboration instead of conflict, we create an atmosphere where mutual respect and progress can flourish. By letting go of our ego-driven desire to be right, we open ourselves up to more enriching, fulfilling relationships—both personally and professionally.

The next time you feel the urge to defend your position or "win" a conversation, pause and ask yourself: *Is it more important to be right, or to understand and connect?* In most cases, the latter will lead to greater happiness and peace for everyone involved.

17. Choosing the Right Problems to Solve

In life, we are constantly presented with problems and challenges. Some are crucial stepping stones toward personal growth, while others can be distractions that drain our energy without contributing to our long-term success or happiness. The key to managing these challenges is to focus on those that align with your values and long-term goals, while letting go of the ones that drain you without offering any real value in return.

When we align the problems, we tackle with what matters most to us, we not only solve them more efficiently but also feel more fulfilled in the process. On the other hand, investing time and energy in problems that are irrelevant or harmful to our well-being can lead to frustration, burnout, and a lack of progress in the areas that truly matter.

Consider Ankita, a professional at a crossroads in her career. She has two major projects to choose from—one that is aligned with her passion for environmental sustainability and another that is purely financially motivated, but doesn't align with her values. While the financially motivated project may seem like an easy win in the short term, Sarah recognizes that her true long-term goal is to contribute positively to the environment.

By focusing on the project that aligns with her values and long-term goals, Sarah not only feels more motivated but also finds herself more creatively engaged and energized. This sense of purpose helps her work through obstacles with more resilience and ultimately leads her to greater professional satisfaction.

On the other hand, if Sarah had chosen to invest her time and energy in the project that didn't align with her values, she might have faced ongoing dissatisfaction, a lack of fulfilment, and the feeling that her work wasn't contributing to something meaningful. This is a classic example of solving problems that align with your core values, which leads to better outcomes and a more rewarding life.

Now, let's take a look at relationships. We all have friends, family, or colleagues who present us with problems. Some of these issues can be opportunities for growth, deeper connection, or the chance to help others. However, not all problems are worth solving, especially when they drain us emotionally without benefiting the relationship.

For instance, Lisa has a friend who constantly seeks validation and attention but never reciprocates emotional support. Lisa finds herself in a pattern of offering advice, listening to complaints, and sacrificing her own well-being to help her friend. Over time, Lisa feels exhausted and unappreciated. She realizes that while she values her friend, the constant emotional drain is no longer serving her.

After reflecting on her values—such as self-care, mutual respect, and balance in her relationships—Lisa decides to set boundaries. She communicates her need for a more balanced dynamic and respectfully distances herself from the emotional drain. This decision allows Lisa to protect her emotional well-being and invest time in relationships that nourish her, creating space for healthier, more fulfilling connections.

Personal development is another area where we are often faced with numerous problems or challenges. Whether it's learning a new skill, managing time better, or improving physical health, the problems that align with your long-term goals will give you a sense of purpose and direction.

For example, Tom is trying to improve his physical health. He has two options: one is to commit to a consistent workout routine that aligns with his long-term goal of becoming healthier and more energetic, while the other is to fall back into old habits of binge-watching TV shows, which temporarily provides comfort but doesn't support his overall goals.

By choosing to focus on solving the problem of sticking to a workout schedule, Tom not only improves his health but also develops discipline and perseverance. The rewards, though small at first, build up over time and align with his broader goal of living a fulfilling, healthy life. On the other hand, if Tom continued to indulge in the comfort of inactivity, he would likely continue to feel frustrated and stuck, as this solution does not align with his long-term vision of self-improvement.

The Power of Saying "No"

One of the most powerful ways to protect your energy and stay aligned with your long-term goals is by learning to say "no" to problems or requests that do not contribute positively to your life. This can be especially difficult when we feel the pressure to say "yes" in order to please others or avoid conflict.

For example, consider a scenario at work where a colleague asks you to take on additional responsibilities that do not align with your job description or personal aspirations. While saying "yes" might temporarily relieve the pressure of disappointing them, it would add to your stress and divert your attention away from the important tasks that contribute to your career growth. By politely saying "no" or offering a compromise, you create the space to focus on your true priorities and avoid getting sidetracked by distractions that do not move you closer to your goals.

Financial decisions are a common area where people struggle to align their problem-solving efforts with their long-term goals. Take the example of Jane, who wants to save for a home but finds herself constantly tempted by immediate gratification, such as frequent shopping trips or dining out. Every time she overspends, it feels like a quick fix for her stress or dissatisfaction, but it ultimately takes her further away from her long-term goal of homeownership.

By re-evaluating her financial goals and values, Jane realizes that her immediate desires are fleeting and do not align with her true aspirations. She begins to redirect her energy toward solving the problem of budgeting, cutting unnecessary expenses, and saving more effectively. Over time, this not only brings her closer to her goal but also fosters a sense of discipline and accomplishment, as she focuses on long-term financial stability.

18. Finding and Vetting Your Mentor

A mentor is an invaluable resource who can guide you through challenges, provide wisdom, and help you achieve your goals more effectively. Finding the right mentor can make all the difference in your personal and professional growth. Here's a deeper look at how you can find a mentor:

Look for Shared Experience

The best mentors are often those who have walked a similar path to yours. Whether you're navigating a new career, developing a business, or working on personal growth, a mentor who has been through similar experiences can offer practical advice, strategies, and insights.

If you're a young entrepreneur starting a tech company, seeking out a mentor who has successfully built and scaled a business in the same industry can be incredibly helpful. This mentor would not only understand the technical aspects of your work but also the emotional and strategic decisions you face. For instance, they might offer advice on funding options, managing a team, or navigating market competition.

Look for a Similar Background

It's important to find someone who understands your unique experiences and challenges. A mentor with a similar background will have an easier time empathizing with your situation and providing advice that resonates with you.

If you come from a background where resources were limited, you might benefit from a mentor who also had to overcome financial barriers to succeed. They can give you actionable steps and emotional support, knowing the hurdles you're facing. They may have advice on how to network effectively without financial resources, or how to make the most of limited opportunities.

Craft Your Ask for Mentorship

When seeking a mentor, it's essential to be clear about what you need. Instead of approaching someone with a vague request like "I need a mentor," take time to reflect on your goals and the areas where you need guidance. This will help the potential mentor understand how they can best assist you and decide if they are the right fit for you.

Let's say you are transitioning into a leadership role in your company. You might approach a senior leader with the request: "I'm looking for guidance on developing my leadership skills, particularly in team management and conflict resolution. Would you be open to meeting with me for an hour each month to discuss challenges and growth in these areas?" This specific ask demonstrates your intent, shows respect for their time, and gives clarity on the kind of mentorship you seek.

Ensure the Relationship Benefits Both of You

Mentorship should be a two-way relationship. While the mentor provides guidance and support, they should also feel that the relationship is mutually enriching. This could be through offering fresh perspectives, being open to learning from you, or building a long-term professional connection.

If you're an emerging social media expert and you're seeking mentorship from someone in a different field, you can offer value by sharing your knowledge on digital marketing and social media trends. This creates a sense of reciprocity where both parties can learn and grow together, reinforcing a stronger, more sustainable mentorship.

Commit to Regular Check-Ins

Consistency is key in mentorship. It's important to schedule regular check-ins and be proactive in your communication. This ensures the relationship stays on track, goals are met, and you remain focused on growth.

After your initial meeting, you might agree with your mentor to meet once a month. In these check-ins, you could review your progress, discuss challenges you've faced, and set new goals. Regular interaction with your mentor helps keep you accountable and continuously sharpens your skills.

In summary, finding the right mentor is about aligning experiences, seeking clarity in your needs, and ensuring the relationship adds value for both of you. When approached thoughtfully, mentorship can provide you with invaluable support and guidance, accelerating your personal and professional growth.

19. Remove Stress by Helping Others

Helping others can be a powerful way to reduce your own stress. By shifting the focus from your own challenges to offering support to others, you not only contribute to their well-being but also experience the emotional benefits of connection, purpose, and fulfilment. Here's how helping others can reduce your stress and enhance your sense of peace:

Assist a Colleague

One of the simplest ways to help reduce your own stress is by assisting a colleague with a task. When you help others, it can shift your focus away from your own stressors, creating a sense of accomplishment and connection.

For example, imagine a colleague is overwhelmed with their workload, and they are juggling multiple deadlines. You notice that they have been struggling with a particular task, like preparing a report. Offering to take that task off their plate for a day or two can not only reduce their stress but also give you a sense of accomplishment and purpose. By alleviating their burden, you foster a collaborative environment that benefits both of you. Plus, seeing their gratitude can create a positive feedback loop that boosts your mood and reduces your own stress.

Support a Team Member

Supporting a team member can be particularly effective when they're facing challenges you might have already dealt with in the past. Your insight and support can ease their stress while also reminding you of your own ability to handle similar situations.

For example, if a team member is struggling to meet a project deadline, offering to help them brainstorm or assist with the workload can make a significant difference. Let's say they're struggling with organizing a presentation for a key client. You can step in by offering suggestions on structure or even help with preparing some slides. This not only helps them stay on track but also gives you a sense of contribution and involvement, which can reduce your own stress. Furthermore, knowing that you've helped someone else succeed can provide a sense of fulfilment that takes your mind off your own concerns.

Share Helpful Resources

Sometimes, the best way to help others is by sharing knowledge or resources that can alleviate their challenges. By doing this, you are helping to resolve a problem and are also indirectly relieving your own stress, as you shift your focus away from personal issues.

For example, if a friend or colleague is dealing with a difficult client or handling a situation that's stressing them out, you could offer helpful resources that might provide them with the tools they need to tackle the issue. Perhaps you know of an article on conflict resolution, a book on time management, or an online course that can assist them. Sharing these resources not only empowers them to handle their challenges but also boosts your own sense of usefulness and satisfaction. When you see the person benefiting from the resource you shared, it can provide a sense of joy and stress relief as it reinforces your role as a positive force in their life.

Offer Emotional Support

Sometimes, stress isn't just about workloads or deadlines. It can also stem from emotional challenges. Offering emotional support can be an effective way to reduce both your stress and that of others.

For example, if a colleague is going through a tough time—whether it's dealing with personal loss, a challenging family situation, or a major life transition—just being there to listen can ease their burden. You don't have to provide solutions; simply offering a compassionate ear can make a world of difference. By providing emotional support, you also create a space for mutual understanding and empathy, which not only helps them navigate their emotional stress but can also put your own concerns into perspective.

Celebrate Others' Successes

Taking the time to genuinely celebrate the successes of others helps shift your focus away from your own challenges and fosters a sense of connection.

For example, if a colleague successfully closes a big deal, takes on a new responsibility, or hits a milestone in their career, acknowledge and celebrate their achievements. Share your congratulations and highlight their hard work. By focusing on others' successes, you not only build stronger relationships but also remind yourself of the positive impact you can have on others, which in turn helps to alleviate any stress or anxiety you may be experiencing. This also cultivates an environment of positivity and support, making it easier for everyone to thrive together.

Offer Constructive Feedback

Sometimes, helping others involves providing feedback. This can help them grow, and it can also give you a sense of purpose and satisfaction.

For example, a teammate might be struggling with a presentation, and they may ask for your feedback. Offering constructive feedback, such as how they could improve their delivery or how to better structure their points, not only helps them improve but also allows you to actively participate in their growth. Knowing that your insights could make a significant impact can shift your attention from your own stress and create a sense of satisfaction from being a valuable contributor to their success.

Helping others is not just an altruistic act—it can also reduce your stress by fostering positive relationships, creating a sense of accomplishment, and shifting your focus away from your own challenges. Whether it's offering practical assistance, emotional support, or simply sharing helpful resources, supporting those around you allows you to build a supportive community that ultimately helps reduce the stress for everyone involved. By lifting others up, you lift yourself as well.

20. The Power of Prayer in Overcoming Stress

Prayer can be a transformative practice, providing not only a sense of peace but also a framework for dealing with stress and adversity. By turning to prayer, we tap into a deeper sense of purpose and connection, which can offer clarity and tranquility when we're facing difficulties. The **Serenity Prayer**, often recited by those navigating tough situations, encapsulates the wisdom of recognizing what is within our control and what is not.

For example, imagine you are in a stressful situation at work, dealing with a difficult deadline or conflict with a colleague. In such moments, reciting the Serenity Prayer can bring a sense of relief. The prayer guides you to focus on what you can change—your actions, reactions, and mindset—while accepting what lies outside your control, like the opinions of others or unexpected circumstances. This shift in focus from external stressors to internal peace can help you feel more grounded and less overwhelmed.

The Serenity Prayer goes as follows: "**God, grant me the serenity to accept the things I cannot change, the courage to change the things I can, and the wisdom to know the difference.**"

The **Saint Francis Prayer**, on the other hand, is a powerful reminder of how we can transform negative emotions and situations into opportunities for healing and peace. It encourages us to be active participants in creating harmony, even when surrounded by discord. For instance, when dealing with an interpersonal conflict, this prayer invites you to become an instrument of peace—by offering love in the face of hatred, or forgiveness where there is injury. This mindset helps you approach challenges with a spirit of compassion rather than frustration, reducing the emotional toll that conflict often brings.

The Saint Francis Prayer goes as follows: "**Lord, make me an instrument of your peace. Where there is hatred, let me sow love; where there is injury, pardon; where there is doubt, faith; where there is despair, hope; where there is darkness, light; and where there is sadness, joy.**"

Prayer is not just a passive request for divine intervention, but an active practice of aligning our hearts and minds with peace, wisdom, and hope. Whether you're facing personal trials, professional obstacles, or navigating the complex emotions of everyday life, turning to prayer can be a powerful tool for reducing stress. It allows you to surrender the need for control, fostering acceptance and resilience as you move through life's challenges.

Moreover, the act of prayer can serve as a daily ritual—a moment of pause amid the chaos of life. This ritual doesn't have to be long or elaborate. Even a few quiet moments of reflection before a challenging situation, like before a presentation or after receiving unsettling news, can provide clarity and calm. It's a gentle reminder that while we may not control every aspect of our lives, we do control our response and our inner peace.

Ultimately, prayer helps us reconnect with our values and higher purpose, grounding us in a sense of tranquility that helps us face whatever comes our way.

Topic 6

SUCCESS FOR DIRECT SELLERS-NETWORK MARKETING INDUSTRY

Chapter 1: Foundational Principles of Network Marketing

Network marketing is a business model, yes, but it is also a mindset. It isn't just about selling products or recruiting people; it's about building relationships, developing leadership, and establishing a culture of trust and mutual growth. When you understand the foundational principles of network marketing, you unlock the potential to create a thriving business that not only generates income but also transforms your life and the lives of others.

The Foundation of Network Marketing

At its core, network marketing is a business of people, relationships, and systems. Unlike traditional employment or retail, where success often depends on individual effort and isolated actions, network marketing thrives on collaboration, mentorship, and duplication. The real power of the model lies in building a network of people—your team—who will in turn build more networks. A leader who trains and empowers others to succeed creates a ripple effect that multiplies success. For example, a distributor who teaches her downline how to conduct effective product demos and close sales is not just increasing her own earnings—she is enabling her entire team to grow. This system of duplication ensures that each level of the network contributes to overall growth, making the business scalable and sustainable.

Your Network is Your Net Worth

In network marketing, the most valuable asset is not the product or the compensation plan—it's your people. Your network—comprised of your clients, prospects, partners, mentors, and even competitors—forms the bedrock of your success. Think of your network as your community. It's not about collecting contacts in your phone; it's about developing meaningful relationships. When you nurture this community with care, you create a loyal ecosystem of people who trust you, refer others to you, and support you during tough **times. One** distributor, for example, built her business by genuinely helping customers improve their health rather than focusing on making sales. Over time, those customers turned into loyal advocates, brought in referrals, and eventually some became business partners themselves. That's how network translates into net worth.

Patience is Key

Patience is more than a virtue in network marketing—it's a strategy. Many newcomers get discouraged when they don't see immediate results. But this is a long-term game. It's like planting a mango tree—you water it, protect it, and give it sunshine, even when you don't see fruit right away. It might take years, but when it bears fruit, the harvest is plentiful. Similarly, in network marketing, your efforts in prospecting, training, and follow-ups may not yield instant rewards, but they build a solid foundation. The ones who succeed are not always the fastest or the flashiest—they're the ones who stay consistent, showing up day after day even when nothing seems to be working. This consistency builds momentum, and soon, the compound effect kicks in, where small daily actions lead to big results over time.

Fear and Inertia Are the Only Real Obstacles

Fear is often the biggest hurdle standing between you and success. It's not just fear of rejection or failure—sometimes it's fear of judgment, or even fear of success itself. A distributor might hesitate to approach a potential client because they worry about being seen as pushy or salesy. But every "no" you hear brings you closer to a "yes." Rejection is not a reflection of your worth; it's simply part of the process. Even more dangerous than fear is inertia—the state of doing nothing because fear paralyzes you. The best way to overcome inertia is by taking imperfect action. Make the call, send the message, host the meeting—even if you don't feel ready. As you take action, confidence replaces fear. One new distributor who was terrified of public speaking forced himself to do a small product presentation to just three people. It wasn't perfect, but it got easier each time. That's how progress is made—through action, not perfection.

Immature Acts When Starting

In the beginning, it's easy to act out of inexperience or unrealistic expectations. One common mistake is expecting your upline to do all the work for you. Your mentor is there to guide and support, but they can't build your business for you. Taking personal responsibility from day one is crucial. Another common trap is expecting quick money. Many newcomers believe that joining a network marketing company is a fast track to riches. But just like opening a traditional business, it requires time, patience, and consistent effort to generate income. Some people fall into the habit of dreaming without doing—they talk about their goals, watch training videos, attend meetings, but never take action. Execution is what separates winners from wishers. Delaying key activities like prospecting or follow-ups is another form of self-sabotage that slows down momentum. Additionally, some people expect financial support from their uplines or the company, but this model is built on personal entrepreneurship. Your growth depends on your efforts, not on someone else's investment.

Immature Decisions

In the early days of building your business, it's easy to make choices that slow down your progress. For instance, many people ignore the tools provided by the company—like presentations, scripts, follow-up systems, or training videos—thinking they can do better on their own. But these tools exist because they work. Using them gives you leverage and speed. Another immature decision is relying solely on external motivation. While it's inspiring to listen to your mentor or attend events, true drive must come from within. You need to stay disciplined and committed even when no one is watching. Some people also fail to reflect on their results. If your business isn't growing, it's not a sign to quit—it's a signal to reassess. Ask yourself what's working, what isn't, and what needs to change. Constant adaptation is key. Many get distracted by the idea of a miracle product or the next big trend, losing focus on the proven fundamentals. And some people, once they have a few team members, try to act like a boss instead of a mentor. This creates resentment and hinders team growth. Real leadership is about guiding, not commanding.

Immature Mindsets

The mindset you carry into network marketing can either empower you or hold you back. A limiting mindset focuses on what you lack—be it money, support, or time. Instead of saying "I don't have resources," shift to "How can I make the most of what I have?" This shift opens up creativity and possibility. Others fall into the habit of constantly looking for negatives—criticizing the company, the product, or the market—without recognizing their own role in the situation. By contrast, successful leaders focus on what they can control and always look for solutions. There's also a tendency to ignore small wins, always chasing the next big milestone. But celebrating progress, however minor, boosts morale and helps you stay engaged.

Doubting Yourself

Self-doubt is a natural part of the journey, but it becomes a problem when it stops you from taking action. Many people entering the business feel like impostors, thinking they lack the skills to succeed. But every expert was once a beginner. Skills can be learned. Confidence grows through doing, not waiting. Blaming the economy, your upline, or your background is another form of avoidance. Success comes when you take full ownership of your results. Negative voices—from within or from others—can also drag you down. That's why it's crucial to surround yourself with a community that uplifts and believes in your potential, even before you do.

Immature Self-Affirmations

The words you repeat to yourself shape your destiny. Saying things like "I can't afford it," "I don't have time," or "I'm not talented" creates a mental barrier that stops progress. Instead of saying you can't afford something, start thinking in terms of prioritization and value. Time, for instance, is never found—it's made. People make time for what matters. Thinking you lack talent ignores the fact that success in network marketing is skill-based, not talent-based. Anyone can learn how to prospect, present, and lead if they're willing to practice. Perhaps the most damaging belief is "I don't deserve success." But the truth is, every human being deserves to grow, prosper, and thrive.

Altitude: Attitude Shift

To thrive in network marketing, you need to change your altitude—your perspective. Thinking bigger opens doors to greater possibilities. Don't just aim to earn a little extra income—envision a future where you lead hundreds, maybe thousands, of empowered individuals. Action is more important than perfection. Waiting to "feel ready" often means waiting forever. Taking small, imperfect steps daily builds momentum. Maintaining a positive mindset, especially when facing rejection or setbacks, is what keeps you moving forward. A growth mindset believes that challenges are opportunities, not roadblocks.

Take That Leap

The beginning of your journey requires a leap of faith. It takes courage to invest in yourself and commit to a business where results are not guaranteed. But every success story begins with a decision—to trust the process and bet on yourself. Choosing the right company and mentors is also crucial. Align yourself with people who believe in ethical growth and personal development. Once you're in, maintain consistent communication with your team. This isn't just about updates—it's about alignment, motivation, and emotional connection. And throughout, stay anchored in a clear vision. When challenges arise—and they will—your vision will be your compass.

Action with Persistence: The Key

Ultimately, success in network marketing boils down to consistent action. A daily routine creates structure and builds habits that lead to results. Prioritizing your tasks ensures that you're spending time on what matters—reaching out, following up, training your team. Regular reflection keeps you honest. If your actions aren't delivering results, tweak your approach. Successful network marketers aren't stuck on one method—they experiment, assess, and adapt constantly.

Considering the Perspective of Others

The final piece of the puzzle is empathy. Network marketing is a people business. The more you understand your prospects' needs, fears, and aspirations, the better you'll serve them. Always ask yourself: What's in it for them? When you focus on helping others achieve their goals—whether it's better health, more income, or personal growth—you'll naturally build stronger, more loyal relationships. And that, ultimately, is the heart of a thriving network marketing business.

Chapter 2: Advancing in Network Marketing through Leadership and Skill Refinement

Once you've laid a solid foundation in network marketing, it's time to focus on refinement—honing your leadership abilities, expanding your skill set, and creating sustainable team growth. In this chapter, we dive deeper into the strategies that allow you to scale your network marketing business and foster a culture of success within your team.

Leadership is the Key to Success

Leadership in network marketing is much more than just giving orders or holding meetings—it's about inspiring and guiding others to unlock their potential. True leaders lead by example. When you demonstrate work ethic, dedication, and integrity, you set the standard for your team. One key aspect of leadership is leading from the front. This means not just training your team but also showing them through your actions how to build a successful business. If you're expecting your team to prospect, follow up, and attend meetings, you must first model these behaviors yourself. Consider the story of a top distributor who grew his business by consistently setting goals and reaching them. He made it a point to share his struggles and victories with his team, creating an environment where transparency and trust were prioritized. As he faced challenges, he took the time to share his learnings with his downline, which in turn empowered them to handle obstacles more effectively.

The Power of Mentorship and Coaching

A strong network marketing business relies on mentorship and coaching. Once you've gained some experience, it's important to pass on the knowledge and skills you've acquired. However, mentorship is not about telling people what to do—it's about empowering them to think for themselves and make decisions. As a mentor, you must ask the right questions and guide your team members toward the answers that align with their goals. One example is how a senior distributor worked closely with her new recruits, not by pushing them to follow a rigid script, but by helping them develop their own style of communication. Over time, these new recruits became successful in their own right, cultivating their personal leadership while also expanding the team's reach.

Effective mentorship also involves offering constructive feedback. It's not enough to tell someone they're doing well—you must also help them identify areas for growth. Constructive feedback should be delivered in a way that is supportive rather than critical. For instance, rather than saying "You're not following the script correctly," a mentor might say, "I noticed you're making great connections with your clients. Let's tweak the way you introduce the product to make it even more effective." This approach makes feedback feel like a positive development opportunity rather than a negative critique.

Skill Building and Mastery

To rise above the competition, network marketers must continually refine their skills. One of the most important skills in this industry is effective communication. Whether you're presenting a product, closing a sale, or simply building rapport, your ability to communicate clearly and persuasively will define your success. It's vital to know your audience—understanding what motivates them, what their pain points are, and how your product or business can offer a solution. This requires active listening, not just speaking.

Additionally, closing skills are essential. This isn't about being pushy or manipulative—it's about knowing when to ask for the sale and confidently offering a solution. It's important to remember that closing is not a single moment; it's a process that begins the moment you start the conversation. Many top distributors take the time to practice these skills regularly, whether through role-playing with teammates or attending communication workshops. They don't wait for opportunities to present themselves; they actively prepare for them by continually improving their communication.

A real-world example of effective communication can be seen with a distributor who shifted from focusing solely on product features to highlighting customer benefits. Instead of simply listing the vitamins and minerals in a health supplement, she began asking questions like, "How would you feel if you had more energy every day?" This approach resonated with her prospects, and her sales dramatically increased. Communication, when mastered, is what allows you to build strong relationships and develop trust within your network.

Time Management for Leaders

In any business, but especially in network marketing, time management is an essential skill. As your business grows, so does your responsibility. You need to balance managing your own team, recruiting new distributors, developing your personal business, and engaging with clients. Without proper time management, it's easy to feel overwhelmed. Effective time management starts with prioritization. Not all tasks are created equal, and successful network marketers focus on what truly moves the needle—whether that's training new recruits, following up with prospects, or closing sales. One distributor might find success by blocking off two hours each morning for prospecting, ensuring that these vital actions get done before other distractions arise.

Another key component of time management is delegation. As your team expands, it becomes impossible to do everything yourself. This is where leadership comes in. A strong leader knows how to delegate tasks based on team members' strengths. For instance, if you have a team member who excels at product knowledge, you might delegate product training to them, allowing you to focus on recruitment and team-building activities. This not only ensures that tasks are completed more efficiently but also empowers your team, giving them the confidence to take on greater responsibility.

Building a Culture of Success

Creating a thriving culture within your team is critical for long-term success. This culture should be one that fosters growth, collaboration, and mutual support. You want your team members to feel like they are part of something bigger than themselves. Celebrating small wins, offering consistent recognition, and building a strong sense of community are all essential elements of a successful culture.

One way to build culture is through regular team meetings. These meetings provide an opportunity to connect with your team, offer training, discuss challenges, and celebrate victories. But even more importantly, they provide a space where your team can bond, share insights, and learn from each other. Over time, this helps create a sense of unity and shared purpose, which in turn drives higher motivation and performance.

Another example is seen in how certain top distributors regularly host recognition events—celebrating those who have reached new ranks or achieved significant sales. By publicly recognizing individuals' hard work, you encourage others to strive for the same success. This culture of recognition can make all the difference, as it shifts the focus from competition to collaboration, helping everyone feel invested in the team's overall growth.

Embracing Challenges as Opportunities

In network marketing, challenges are inevitable. From dealing with rejection to facing periods of stagnation, obstacles are part of the journey. However, the way you react to these challenges is what separates successful marketers from those who give up. It's important to see challenges as opportunities to learn and grow. For example, when faced with a particularly tough rejection, instead of feeling discouraged, view it as a learning experience. What could you have done differently in your approach? How can you refine your pitch or presentation next time?

One distributor in a large organization had a rough period of low sales and no new recruits. Instead of giving up, she took that time to refine her pitch and focus on the needs of her clients. She found new ways to connect emotionally with her prospects and honed her closing techniques. Within a few months, her sales skyrocketed, and she recruited a team of motivated individuals who were inspired by her resilience.

Developing Your Personal Brand

Finally, a crucial aspect of growing your network marketing business is personal branding. In a competitive industry, standing out is important. What makes you unique? How do you present yourself to the world? Your personal brand should be a reflection of your values, your mission, and the value you offer to others. Whether it's through social media, your website, or in person, your personal brand communicates who you are and what you stand for. For example, if you are passionate about health and wellness, make sure that passion shines through in your communications. Your authentic self will attract the right people to you, and when people resonate with your message, they're more likely to become loyal customers or team members.

A network marketer who consistently posted motivational content on social media, shared success stories, and offered advice on overcoming challenges developed a strong personal brand. As a result, people began **reaching out to her for advice and to join her team. She didn't rely on traditional advertising—her brand became her marketing strategy.**

Chapter 3: Preparing for Success in Network Marketing

Network marketing presents vast opportunities for personal and financial growth, but like any business, it comes with its challenges. Success doesn't come easily, but those who approach it with the right mindset, sound strategies, and consistency can experience life-changing rewards. This chapter delves into the foundational principles and strategies essential for success in network marketing, focusing on preparation, mindset, and long-term growth.

Setting Realistic Expectations

The first step in achieving success in network marketing is setting realistic expectations. It's vital to recognize that while the rewards can be significant, success in this field is a gradual process. Network marketing requires dedication, persistence, and a clear understanding of the effort involved. Many are drawn to the allure of passive income or financial freedom, but it's essential to realize that these rewards come over time, built on consistent effort and perseverance. The journey is not about instant success but about the small steps taken daily, which collectively lead to achieving larger goals.

The Power of Consistency

In network marketing, consistency is the key to building momentum. Whether you're reaching out to new prospects, following up with leads, or engaging with your team, consistent action is what drives steady growth. It's easy to become distracted by new opportunities or tempting shortcuts, but long-term success demands a commitment to your daily actions. Dedicate yourself to building relationships, producing valuable content, and interacting with prospects regularly. Over time, these consistent actions will build your presence in the market and help you achieve significant results.

Educating Yourself and Your Team

Continuous learning is essential in network marketing, as the industry is constantly evolving. New tools, strategies, and techniques emerge regularly, making it important to stay updated and ahead of the curve. Attending trainings, reading books, and staying informed about the latest trends are essential to enhance your knowledge and effectiveness. Equally important is educating **your** team—your downline. Share your insights with them and equip them with the tools they need to succeed. Fostering a culture of learning ensures that everyone grows together, benefiting from the knowledge and skills that drive success.

Creating a Promotion Plan for Network Marketing Success

To achieve success in network marketing, effective promotion and recruitment are crucial. A well-organized promotion plan can help you manage tasks and avoid feeling overwhelmed. Breaking down your activities into manageable tasks will keep you on track and foster consistent growth.

Daily tasks should include maintaining a strong social media presence by posting helpful, engaging content regularly. Engaging with your audience and responding to queries is essential in building and maintaining connections. Focusing on your audience is critical—avoid distractions and ensure your interactions remain purposeful and consistent. On a weekly basis, collaborate with colleagues for joint promotions and network-building efforts. This not only extends your reach but also nurtures a sense of community within your team. Monthly tasks should involve checking in with your customers to ensure their satisfaction and preparing for upcoming events like product launches or promotions. These actions build anticipation and create excitement, driving future sales.

Effective Selling Strategies in Network Marketing

Selling effectively is at the heart of success in network marketing. Implementing a few powerful strategies can make a significant difference in increasing sales and growing your business. Upselling, cross-selling, and presenting post-sale offers are three key tactics that can help.

Upselling involves suggesting a higher-tier version or an additional product when making a sale. For example, after a customer purchases a product, you might offer them an upgraded version. Cross-selling is another technique, where you suggest complementary products to enhance the customer's experience. If someone buys a skincare product, you can recommend related items that other customers have enjoyed. Additionally, presenting a special post-sale offer can create urgency and encourage repeat purchases.

Building an Authentic Online Presence

Authenticity is crucial in network marketing. Building a personal brand that reflects your true self will foster trust and deeper connections with potential customers and team members. Share your journey, including both successes and challenges, to humanize your brand and show that you are genuine. People are more likely to connect with someone who is open and transparent. This authenticity builds stronger relationships and attracts individuals who resonate with your message, fostering a loyal customer base and a motivated downline.

Traditional Franchises vs. Network Marketing

A key advantage of network marketing over traditional franchises is the level of flexibility it offers. Traditional franchises often require significant upfront investment, adherence to strict rules, and a relinquishment of some degree of control. On the other hand, network marketing allows you to build your business on your terms. There are no large startup costs, and you have the freedom to work at your own pace, make independent decisions, and set your own schedule. This flexibility is a major draw for many individuals seeking a business model that offers both autonomy and scalability.

Monitoring Your Direct Selling Business

To effectively manage and grow your network marketing business, it's essential to track the right metrics. Focus on key performance indicators that will provide insight into the health of your business. For instance, tracking daily sales, website visitors, and the average order value will give you a clear sense of how your business is performing. In addition, regular biweekly or monthly reviews of metrics like sales conversion rates, customer satisfaction, and lead generation will help you identify trends, improve strategies, and ensure consistent growth.

Developing the Right Mindset for Success

Network marketing requires more than just practical strategies; it's a mindset-driven business. Without the right mental framework, setbacks and slow progress can be discouraging. Cultivating a success-oriented mindset is critical to maintaining momentum. Taking action, even in small steps, is an essential part of moving forward. As Brian Tracy suggests, clarity and immediate action are powerful tools—don't wait for the "perfect" moment, start now and adjust as you go. Embrace imperfection, as perfect timing rarely exists. Instead, focus on starting small and thinking big. Network marketing offers great opportunities for those who are willing to disrupt the status quo and think creatively about their approach.

The Mindset of Highly Successful Network Marketers

Highly successful network marketers share common traits that set them apart. These individuals treat their businesses with the same dedication and professionalism as any other successful enterprise. The four "D's" of success—desire, determination, decisiveness, and discipline—are essential qualities for anyone looking to thrive in network marketing.

Desire is the foundation of success; you must have a genuine passion for your business and a clear vision of where you want to go. Determination helps you push through setbacks and challenges, ensuring you stay the course even when things get tough. Decisiveness is about making quick, confident decisions, avoiding hesitation and doubt. Finally, discipline is the ability to stay focused and continue working towards your goals, even when immediate results are not visible.

By embodying these four principles, you can build a strong foundation for long-term success in network marketing.

Topic 7
A WORD ON PROJECT MANAGEMENT-TURNING IDEAS INTO REALITY

In the realm of professional and personal growth, project management often stands misunderstood as a skill relevant only to certified professionals or corporate managers. Yet, in truth, it is a universal discipline—one that applies to everyone, regardless of job title, industry, or background. At its heart, project management is the ability to take an idea and bring it to life through structure, planning, and execution. It is not merely about handling complex charts or using sophisticated software; it is about organizing thought, channeling effort, and driving outcomes with intention and clarity.

Every individual, knowingly or unknowingly, is a project manager in some capacity. Whether one is planning a wedding, launching a product, leading a marketing campaign, organizing a home renovation, or simply managing daily routines, the principles of project management are at play. The ability to clearly define what needs to be done, break it into manageable parts, align resources, anticipate challenges, maintain timelines, and deliver results—this is what transforms busyness into meaningful productivity. In jobs, applying project management principles enhances one's ability to prioritize, coordinate with others, and meet deadlines without last-minute panic. It brings focus to the day-to-day and ties even the smallest task to a larger goal, offering a sense of purpose and progress.

For entrepreneurs and business leaders, project management becomes even more crucial. A business is essentially a series of projects in motion—developing new offerings, expanding into markets, recruiting teams, launching promotions, or improving customer experience. Without a system to manage these moving parts, even the best ideas risk failure. Project management in this context ensures that the visionary energy of a leader is supported by a disciplined structure. It helps entrepreneurs stay grounded, make informed decisions, and execute swiftly without being consumed by chaos. It also enables them to delegate effectively, track progress, and adapt to change while maintaining the integrity of the original vision.

Leadership, too, finds its backbone in project management. Great leaders are not just people who inspire; they are individuals who can translate vision into reality. They understand how to mobilize teams, align actions with goals, and create momentum through clarity and coordination. A leader who manages projects well ensures that people are not just busy, but moving forward in a deliberate direction. They prevent energy from being scattered and focus it toward meaningful achievements. In this way, project management becomes an invisible thread running through successful leadership—it is the act of leading with intent, foresight, and executional excellence.

Beyond the workplace, project management seeps into personal life in profound ways. Consider a family planning a holiday. From selecting dates and booking tickets to organizing activities and managing expenses, the entire effort mirrors a well-executed project. Or imagine someone renovating their house—coordinating with contractors, sourcing materials, sticking to budgets, and managing disruptions. These everyday scenarios become smoother, less stressful, and more fulfilling when approached with the mindset of a project manager. It transforms a reactive life into a proactive one. Instead of simply responding to events, we learn to anticipate, prepare, and act with purpose.

The essence of project management lies in bringing order to complexity. Every project, no matter how small or grand, begins with an intention—an outcome we want to see. The first step, therefore, is to start with clarity: What do we want to achieve, and why does it matter? This initial phase, often referred to as the project kick-off, is not about diving into action but about aligning minds. It is a time for defining expectations, roles, and communication protocols. When everyone involved understands the purpose and direction from the outset, the path ahead becomes clearer, smoother, and less prone to confusion.

From there, the challenge becomes about breaking the larger goal into smaller, actionable steps. This process creates clarity by eliminating overwhelm. A project that seems insurmountable when viewed as a whole becomes achievable when divided into meaningful components. Each task, when well-defined, carries its own deadline, responsibility, and outcome. This structure is what brings flow to the execution. It ensures that every person knows their part and is empowered to move forward without waiting for micromanagement or chasing approvals.

Of course, even the best plans require resources—people, time, tools, and money. A thoughtful project manager understands the importance of matching the right resources to the right tasks. Overburdening one team member while another is underutilized leads to burnout and inefficiency. Similarly, tools and budgets must be aligned with the complexity and needs of the project. Effective resource allocation becomes the quiet force behind seamless execution. It allows teams to move with rhythm, knowing that they have what they need to succeed.

Time is another critical element. Projects are always bound by time, and yet this is the resource most often mismanaged. Instead of working reactively against deadlines, project management offers the tools to work with time—through planning, tracking, and adjustments. Timelines bring accountability, but they also offer room for flexibility when backed by foresight. A delay in one task doesn't need to derail the entire project if interdependencies are known and alternative paths are available. This is where tools like Gantt charts or simple visual schedules can be powerful—not just as management devices, but as clarity tools for the team.

And then comes the element of risk. No project is ever immune to surprises. Deadlines get missed, people fall sick, budgets stretch, external situations shift. What separates a successful project from a failed one is not the absence of problems, but the presence of preparedness. Good project management teaches us to identify potential risks in advance and develop contingency plans. It encourages us to ask, "What if?" before we're forced to. This proactive mindset saves time, protects reputation, and prevents panic when things inevitably go off-script.

Yet, none of this would work without communication. It is the lifeblood of every project. Without consistent and transparent communication, even the most brilliant plans can collapse. Project management emphasizes clear updates, timely feedback, and open channels. Everyone should know who to reach out to, when updates are expected, and how decisions will be made. This reduces friction and fosters collaboration, which in turn enhances trust and speed.

As the project unfolds, it becomes equally important to stay within the original intent. There is always a temptation to keep adding new features, requests, or changes—what professionals call "scope creep." But expanding the scope without re-evaluating timelines, budgets, and resources can be dangerous. It leads to diluted focus and missed deadlines. Managing the scope with discipline is not about resisting innovation; it is about honoring the project's core promise.

Financial discipline also plays a key role. Budgets reflect not only cost estimates but also the values of a project. Staying within budget requires constant vigilance, smart decisions, and honest conversations. And at the heart of it all lies quality. A project completed on time and under budget is still a failure if it doesn't meet the expected standard. Quality control ensures that what is delivered is not just done, but done right.

None of this, however, is possible without people. Motivated, engaged team members bring energy and creativity to a project. A skilled project manager knows that people are not just resources—they are the engine. Recognizing their efforts, providing regular feedback, and celebrating milestones creates an environment where excellence can thrive. Delegation becomes a strength here. Leaders who delegate effectively free up their own bandwidth and allow others to grow.

When the project nears completion, many make the mistake of simply moving on to the next task. But wise project managers pause to reflect. What went well? What could have been done better? What lessons should be carried forward? This stage, often called the project review or post-mortem, is vital for continuous improvement. It builds a culture of learning and refinement.

Conflict, too, is a reality of collaborative work. Differing opinions, unclear responsibilities, or competing priorities can create tension. A mature project manager doesn't ignore conflict but addresses it early, listens deeply, and navigates toward resolution. By doing so, they protect team morale and preserve forward momentum.

In the end, project management is much more than a technique—it is a way of thinking, planning, and acting. It teaches us to move through the world with intention, to pursue our goals with structure, and to collaborate with empathy. It empowers individuals to become more organized, more reliable, and more impactful. Whether you're leading a corporate strategy, growing a business, or planning your next move in life, mastering the mindset of project management equips you to turn vision into reality with confidence and grace.

Topic 8

THE PHILOSOPHY OF A FULFILLED LIFE

What does it mean to live a happy and fulfilled life? For thousands of years, philosophers and spiritual teachers across the world have sought to answer this question. From the wisdom of ancient Greece to the spiritual depths of the East, one truth remains constant—happiness is not something to be found outside, but something to be cultivated within. The journey to fulfilment is a deeply personal one, shaped by self-awareness, virtue, purpose, and connection to the greater whole.

The great Socrates once said, "*Know thyself.*" This simple yet profound idea is the beginning of all wisdom. When we take the time to reflect inward—on our thoughts, emotions, values, and desires—we begin to understand who we truly are. In that understanding lies freedom: freedom from societal pressures, from the need to constantly prove ourselves, and from the fear of judgment. This self-knowledge becomes the foundation of authenticity and emotional resilience.

Aristotle built upon this with his idea of the *Golden Mean*—that true virtue lies in balance. Courage is not the absence of fear, nor reckless daring; it is the calm strength that lies between cowardice and foolishness. Temperance, or emotional balance, is not about suppressing feelings, but learning to regulate them. A life lived in moderation—free from extremes of desire and aversion—creates harmony in both our inner and outer worlds. It is this harmony that Aristotle called *eudaimonia*—a flourishing life of purpose, virtue, and well-being.

Plato, in his own vision of the Good, saw happiness as a result of aligning oneself with higher ideals. When our actions reflect our deepest truths—when we live with integrity—we feel fulfilled. Plato believed that contemplation and the pursuit of wisdom lift us beyond the chaos of everyday life and connect us to something eternal. Through this connection, we begin to find meaning in even the smallest of moments.

The Stoic philosophers, such as Epictetus and Marcus Aurelius, offered us a practical path to peace. They taught that while we cannot control what happens to us, we can always choose how we respond. By focusing only on what lies within our control—our thoughts, decisions, and actions—we become free from the tyranny of circumstances. Acceptance, they believed, is not weakness but wisdom: the art of surrendering to fate with grace and strength. In that surrender, we find serenity.

Eastern philosophies echo similar truths. In the *Bhagavad Gita*, Krishna advises Arjuna to act without attachment to outcomes. This detachment is not indifference—it is freedom from obsession, anxiety, and expectation. When we are fully present in our duties and let go of craving for results, we find peace. The Gita also speaks of the *Atman*—the divine spark within us all. Connecting to this inner self through self-realization leads to a deeper understanding of our place in the universe, and with it, an enduring calm.

Buddhism teaches that desire is the root of suffering. The Buddha's *Middle Way* is a life of balance, avoiding both indulgence and extreme denial. Through mindfulness, compassion, and meditation, we train the mind to let go of attachments. In the stillness of the present moment, we find freedom from suffering and awaken to true peace. Meditation is not just a technique—it is a path to clarity, inner balance, and compassion for all beings.

Christianity and Sufi mysticism remind us of the transformative power of love and forgiveness. Jesus taught that forgiving others is not just for their sake, but for our own healing. Holding on to resentment binds us to pain, while forgiveness releases us into peace. The mystics speak of love as the ultimate spiritual act—a love that transcends ego, that heals, that connects. When we love unconditionally, we align ourselves with the divine.

Vedic philosophy speaks of *Dharma*—one's righteous duty—as the key to fulfilment. Living according to our inner calling and moral responsibilities brings inner contentment. When our actions reflect our purpose, life becomes meaningful. Alongside this, the Vedic virtue of *Karuna*, or compassion, teaches us to see ourselves in others. Through kindness, we expand our well-being beyond the personal and into the collective.

Immanuel Kant adds another layer by encouraging us to live by moral reason. Happiness, according to him, comes when we act not out of impulse but from a place of ethical clarity—choosing what is right even when it's not easy. This commitment to integrity fosters a strong sense of self-respect and peace of mind.

Thinkers like Ralph Waldo Emerson and Henry David Thoreau believed that nature and solitude are vital for self-discovery. When we disconnect from noise and immerse ourselves in the natural world, we reconnect with something essential and pure. Nature becomes a mirror of the soul, reminding us of simplicity, beauty, and the quiet joy of just being.

Finally, Advaita Vedanta brings us back to oneness. It teaches that all separation is illusion—that every being, every particle, every breath is part of one unified consciousness. When we realize this, the ego begins to dissolve, and we experience a love that is universal and unconditional. In this awareness, conflict fades, fear dissolves, and a deep, abiding peace settles in our hearts.

In the end, a fulfilled life is not defined by wealth, fame, or comfort. It is shaped by clarity of mind, strength of character, and depth of connection—to self, to others, to nature, and to the divine. It is a life where we know ourselves, live by our values, let go of what we cannot control, and walk each day with presence, love, and wisdom.

This is the true philosophy of a fulfilled life—not a single teaching or path, but a tapestry of timeless wisdom that gently guides us back home to ourselves.

BORN TWICE, BUILT ONCE: THE FINAL MESSAGE

As I reach the final pages of this book, I reflect on the journey we've travelled together. The lessons shared, the strategies unveiled, and the personal insights offered have all been a part of a larger vision—to guide you toward living a life of purpose, authenticity, and success. But the real work, the transformation, happens beyond these words. It happens in your actions.

I stand before you as someone who has experienced the highs and lows of life, someone who was born twice: once by birth, and once again through self-realization, growth, and the choice to change. The first birth gave me life, but it was the second birth—the conscious decision to reshape my mindset and my approach to life—that truly made me who I am today. It is through this process that I realized the importance of "building once," focusing on lasting principles, values, and systems that can withstand the challenges of life.

I want to leave you with a simple yet powerful truth: You must *build* your life on your own terms, based on your unique strengths, values, and vision. But this building doesn't happen in isolation or in haste. It requires self-awareness, persistence, and the ability to adapt to change. It requires consistency, resilience, and an unwavering belief in yourself, even when things seem difficult.

Now is the time for you to take responsibility. Take control of your future. It doesn't matter where you've been; what matters is where you choose to go from here. Ask yourself: What do I want my life to stand for? What legacy do I want to create? How will I grow through the challenges ahead?

If there's one thing, I want you to take away from this book, it's this: Transformation begins with *choice*. You have the power to change your mindset, to change your habits, and to change the course of your life. There's no magic formula—just daily actions aligned with your values, a commitment to learning, and a mindset of resilience.

The road ahead may not always be smooth, but it is your journey to walk. Stay true to yourself. Build once, and build wisely.

You were born with potential; now it's time to build the life you truly deserve.

– Siddharth Sharma

www.ingramcontent.com/pod-product-compliance
Ingram Content Group UK Ltd.
Pitfield, Milton Keynes, MK11 3LW, UK
UKHW041831200726
13854UKWH00002BA/982

9 798899 293467